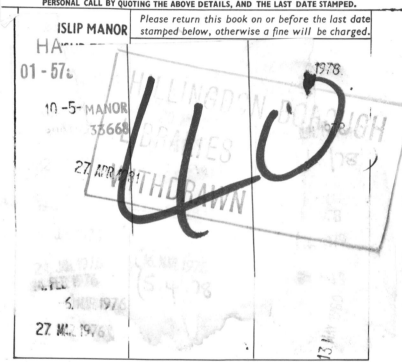

Austin Morris 10/12 cwt. J4 Van 1960-74 Autobook

By Kenneth Ball
Associate Member, Guild of Motoring Writers
and the Autopress Team of Technical Writers.

Austin 10/12 cwt Van and Pick-up
   Series J4/VA, J4/PA, J4/M10 1960-67
Morris Commercial 10/12 cwt Van and Pick-up,
   Series J4/VM, J4/PM, J4/M10 1960-67
BMC 10/12 cwt Van and Pick-up,
   Series 180J4, 190J4, 200J4 1968-70
Austin Morris 10/12 cwt Van and Pick-up,
   Series 180J4, 200J4 1970-74

Autopress Ltd. Golden Lane Brighton BN1 2QJ England

The AUTOBOOK series of Workshop Manuals is the largest in the world and covers the majority of British and Continental motor cars, as well as all major Japanese and Australian models. For a full list see the back of this manual.

CONTENTS

ISBN 0 85147 530 2

First Edition   1972
Second Edition, fully revised   1974

© Autopress Ltd 1974

846

Printed and bound in Brighton England for Autopress Ltd by G Beard & Son Ltd   A

ACKNOWLEDGEMENT

My thanks are due to British Leyland Motor Corporation Ltd. for their unstinted co-operation and also for supplying data and illustrations.

I am also grateful to a considerable number of owners who have discussed their vehicles at length and many of whose suggestions have been included in this manual.

Kenneth Ball
Associate Member, Guild of Motoring Writers
Ditchling Sussex England.

INTRODUCTION

This do-it-yourself Workshop Manual has been specially written for the owner who wishes to maintain his vehicle in first class condition and to carry out his own servicing and repairs. Considerable savings on garage charges can be made, and one can drive in safety and confidence knowing the work has been done properly.

Comprehensive step-by-step instructions and illustrations are given on all dismantling, overhauling and assembling operations. Certain assemblies require the use of expensive special tools, the purchase of which would be unjustified. In these cases information is included but the reader is recommended to hand the unit to the agent for attention.

Throughout the Manual hints and tips are included which will be found invaluable, and there is an easy to follow fault diagnosis at the end of each chapter.

Whilst every care has been taken to ensure correctness of information it is obviously not possible to guarantee complete freedom from errors or to accept liability arising from such errors or omissions.

Instructions may refer to the righthand or lefthand sides of the vehicle or the components. These are the same as the righthand or lefthand of an observer standing behind the vehicle and looking forward.

CHAPTER 1

THE PETROL ENGINE

1 : 1 Description

The petrol engine fitted in these vehicles is in two sizes, the smaller, or type 15JE, being of 1489cc and the larger type, or 16JE, being 1622cc. The stroke in each case is 3.5 inch (88.9 mm), the capacity difference being obtained by increasing the bore from 2.875 inch (73.02 mm) to 3.0 inch (76.2 mm). Apart from a few dimensional differences, which will be tabulated in Technical Data at the end of this manual, the two engines are identical.

It is a four cylinder in-line unit, built in unit construction with a single dry plate clutch. The valves are set in line in the detachable cylinder head and are operated by rockers and pushrods from the camshaft in the lefthand side of the engine. Oil seals are fitted to the valves and there is normal provision for clearance adjustment.

The camshaft, running in three steel-backed, whitemetal bearings, is chain driven and the timing chain is provided with synthetic rubber slipper-type tensioner. The oil pump, distributor, and when fitted, engine revolution counter are driven from the camshaft, each having its own drive shaft.

The pistons are of aluminium alloy with anodized finish, and carry three compression rings and a slotted oil control ring. The gudgeon pins are clamped in connecting rods which have steel-backed renewable big-end bearings.

Three steel-backed whitemetal bearings support the forged steel counterbalanced crankshaft. The thrust is taken by special washers at the centre main bearing. The renewable element oil filter is secured by its centre bolt to the righthand side of the engine.

A centrifugal water pump and fan are driven from the crankshaft pulley by the dynamo belt.

An eccentric type oil pump inside the crankcase is driven from the camshaft by a short vertical shaft. Oil is drawn into the pump through a gauze strainer and is delivered through crankcase drillings to a non-adjustable plunger-type relief valve located at the rear of the engine. From the relief valve oil passes to the main oil gallery. Drillings from the main oil gallery supply oil to the main, big-end, and camshaft bearings. The connecting rod ends are drilled and supply oil to the cylinder walls.

From the rear camshaft bearing oil passes through the block and a drilling in the rear rocker shaft bracket to lubricate the rockers, returning to the sump via the push-rod holes. Sectioned views of the engine and the engine components can be seen in **FIGS 1 : 1, 1 : 2** and **1 : 3**.

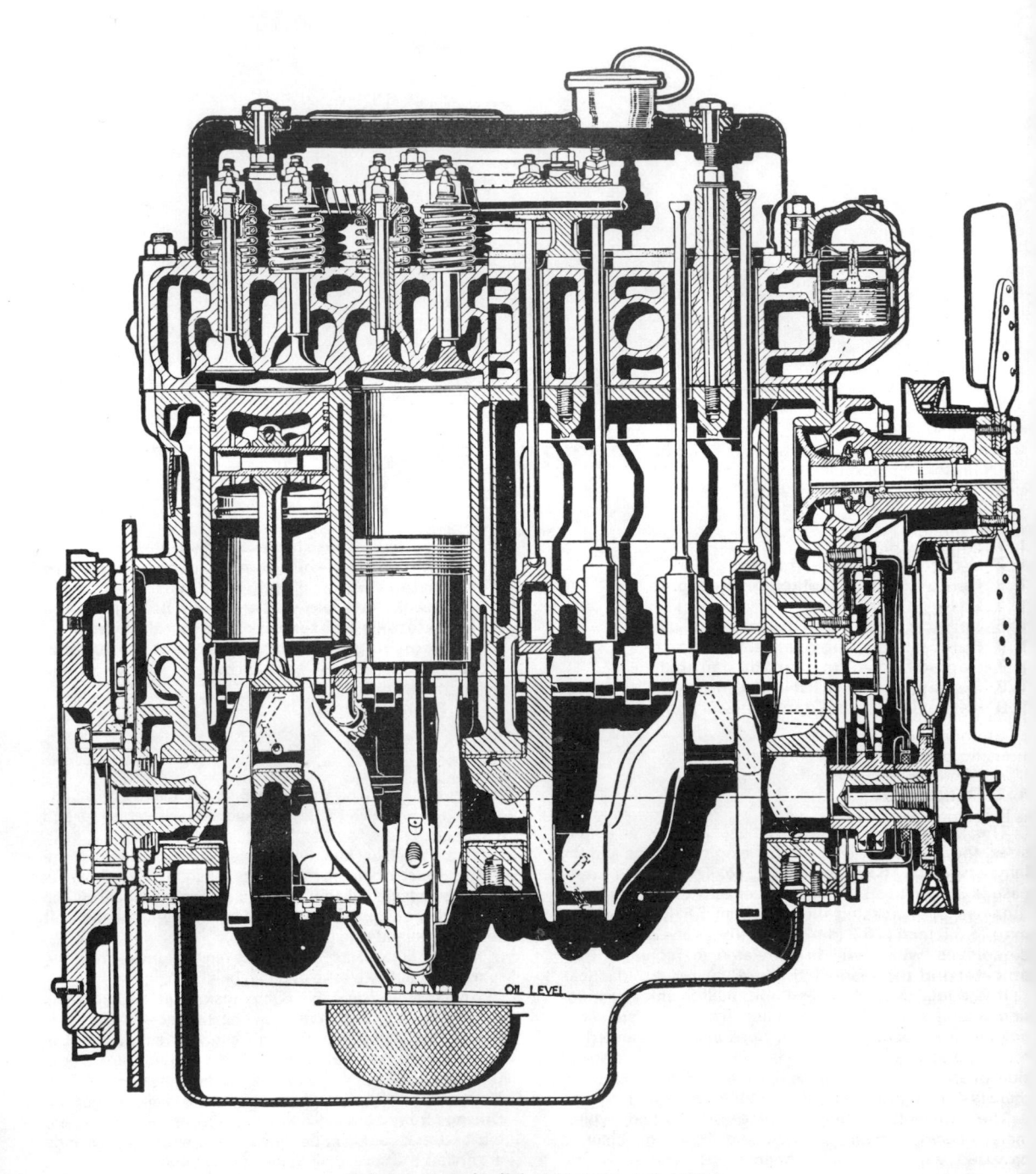

FIG 1:1 Longitudial section through engine

1 : 2 Working on engine in car

If the operator is not a skilled automobile engineer it is suggested that before starting work he should read the 'Hints on Maintenance and Overhaul' to be found at the end of this manual. The need for cleanliness must be stressed and the operator will save himself much time and trouble by carrying out the operations in an orderly manner, and by marking each part before dismantling to facilitate easier reassembly. Always use the approved grades of lubricant.

The operations of decarbonizing, top overhaul, the removal of clutch, transmission, oil sump, oil pump and front cover and all subsequent refitting operations can be done without removing the engine from the car.

For working under the car it is often helpful to have the car raised on jacks or blocks, but ensure always that any such supports are firmly based and not likely to collapse or serious injury could result.

1 : 3 Removing and replacing the engine

Unfasten the door check to facilitate engine removal, then remove the seats and under-seat inspection plates.

Lift off the engine cowling. Disconnect the battery cables and remove the battery. Remove the engine cowling floor base.

Drain the radiator, on later vehicles with an expansion tank, disconnect the pipe from the radiator neck, disconnect the radiator upper tie-bars. Remove the radiator lower support brackets or disconnect the radiator from the former. Disconnect the hose clips and remove the radiator.

Disconnect the choke and throttle cables and the heater connections when fitted. Disconnect the petrol feed pipe to the fuel pump.

Remove the cables from the generator, distributor and starter.

Remove the fan unit. Disconnect the exhaust downpipe. Remove the starter.

Support the gearbox on a jack and remove all the bellhousing bolts.

Attach suitable lifting tackle to two lifting bolts on the cylinder head and take the weight of the engine. This is best done with a jib crane through the passenger doorway (see FIG 1 : 4).

Remove the engine mounting bolts. Then swing the engine forward to withdraw the first motion shaft and lift the engine out through the car doorway.

Replacing the engine is a reversal of the above procedure.

1 : 4 Lifting the head

1 Drain the water from the cooling system. One drain tap is at the base of the radiator and the other is at the rear of the engine on the righthand side. If antifreeze is being used it should be drained into a suitable container and placed aside for future use.
2 Remove the top water hose. Remove the three thermostat housing securing nuts and washers and remove the housing and the thermostat.
3 Remove the air cleaner and the carburetter.
4 Remove the inlet and exhaust manifolds. The heater pipe, if fitted, should be withdrawn from the studs.
5 Unscrew the two nuts and lift off the rocker cover, taking care not to damage the cork gasket or lose the washers and rubber seals.

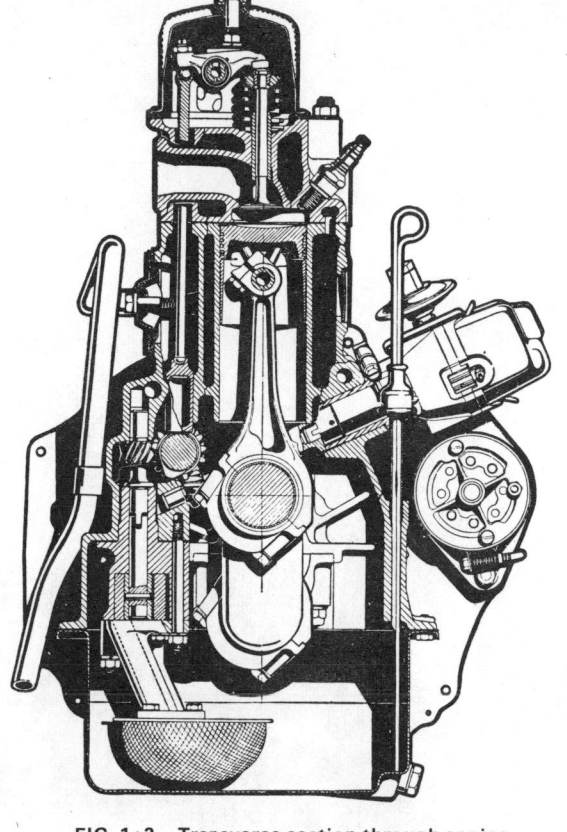

FIG 1 : 2   Transverse section through engine

6 Notice that under the righthand rear rocker stud nut there is a special locking plate (see FIG 1 : 5).
7 Unscrew the 11 cylinder head retaining nuts gradually a turn at a time, in the order shown in FIG 1 : 6, until the load has been released. As four of the rocker shaft bracket fixing nuts also serve to retain the cylinder head, it is essential, even if only removing the rocker shaft, to slacken all 11 cylinder head nuts to avoid distortion of the cylinder head and the possibility of water entering the cylinders and sump.
8 Unscrew the remaining four rocker shaft bracket nuts and remove the rocker assembly complete with brackets and rockers. Withdraw the eight pushrods, storing them carefully so that they may be replaced in their original positions.
9 Detach the high-tension cables and remove the sparking plugs.
10 Unscrew and remove the thermal transmitter from the front of the cylinder head.
11 Release the ignition vacuum control pipe from the rear cylinder head stud and remove the cylinder head. To facilitate breaking the joint, tap each side of the cylinder head with a hammer, using a block of wood interposed to break the blow. When lifting the head a direct pull should be given to withdraw it evenly up the studs.

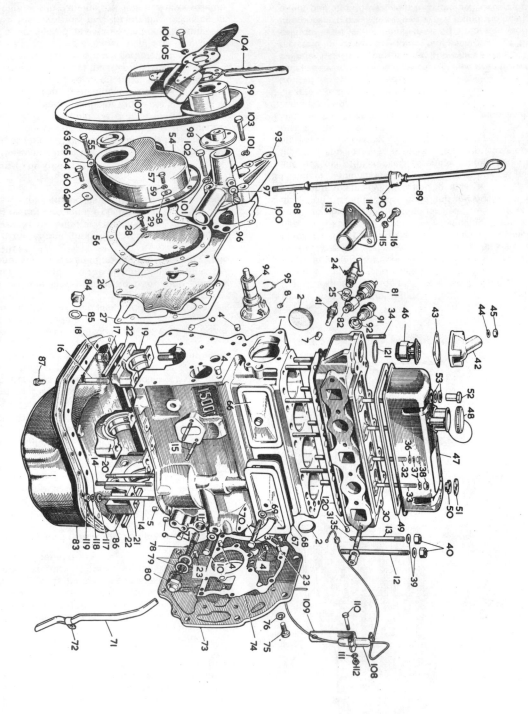

FIG 1:3   External components of engine

Key to Fig 1:3

1 Cylinder block 2 Plug (welch)—large 3 Plug—crankcase oil gallery 4 Plug—crankcase oil gallery 5 Plug—taper—crankcase oil hole 6 Plug—oil relief valve vent hole 7 Plug for oil hole—oil filter boss 8 Plug—oil dipper rod boss 9 Plug for chain tensioner oil feed 10 Plug for oil hole (screwed) 11 Washer for screwed plug 12 Stud for cylinder head (long) 13 Stud for cylinder head (short) 14 Stud for oil pump (short) 15 Stud—petrol pump to crankcase 16 Stud—main bearing cap 17 Washer for main bearing stud 18 Nut for main bearing stud 19 Cap—main bearing (front) 20 Cap—main bearing (centre) 21 Cap—main bearing (rear) 22 Joint for front and rear main bearing caps 23 Dowel for gearbox mounting plate 24 Tap—cylinder block—drain 25 Washer for drain tap 26 Plate—engine mounting (front) 28 Screw—mounting plate to crankcase 29 Washer for screw (spring) 30 Cylinder head 31 Plug for oil hole 32 Joint washer for mounting plate 33 Stud for rocker bracket (short) 34 Stud for water outlet elbow 35 Stud for water outlet elbow 36 Washer for cylinder head 37 Washer for rocker bracket stud (plain) 38 Nut for rocker bracket stud 39 Washer for cylinder head stud 40 Nut for cylinder head stud 41 Thermal transmitter 42 Elbow—water outlet 43 Joint washer for elbow 44 Washer for elbow stud in cylinder head 45 Nut for stud 46 Thermostat 47 Cover—valve rocker 48 Cap and cable—oil filler 49 Joint washer—rocker cover to cylinder head 50 Bush for cover (rubber) 51 Washer (cup) 52 Nut for rocker cover (cap) 53 Washer for rocker cover nut (plain) 54 Cover (front) 55 Ring—crankcase front cover (felt) 56 Joint washer for crankcase front cover 57 Screw—cover to front plate 58 Washer for screw 59 Washer for screw (spring) 60 Screw—cover and front plate to crankcase 61 Washer for screw (plain) 62 Washer for screw (spring) 63 Screw—front cover to bearing cap 64 Washer for screw 65 Washer for screw (spring) 66 Cover—cylinder side (front) 67 Cover—cylinder side—rear (with elbow) 68 Joint washer—cylinder side cover 69 Washer for screw 70 Screw—side cover to crankcase 71 Pipe—crankcase vent 72 Clip for crankcase vent pipe 73 Plate—gearbox mounting 74 Joint washer—mounting plate to crankcase 75 Screw—mounting plate to crankcase 76 Washer for screw (spring) 77 Valve—oil release 78 Spring for valve 79 Washer for oil release valve spring 80 Cap nut—oil release valve cap nut 81 Switch—oil pressure 82 Adaptor—oil pressure switch 83 Reservoir—oil 84 Plug—drain 85 Washer for drain plug 86 Joint washer for oil reservoir 87 Screw with captive washer—reservoir to crankcase 88 Tube—oil level indicator rod 89 Rod—oil level indicator 90 Cover—dust for rod 91 Adaptor—fullflow filter connection 92 Joint washer for adaptor 93 Pump body 94 Vane—water pump/Seal—water pump/Bearing assembly (complete with spindle) 95 Wire—bearing locating 96 Screw—lubricating point 97 Washer for screw (fibre) 98 Hub for pulley 99 Pulley—fan and water pump 100 Joint washer—water pump to crankcase 101 Washer for screw (spring) 102 Screw—water pump to crankcase (long) 103 Screw—water pump to crankcase (short) 104 Fan—water pump 105 Joint washer for fuel trap 106 Screw—fan to pulley 107 Belt—fan 108 Pipe—vacuum control (with fuel trap) 109 Clip for fuel trap 110 Bolt for mounting clip 111 Washer for bolt (spring) 112 Nut for bolt 113 Housing—distributor 114 Screw—distributor housing to crankcase 115 Washer for screw (spring) 116 Screw—distributor to distributor housing 117 Washer for stud (plain) 118 Washer for stud 119 Nut for stud—oil pump to crankcase 120 Joint washer—cylinder head to block 121 Joint washer—cylinder head to thermostat

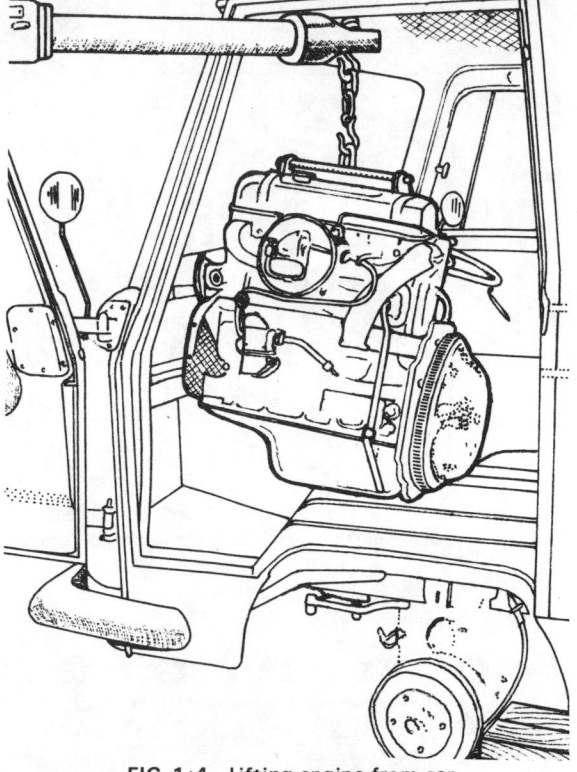

FIG 1:4 Lifting engine from car

Refitting the head:

Make sure that the surfaces of both the cylinder head and the cylinder block are clean. It will be noticed that the cylinder head gasket is marked 'TOP' and 'FRONT' to assist in replacing it correctly.

With the gasket correctly positioned over the studs, lower the cylinder head into position. Replace the vacuum control pipe clip and fit the seven external cylinder head nuts finger tight.

Replace the pushrods in the positions from which they were removed. Replace the rocker assembly and tighten the securing nuts finger tight. Tighten the 11 nuts securing the cylinder head a turn at a time in the order shown in **FIG 1:6,** finally tightening them to a torque of 40 lb ft (5.5 kg m). Tighten the four remaining rocker bracket nuts.

The assembly now continues in the reverse order to the dismantling procedure. On completion refill the cooling system and run the engine to check for leaks.

1:5 Servicing the head, attention to valves

With the cylinder head removed as in **Section 1:4,** refer to **FIG 1:7** and remove the valve circlip. Compress the valve spring using a spring compressing tool, and remove the two valve cotters. Release the valve spring and remove the compressor, valve spring cap, shroud, spring and bottom collar if fitted. Remove the valve packing ring from the cotter groove and withdraw the valve from the guide.

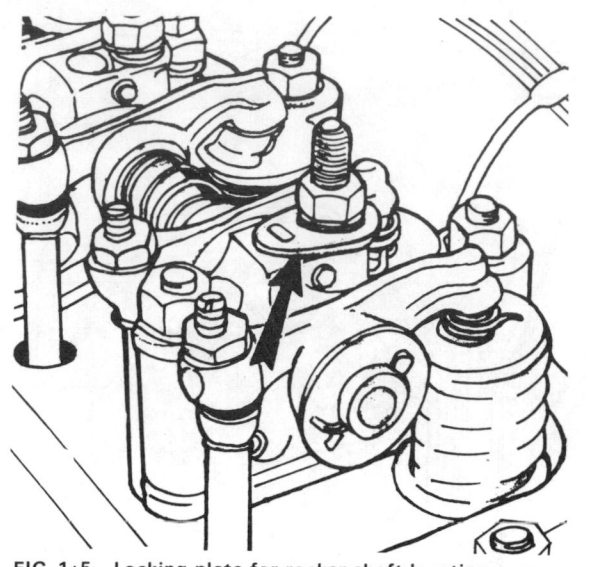

FIG 1:5 Locking plate for rocker shaft locating screw

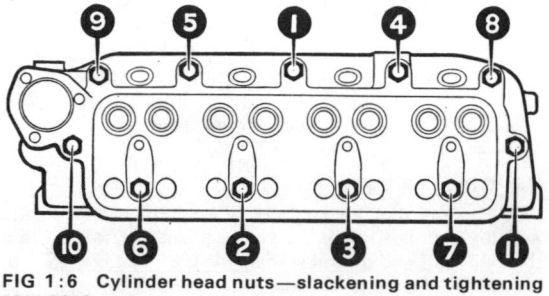

FIG 1:6 Cylinder head nuts—slackening and tightening sequence

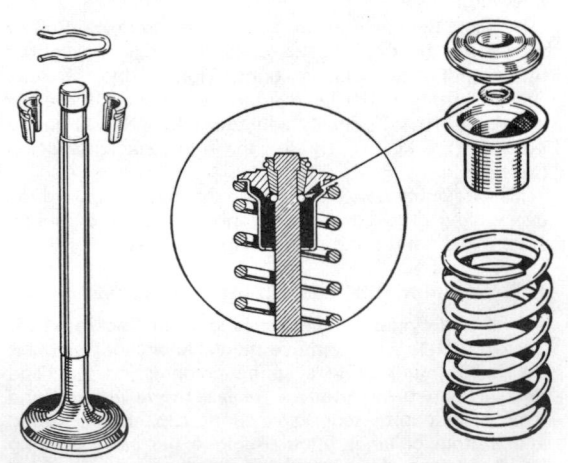

FIG 1:7 A valve assembly. Inset shows valve packing ring correctly fitted below the cotters

Keep the valves in their relative positions when removed from the engine to ensure replacements in their original valve guides. The exhaust valve heads are concave and are smaller in diameter than the inlet valves. Each valve must be cleaned and carefully inspected for pitting. Valves that are pitted should be refaced with a suitable grinder or new valves should be fitted.

When grinding a valve onto its seating, the valve face should be smeared lightly with fine or medium grade carborundum paste and then lapped in with a suction type grinding tool (see FIG 1:8). The valve must be ground to its seat with a semi-rotary motion. A light coil spring interposed between the valve head and the port will assist considerably when lifting the valve to rotate the face to a different position. This should be done frequently to spread the grinding paste evenly.

The grinding process must be continued until an even, matt surface is produced on the seating and the valve face. On completion, the valve seats and ports should be thoroughly cleaned with a fuel-soaked rag, dried, and subjected to a compressed air blast. The valves should be washed in fuel and all grinding paste removed.

Removing and replacing valve guides:

Rest the cylinder head with its machined face downwards on a clean surface and drive the valve guide downwards into the combustion space with a drift. The drift should be a hardened steel punch $\frac{9}{16}$ inch in diameter and not less than 4 inches in length, with a locating spigot $\frac{5}{16}$ inch diameter machined on one end for a length of 1 inch to engage the bore of the guide. Note that the exhaust valve guide is longer than the inlet.

New valve guides should be pressed in from the top of the cylinder head. The inlet valve guides must be inserted with the end having the largest chamfer at the top, and the exhaust valve guides should have their counterbored ends to the bottom. The guides should be driven into the cylinder head until they are $\frac{5}{8}$ inch (15.8mm) above the machined surface of the valve spring seating (see FIG 1:9).

Decarbonizing:

If special equipment is not available for decarbonizing it will be necessary to scrape the carbon deposit from the piston crowns, cylinder block, and cylinder head, using a blunt scraper. A ring of carbon should be left around the periphery of the piston crown and the ring of carbon around the top of the cylinder bore should not be disturbed. To facilitate this an old piston ring can be sprung into the bore so that it rests on the piston crown.

The cylinder head is next given attention. Clean off the carbon deposit from the valve stems, valve ports, and combustion spaces of the cylinder head. Remove all traces of carbon dust with compressed air and then thoroughly wash with paraffin and dry off.

Fit a new cylinder head gasket when replacing the head if the old one has been damaged, noting that it is marked to indicate the top face and front end.

To replace the valves, place each valve into its guide and fit the bottom collars (if fitted), valve springs shrouds and caps. Compress the valve spring and push new synthetic rubber packing ring over the tip of the valve stem down to the bottom of the cotter groove (see FIG 1:10). Refit the two valve cotters and remove the

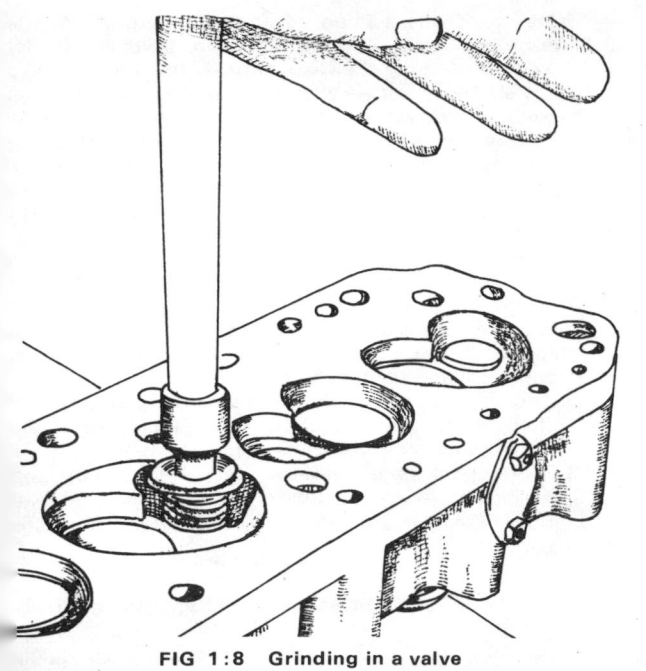

FIG 1:8 Grinding in a valve

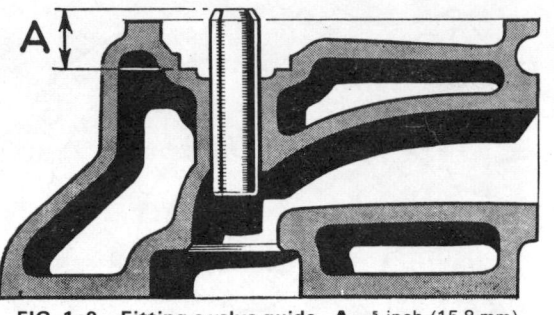

FIG 1:9 Fitting a valve guide. **A** = $\frac{5}{8}$ inch (15.8 mm)

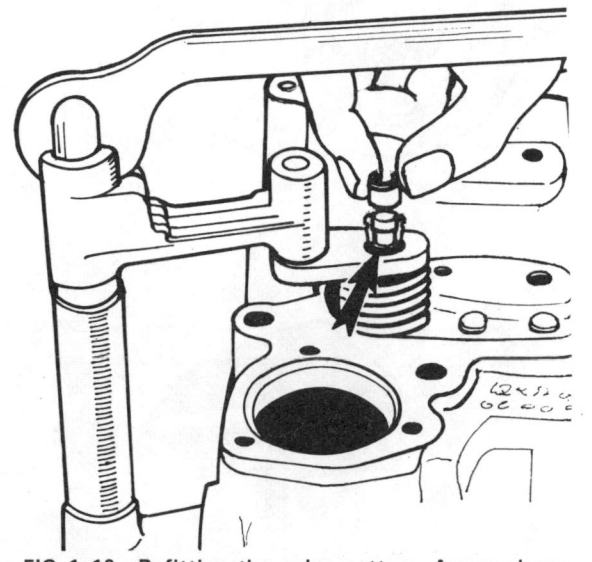

FIG 1:10 Refitting the valve cotters. Arrow shows position of packing ring

compressor, then refit the valve circlip. When replacing the valves, do not fit old valve packing rings or oil leakage may occur. The rings are fitted more easily if they have been soaked in clean engine oil for a short period before use.

1:6 Removing timing gear and camshaft

1 Straighten the tab on the starting dog nut lockwasher. Unscrew the starting dog nut. A few sharp blows in an anticlockwise direction will slacken the nut. Remove the crankshaft pulley.

2 The timing cover is secured by nine bolts, each with a spring washer and an elongated 'plain washer. Remove all nine bolts and washers and remove the timing cover. Care should be taken not to damage the timing cover gasket. If it is damaged, clean the face of the cover flange and the front face of the engine mounting plate and fit a new gasket on reassembly.

3 Remove the bottom plug from the chain tensioner body. Insert a $\frac{1}{8}$ inch (3 mm) Allen key to engage the cylinders and turn the key clockwise until the rubber slipper is fully retracted behind the limit peg (see **FIG 1:11**). To remove the tensioner assembly complete, unlock and remove the two securing bolts, and the assembly and backplate may be removed from the engine.

4 Unlock and remove the camshaft chain wheel nut and lockwasher. Note that the locating tag on the lock-washer fits into the keyway of the camshaft chain-wheel. The camshaft and crankshaft chainwheels may now be removed, together with the timing chain, by easing each wheel forward, a fraction at a time, with suitable small levers. As the crankshaft gearwheel is withdrawn, care must be taken not to lose the gear packing washers immediately behind it.

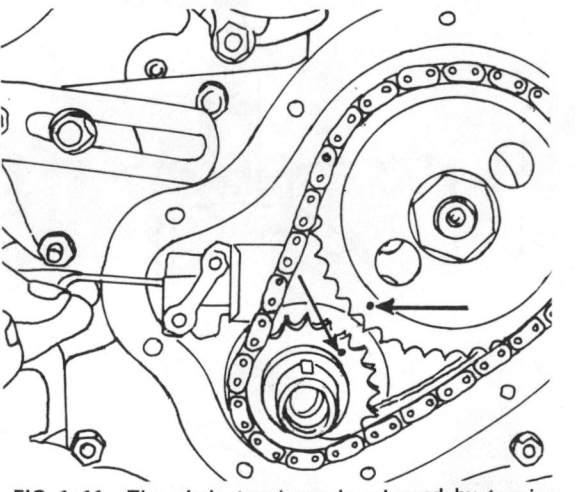

FIG 1:11 The chain tensioner is released by turning Allen key clockwise. The timing marks indicated by arrows must be in line to give correct valve timing

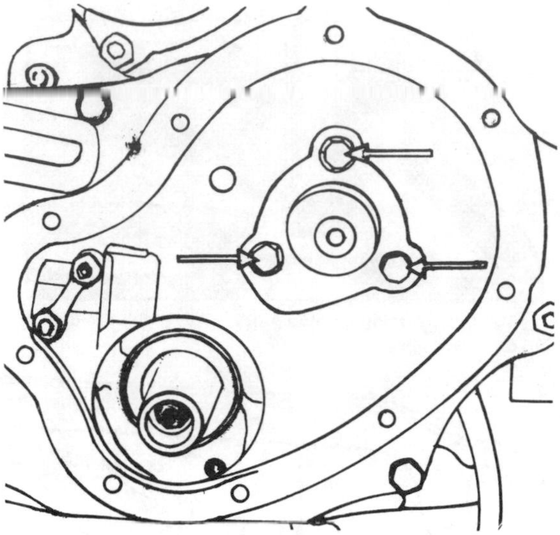

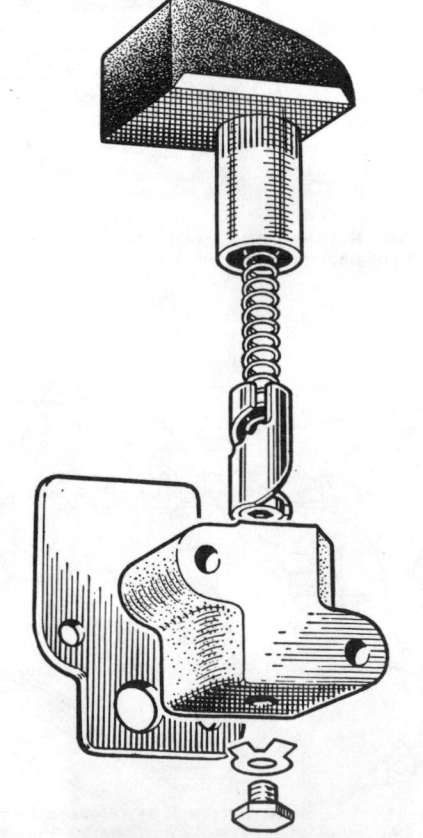

FIG 1:12 Three camshaft locating plate securing screws

5 Disconnect the suction advance unit pipe from the distributor and take out the two bolts with flat washers securing the distributor to the housing. Do not slacken the clamping plate bolt or the ignition timing setting will be lost. Withdraw the distributor.

6 Take out the screw securing the distributor housing to the cylinder block and withdraw the housing. Using a $\frac{5}{16}$ inch UNF bolt $2\frac{1}{2}$ inches long as an extractor, screw it into the tapped end of the distributor drive spindle and withdraw the spindle.

7 Remove the sump, the oil pump, and the oil pump drive shaft.

8 To remove the camshaft the engine must be removed from the vehicle, and the gearbox separated from the engine. Remove the inlet and exhaust manifolds, cylinder head, pushrods and tappets.

9 Disconnect the engine revolution indicator drive (if fitted), remove the securing nuts and washers and withdraw the indicator drive gear.

10 Take out the three setscrews (see **FIG 1:12**), and shakeproof washers which secure the camshaft locating plate to the cylinder block and withdraw the camshaft.

Dismantling and reassembling the timing chain tensioner:

With the tensioner removed from the engine as detailed in the previous section, withdraw the plunger and slipper assembly from the tensioner body and engage the lower end of the cylinder with the Allen key. The tensioner components can be seen in **FIG 1:13**. Turn the key clockwise, holding the key and plunger securely until the cylinder and spring are released from the inside of the plunger.

Check the bore of the tensioner body for ovality. If the ovality is greater than .003 inch (.076 mm) near the mouth of the bore then the complete chain tensioner must be renewed. Inspect the slipper head for wear. If it is worn, a new slipper head and cylinder assembly can be fitted to the existing body.

The components should be thoroughly cleaned in fuel and the inlet oil hole in the spigot and the outlet oil hole in the slipper should be blown through with compressed air.

When reassembling, insert the spring in the plunger and place the cylinder on the other end of the spring. Compress the spring until the cylinder enters the plunger bore, engaging the helical slot with the peg in the plunger. Hold the assembly compressed in this position and engage the Allen key. Turn the cylinder clockwise until the end of the cylinder is below the peg and the spring is held compressed. Withdraw the key and insert the plunger assembly in the body. Replace the backplate and secure the assembly to the cylinder block. After fitting, check the slipper head for freedom of movement and ensure that it does not bind on the backplate when it is moved in the body.

When the timing chain is in position, the tensioner is released for operation by inserting the key and turning clockwise until the slipper head moves forward under spring pressure against the chain.

Do not attempt to turn the key anticlockwise or force the slipper head into the chain by external pressure.

FIG 1:13 Components of chain tensioner

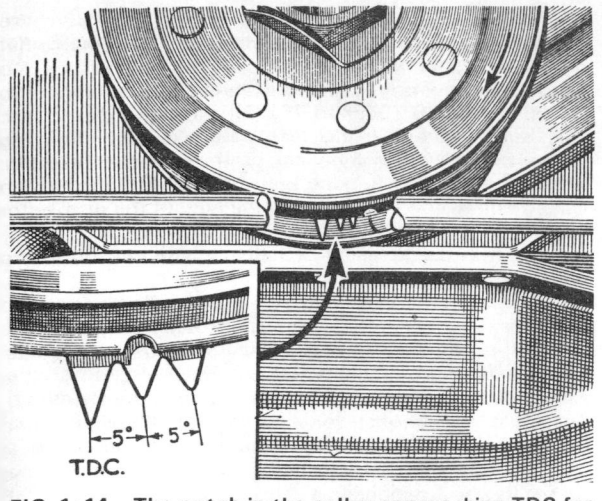

FIG 1:14 The notch in the pulley approaching TDC for No. 1 and 4 pistons

1:7 Replacing timing gear and camshaft

Refitting the camshaft is a reversal of the removal instructions given in **Section 1:6**.

When replacing the timing chain and wheels, set the crankshaft with its keyway at TDC, and the camshaft with its keyway at approximately the one o'clock position when seen from the front. Assemble the wheels into the timing chain with the two dimples on the chainwheels opposite to one another as seen in **FIG 1:11**. Keeping the wheels in this position, engage the crankshaft wheel keyway with the key on the crankshaft and rotate the camshaft until the camshaft wheel keyway and the key are aligned. Push the gears onto the shafts as far as they will go and secure the camshaft wheel with the lockwasher and nut.

If the chain tensioner has been removed from the engine, replace the backplate and secure the assembly to the cylinder block. The tensioner is released for operation by inserting the Allen key and turning it clockwise until the slipper head moves forward under spring pressure against the chain. Secure the bolts with the locking plate, replace the bottom plug, and lock with the tabwasher.

Inspect the timing cover gasket. If it is damaged, clean the face of the cover flange and the front engine mounting plate and fit a new gasket. The oil seal in the cover must be renewed if it shows signs of damage or deterioration. A service tool 18G.134 together with adaptor 18G.134.BD is used for this.

Ensure that the oil thrower behind the crankshaft pulley is fitted with the face marked 'F' away from the engine. When refitting the cover it is essential to ensure that the rubber seal is centralized on the crankshaft, and a service tool 18G.1046 is available for this purpose.

Insert the setscrews and tighten up evenly, then refit and tighten the pulley securing nut.

The early type front cover and oil thrower must be used together. When refitting, ensure that the oil thrower is fitted with its concave side facing away from the engine. Use service tool 18G.3 to centralize the seal (rubber or

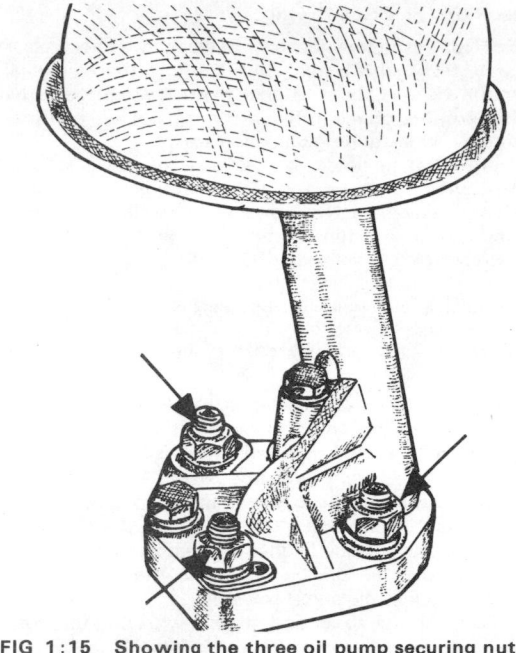

FIG 1:15 Showing the three oil pump securing nuts

felt) on the crankshaft, or alternatively use the crankshaft pulley as follows:

If a rubber seal is fitted, fill the annular groove between the lips with grease. Lubricate the hub of the pulley and push it into the seal, at the same time turning it to avoid damaging the felt or the lips of the rubber seal. Slide the pulley onto the shaft with the keyway in line with the key in the crankshaft. Turn the cover as necessary to align the setscrew holes with those in the crankcase, taking care not to strain the cover against the flexibility of the seal.

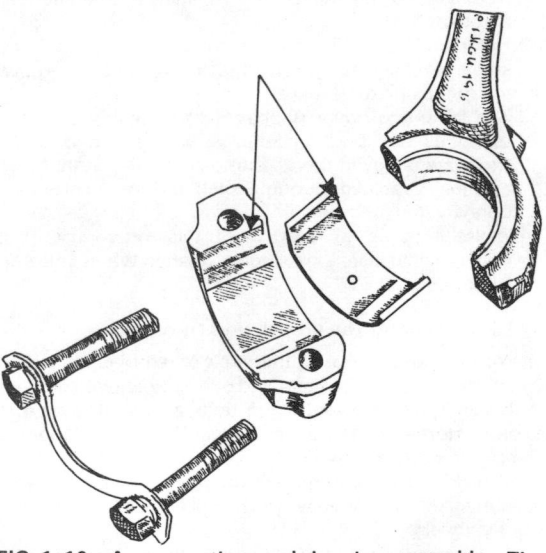

FIG 1:16 A connecting rod bearing assembly. The bearing locating tab is arrowed

Checking the valve timing:

Set No. 1 cylinder inlet valve to the timing check clearance of .021 inch (.5 mm) and then turn the crankshaft until the valve is about to open. This clearance is for valve timing check only and must not be confused with the normal running tappet clearance.

The indicating notch in the flange of the crankshaft pulley, should then be opposite the required pointer on the timing cover, i.e. No. 1 inlet valve should be about to open and No. 4 piston will be at the required setting on its compression stroke (see **FIG 1 : 14**).

Do not omit to reset the inlet valve to its correct running clearance when the timing check is complete.

1 : 8 Removing and refitting the sump and oil strainer

1 Remove the hexagonal drain plug on the righthand side of the sump and drain the contents.
2 Remove the 19 bolts and washers and lower the sump. If the sump will not pass the crossmember, remove the eight engine mounting to crossmember bolts and lift the engine slightly. Turn the crankshaft to clear the balancing lobes and remove the sump.
3 To remove the oil strainer, undo the three screws securing it to the pump cover.

Clean out the sump and strainer with paraffin and a stiff brush; never use rag. When refitting the sump to the engine give particular attention to the sealing gaskets for the crankcase face and the two oil seal packings for the crankshaft which fit into recesses in the crankcase.

If the gaskets are in good condition they may be used again, but if new ones are available it is advisable to fit them. Before fitting new gaskets, clean off the sump and crankcase faces. Smear the faces of the crankcase joint with grease and fit the two halves of the large gasket. Lift the sump into position on the crankcase, insert the 19 bolts, and tighten them evenly.

1 : 9 Removing and refitting the oil pump

1 Remove the oil sump and strainer as detailed in **Section 1 : 8.**
2 Refer to **FIG 1 : 15,** unscrew the three nuts from the studs securing the pump to the crankcase and remove the pump and drive shaft.
3 The oil pump cover is attached to the body of the pump by two bolts and spring washers, and when these are removed the oil pump cover, the outer rotor, and the combined oil pump shaft and inner rotor may be extracted.
4 Reassembly is a reversal of this procedure, but remember to use a new joint washer when refitting the pump.

1 : 10 Removing the clutch and flywheel

With the engine out of the vehicle, remove the clutch by unscrewing the six bolts and spring washers securing it to the flywheel. Release the bolts a turn at a time to avoid distortion of the cover flange. Two dowels locate the clutch cover on the flywheel.

Unlock and remove the six nuts and three lockplates which secure the flywheel to the crankshaft and remove the flywheel.

To remove the old starter ring from the flywheel flange, split the ring with a cold chisel, taking care not to damage

the flywheel. Make certain that the bore of the new ring and its mating surface on the flywheel are free from burr and are perfectly clean.

To fit the new ring it must be heated to a temperature of 300° to 400°C (575° to 752°F), indicated by a light blue surface colour. If this temperature is exceeded the temper of the teeth will be lost, so the use of a thermostatically controlled furnace is recommended. Place the heated ring on the flywheel with the lead of the ring teeth uppermost. The expansion will allow the ring to be fitted without force by pressing or tapping it lightly until the ring is hard against its register.

The operation should be followed by natural cooling when the 'shrink fit' will be permanently established.

When refitting the flywheel, ensure that the 1/4 mark on the periphery of the flywheel is in line with and on the same side as the first and fourth throws of the crankshaft. To assist the correct location of the flywheel, the depression in the crankshaft flange is stamped with a similar timing mark, which should be in line with the one on the flywheel periphery.

1 : 11 Splitting big-ends, removing rods and pistons

1 Remove the cylinder head (see **Section 1 : 4**). Drain and remove the sump and oil strainer (see **Section 1 : 8**).
2 The pistons and connecting rods must be withdrawn from the top of the cylinder block. Unlock and remove the big-end bolts and remove the bearing caps (see **FIG 1 : 16**). Release the connecting rod from the crankshaft.
3 Withdraw the piston and connecting rod from the top of the cylinder block and refit the bearing cap.

The big-end bearing caps are offset, and the caps of the big-ends in Nos. 1 and 3 cylinders are interchangeable when new, as are those for Nos. 2 and 4 cylinders. When used parts are replaced after dismantling, it is essential that they are fitted in their original positions. In order to ensure this, mark the caps and connecting rods on the sides which are fitted together with the number of the cylinder from which each was taken.

Refitting of the piston and connecting rod is a reversal of the above procedure, but the piston ring gaps must be set at 180 deg. to each other. Compress the piston rings with service tool 18G.55A and gently tap the crown of the piston with the end of a hammer handle until the piston is clear of the piston ring clamp (see **FIG 1 : 17**).

It is essential that the connecting rod and piston assemblies are replaced in their own bores and fitted the same way round, i.e. with the gudgeon pin clamp screw on the camshaft side of the engine. The piston crowns are marked 'FRONT' to assist correct assembly to the connecting rods.

Refit the big-end bearings in their original positions.

1 : 12 Pistons, rings and gudgeon pins

Piston and connecting rod assembly:

The gudgeon pin is rigidly held in the split little-end of the connecting rod by a clamp bolt engaging the central groove of the gudgeon pin.

Before the piston and gudgeon pin can be dismantled from the connecting rod it is necessary to remove the clamp screw. To enable the assembly to be held in a vice for this operation without damage, holding plugs should be inserted in each end of the gudgeon pin.

Unscrew the gudgeon pin clamp screw and remove it completely. Push out the gudgeon pin.

Reassembly is the reversal of the above operation, but attention must be given to the following points when assembling the piston to the connecting rod.

1 That the piston is fitted the correct way round on the connecting rod. The crown of the piston is marked 'FRONT' to assist this, and the connecting rod must be fitted with the gudgeon pin clamp screw on the camshaft side.

2 That the gudgeon pin is positioned in the connecting rod so that its groove is in line with the clamp screw hole.

3 That the clamp screw spring washer has sufficient tension.

4 That the clamp screw will pass readily into its hole and screw freely into the threaded portion of the little end, and also that it will hold firmly onto the spring washer.

A certain amount of selective assembly must be used when fitting a new gudgeon pin. It must be a thumb fit for three-quarters of its travel, and finally tapped in with a rawhide mallet. This operation must be carried out with the piston and the gudgeon pin cold.

Removing and replacing piston rings:

If no special ring expander is available use a piece of thin steel such as a smoothly ground hacksaw blade or a disused feeler gauge.

Raise one end of the ring out of the groove and insert the steel strip between the ring and the piston (see **FIG 1:18**). Rotate the strip around the piston, applying slight upward pressure to the raised portion of the ring until it rests on the land above the ring grooves. It can then be eased off the piston. Never remove or replace piston rings over the piston skirt, but always over the top of the piston.

Before fitting new rings clean the grooves in the piston to remove any carbon deposit. Care must be taken not to remove any metal, or side play will result between the ring and the groove, with consequent excessive oil consumption and loss of gas-tightness. The correct clearance of the ring in the groove is .002 to .004 inch (.051 to .102 mm).

The second and third compression rings are tapered and marked 'T' (top) for correct assembly.

Pistons and rings are available in .010, .020, .030 and .040 inch (.254, .508, .762 and 1.016 mm) oversizes, and when fitting new rings it is advisable to test them in the cylinder bore to ensure that the ends do not butt together. To do this, insert the piston approximately 1 inch into the cylinder bore, insert the ring above it, and press it down onto the top of the piston to ensure that the ring is square with the bore. The gap between the piston ring ends may now be measured with a feeler gauge and should be between .008 to .013 inch (.20 to .33 mm) for 1489 cc engine, or .012 to .017 inch (.305 to 432 mm) for 1622 cc engine.

Piston sizes and cylinder bores:

In production, pistons are fitted by selective assembly, and to facilitate this the pistons are stamped with identification figures on their crowns.

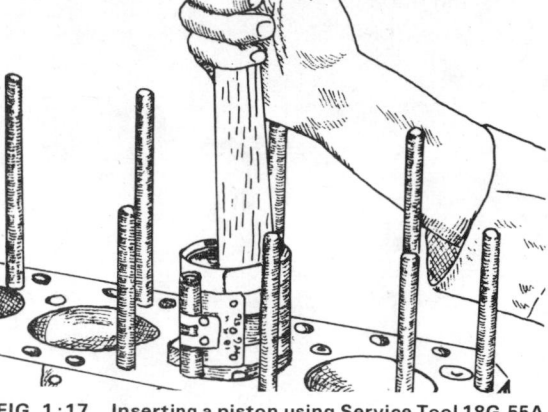

FIG 1:17   Inserting a piston using Service Tool 18G.55A to compress the piston rings

The number enclosed in a diamond, e.g. a piston stamped with a figure 2, is for use with a block having a similar stamp adjacent to the bore.

In addition to the standard pistons there is a range of four oversize pistons available, i.e. .010, .020, .030 and .040 inch oversize.

Oversize pistons are marked with the actual oversize dimensions enclosed in an ellipse. A piston stamped .020 is only suitable for a bore .020 inch (.508 mm) larger than the standard bore, similarly, pistons with other markings are only suitable for the oversize bore indicated.

The piston markings indicate the actual bore size to which they must be fitted, the requisite running clearance being allowed for in the machine.

After reboring engine, or whenever fitting pistons differing in size from those removed during dismantling ensure that the size of the piston fitted is stamped clearly on the top of the cylinder block alongside the appropriate cylinder bore.

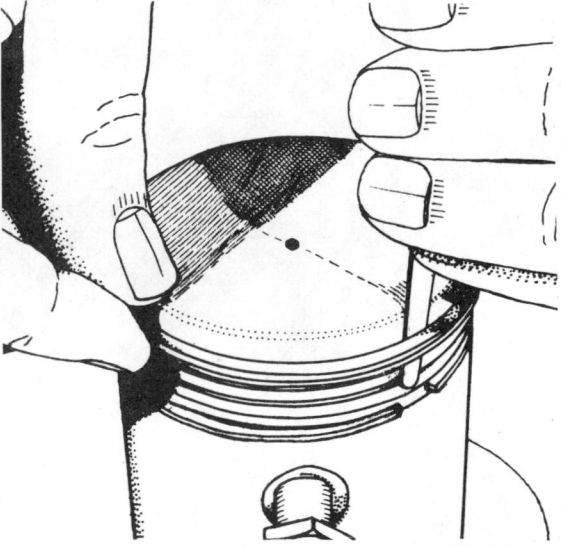

FIG 1:18   Removing a piston ring using a disused feeler gauge

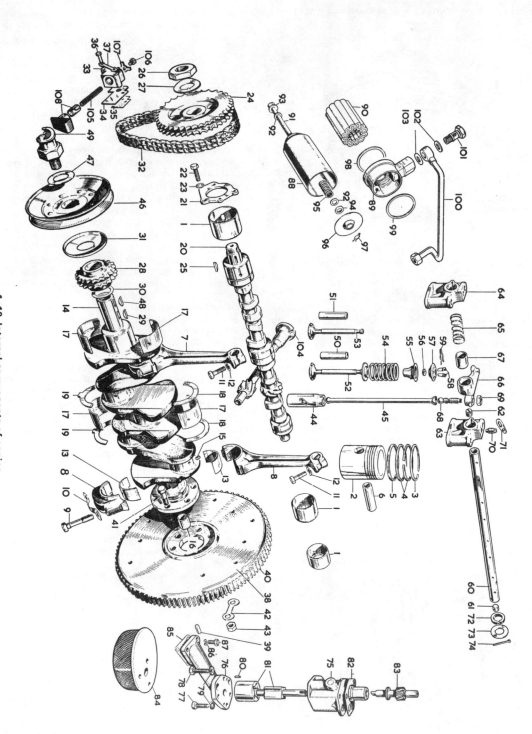

1 : 19 Internal components of engine

20

Key to Fig 1:19
1 Liner—camshaft bearing
2 Piston
3 Ring—compression—top
4 Ring—compression—2nd and 3rd
5 Ring—scraper
6 Pin—gudgeon
7 Connecting rod and cap for Nos. 1 and 3 cylinders
8 Connecting rod and cap for Nos. 2 and 4 cylinders
9 Screw for cap
10 Washer for screw (locking)
11 Screw—clamping
12 Washer for screw (spring)
13 Bearing—connecting rod
14 Crankshaft
15 Restrictor—oil
16 Bush—first motion shaft
17 Bearing—main
18 Washer—thrust (upper)
19 Washer—thrust (lower)
20 Camshaft
21 Plate—camshaft locating
22 Screw—plate to crankcase
23 Washer for screw (shakeproof)
24 Gear—camshaft
25 Key to camshaft gear
26 Nut for gear
27 Washer for nut (locking)
28 Gear—crankshaft
29 Key for crankshaft gear
30 Washer for crankshaft gear (packing)
31 Thrower—oil—crankshaft
32 Chain—timing
33 Tension body—chain
34 Backplate
35 Joint washer for tensioner
36 Screw for tensioner
37 Washer for screw (locking)
38 Flywheel
39 Dowel—clutch to flywheel
40 Ring gear—starting
41 Bolt—flywheel to crankshaft
42 Washer for flywheel bolt
43 Nut for bolt
44 Tappet
45 Pushrod
46 Pulley—crankshaft
47 Washer for starting nut (locking)
48 Key for crankshaft pulley
49 Nut—starting
50 Guide—valve—inlet
51 Guide—valve—exhaust
52 Valve—inlet
53 Valve—exhaust
54 Spring—valve
55 Shroud—valve guide
56 Ring—valve packing
57 Cup—valve spring
58 Cotter for valves (halves)
59 Circlip for valve cotter
60 Shaft—valve rocker
61 Plug—rocker
62 Plug—rocker shaft (screwed)
63 Bracket—rocker shaft (tapped)
64 Bracket—rocker shaft (plain)
65 Spring—rocker spacing
66 Rocker—valve (bushed)
67 Bush—valve rocker
68 Screw—valve rocker
69 Nut for tappet adjusting screw (locking)
70 Screw—rocker shaft (locating)
71 Plate—locating screw (locking)
72 Washer for rocker shaft—D/C (spring)
73 Washer for rocker shaft
74 Splitpin—rocker shaft
75 Body with plug
76 Cover
77 Screw for cover (short)
78 Screw for cover (long)
79 Washer for screw (spring)
80 Dowel
81 Shaft with rotors—driving
82 Joint—pump to crankcase
83 Spindle—oil pump driving
84 Strainer—oil
85 Joint washer—strainer to oil pump
86 Washer for screw—strainer to pump (spring)
87 Screw—strainer to pump
88 Container—oil filter
89 Head assembly
90 Element
91 Centre bolt
92 Washer—sealing
93 Washer (felt)
94 Washer (steel)
95 Spring
96 Plate—pressure
97 Circlip
98 Joint ring—body to filter head
99 Joint washer—oil filter to crankcase
100 Pipe assembly—filter to crankcase
101 Screw for banjo union
102 Washer for screw (outer)
103 Washer for screw (inner)
104 Spindle—distributor driving
105 Spring—tensioner
106 Bottom plug
107 Tabwasher
108 Chain tensioner

Cylinder liners:

Should the condition of the bore be such that it cannot be cleaned up to accept the recommended oversize pistons, it is possible that dry cylinder liners can be fitted. This operation requires the use of specialized equipment and must be left to a fully equipped service station.

1:13 Crankshaft, big-end and main bearings

Unless the bearing journals are badly worn the big-end bearings may be renewed without removing the crankshaft. To renew the main bearings it is necessary to remove the crankshaft. Liners are used for the main and big-end bearings, which are of the shimless type and therefore non-adjustable. The arrangement of the crankshaft and bearings can be clearly seen in **FIG 1:19**.

Big-end bearings:

Drain the engine oil and remove the sump as detailed in **Section 1:8**.

As the bearings are of the shimless type it is essential that no attempt should be made to adjust bearings that are worn. If the crankshaft journals are found to be in a worn condition, it is advisable to fit a service reground crankshaft, complete with main and big-end bearings, available from service agents.

Both the big-end and main bearing liners are located in position in the bearing housings by a small tag on one side of each half bearing, and it should be noted that the bearings are fitted so that the tags come on the same joint edge of the bearing housing, although on opposite corners.

To detach the big-end bearings, bend down the locking strips so that the bolts may be removed. Remove the connecting rod caps and extract the bearings. Care must be taken to see that the bearing journals, etc. are thoroughly cleaned before installing new bearings. No scraping is required, as the bearings are machined to give the correct diametrical clearance.

Main bearings:

Remove the engine from the vehicle and remove the clutch and flywheel, the timing chain, the sump and strainer, and the rear engine mounting plate.

Remove the self-locking nuts securing the main bearing caps to the cylinder block and the two bolts securing the front cap to the front engine bearer plate.

The removal of the main bearing caps is made easier by the use of the impulse extractor 18G.284 together with the adaptor 18G.284A, shown in use in **FIG 1:20**.

Note that a thrust washer is fitted on each side of the centre main bearing to take the crankshaft end thrust (see **FIG 1:19**). These thrust washers consist of two semi-circular halves, one half having a lug which is located in a recess in the detachable half of the bearing and the other being plain.

When fitting new bearings, no scraping is required as the bearings are machined to give the correct diametrical clearance.

In the case of a 'run' bearing it is always essential to clean out thoroughly all the oilways in the crankshaft and block, wash out the engine base in paraffin and clean the oil pump and oil strainer, to ensure that no particles of whitemetal are left anywhere in the lubrication system.

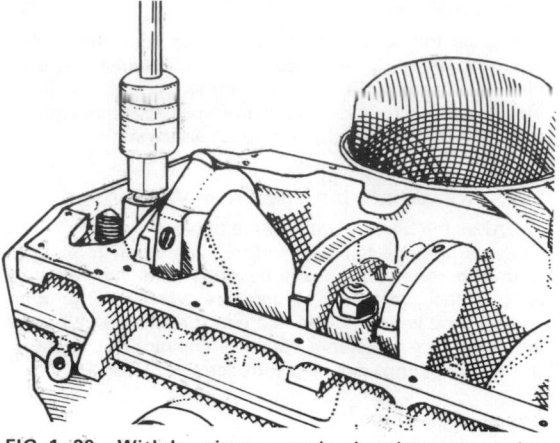

FIG 1:20 Withdrawing a main bearing cap using impulse extractor 18G.284 and adaptor 18G.284A

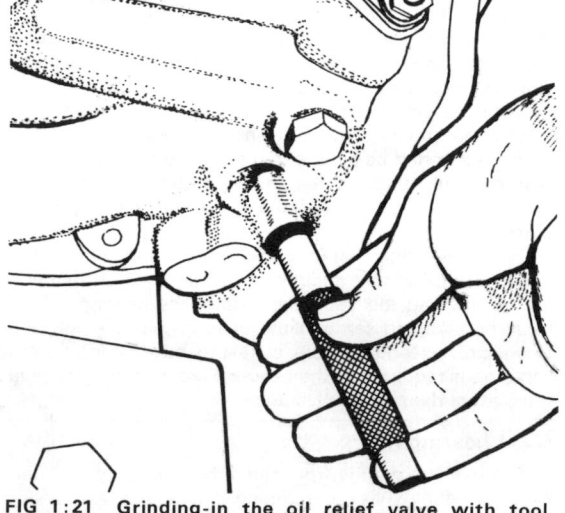

FIG 1:21 Grinding-in the oil relief valve with tool 18G.69

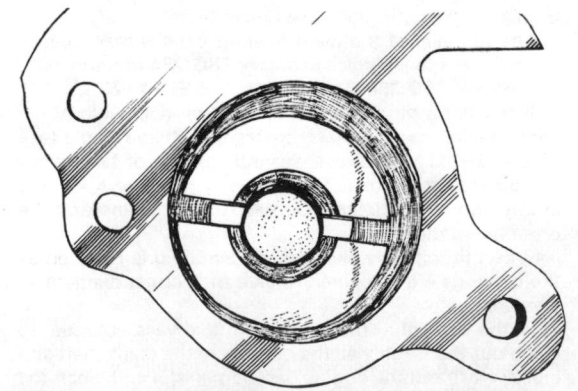

FIG 1:22 Refitting the distributor drive. Note the slot angle with the longer offset uppermost

The rear main bearing cap horizontal joint surfaces should be thoroughly cleaned and lightly covered with 'Wel-Seal' sealing compound before the cap is fitted to the cylinder block. This will ensure a perfect oil seal when the cap is bolted down to the block.

Replace each main bearing cap, replacing the thrust washers in their correct positions at the centre main bearing, with the oil grooves away from the bearing. refit the locking strips or plates to each bearing cap and bend them to lock the bolts after tightening them to the recommended torque of 70 lb ft (9.7 kgm).

The two bolts securing the front main bearing cap to the front bearer plate are locked by a common plate.

Removing and refitting the crankshaft:

With the engine out of the vehicle, take off the clutch and the flywheel, the timing cover, the timing wheels and chain, the sump and oil pump strainer, and finally the rear engine mounting plate.

Disconnect the big-end bearings and remove the main bearing caps. Mark each big-end bearing and bearing cap to ensure that they are replaced onto their correct journals. Take care when marking the bearings that they are not damaged in any way. On no account use a punch for this purpose. Note that each main bearing cap is stamped with a number which is also stamped on the centre web of the crankcase near each main bearing.

Lift the crankshaft out of the bearings.

Replacement is a reversal of these instructions. Do not forget to refit the thrust washers in their correct positions at the centre main bearing with the oil grooves away from the bearings. Also remember the packing washers behind the crankshaft timing chainwheel.

1:14 External oil filter, oil pressure relief valve

Oil filter:

The external oil filter is of the fullflow type, thus ensuring that all oil in the lubrication system passes through the filter before entering the bearings. The element of the filter is of star formation in which a special quality felt, selected for its filtering qualities, is used.

Oil is passed through the filter from the pump at a pressure controlled by a relief valve at 50 lb/sq inch. This pressure will, of course, be somewhat higher until the oil reaches a working temperature. Some pressure is lost in passing the oil through the filter element. This will only be a pound or two per square inch with a new element, but will increase as the element becomes progressively contaminated by foreign matter removed from the oil.

Should the filter become blocked due to neglect, a balance valve is provided to ensure that oil will still reach the bearings. This valve, non-adjustable, is located in the filter head casting. When the valve is opened, unfiltered oil will bypass the filter element and reach the bearings.

Changing the filter element:

The filter element is released by unscrewing the centre fixing bolt and withdrawing the filter complete. Wash out the filter bowl in fuel and allow to dry. Install a new element, ensure that the filter bowl to head joint washer is correctly positioned, clean and serviceable, and replace the filter bowl. Hold the bowl against the spring pressure before finally tightening up the central fixing bolt, and ascertain that the bowl is seating centrally on its seat.

Oil pressure relief valve:

The non-adjustable oil pressure relief valve is situated at the rear of the lefthand side of the cylinder block and is held in position by a domed hexagon nut sealed by two fibre washers. The relief valve spring maintains a valve cup against a seating machined in the block.

The valve should be examined to ensure that the cup is seating correctly and that the relief spring has not lost its tension. This can be checked by measuring the length of the spring, the free length of which should be 2.859 inch (72.638 mm).

The valve seating can be checked by applying engineers blue to the valve surface and testing for continuous marking. Should the seating be damaged, the valve must be lapped in, using service tool 18G.69, (see **FIG 1 : 21**). The small knurled knob on the end of the tool is turned to compress the rubber sleeve and increase the diameter until, when pressed into the valve, it will hold it securely while it is lapped to its seat.

1 : 15 Removing and replacing the distributor drive gear

1 Withdraw the distributor as detailed in **Chapter 3**.
2 Take out the special screw securing the distributor housing to the cylinder block. Using a $\frac{5}{16}$ UNF bolt, $2\frac{1}{2}$ inches or more long as an extractor, screw it into the tapped end of the distributor drive spindle and withdraw the spindle.
3 To refit the drive gear, turn the engine until No. 1 piston is at TDC on its compression stroke. When the valves on No. 4 cylinder are 'rocking' (i.e. exhaust just closing and inlet just opening), No. 1 piston is at the top of its compression stroke. If the engine is set so that the notch in the crankshaft pulley is in line with the longest pointer on the cover, or the 'dimples' in the crankshaft and camshaft gears are in line, the piston is exactly at TDC.
4 Screw the extractor bolt in the threaded end of the distributor drive gear and, holding the drive gear with the slot just below the horizontal position and the large offset uppermost, insert the gear (see **FIG 1 : 22**).
5 As the gear engages with the camshaft the slot will turn in an anticlockwise direction until it is approximately in the one o'clock position.
6 Remove the bolt from the gear, insert the distributor housing and secure it with the special bolt. Ensure that the correct bolt is used and that the head does not protrude above the face of the housing.
7 Refit the distributor (see **Chapter 3**).

1 : 16 Reassembling the stripped engine, valve clearances

All dismantling and reassembling operations have been given in detail in the various Sections, so that it is simply a matter of tackling the tasks in the correct sequence. Always fit new gaskets, which are available in complete sets and always lubricate all running surfaces with clean engine oil.

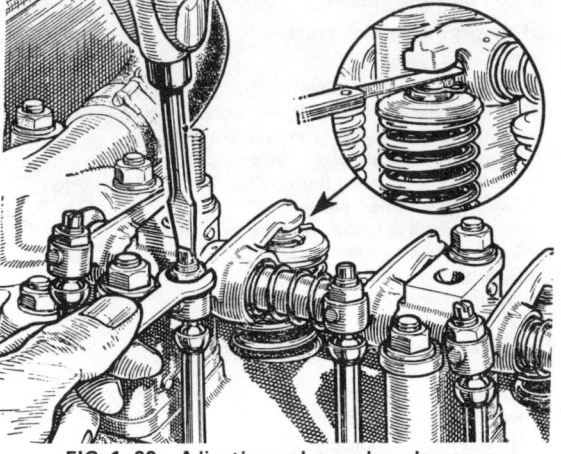

FIG 1 : 23   Adjusting valve rocker clearance

Start by fitting the crankshaft, then the flywheel and clutch. Continue by fitting the connecting rods and pistons, camshaft, timing gear, oil pump, tappets, pushrods, cylinder head and manifolds. Any engine auxiliaries which will not be in the way when fitting the engine back into the car can now be fitted.

Adjusting the valve rocker clearances:

The correct clearance for the exhaust and inlet valves is .015 inch (.38 mm). The engine has been designed to operate with this clearance and no departure from this is permissible. Always set the clearances with the engine cold.

Provision for adjusting the clearance is made in the rocker arm by an adjustable screw and locknut (see **FIG 1 : 23**).

The adjusting screw is released by slackening the hexagonal locknut with a spanner while holding the adjusting screw against rotation with a screwdriver. The valve clearance can then be set by carefully rotating the rocker screw in the desired direction until the correct clearance is obtained, that is, when the feeler gauge can just be pushed between the rocker face and the valve stem. The adjusting locknut is then tightened while the screw is held against further rotation with the screwdriver. Recheck the gap after the locknut has been tightened.

It is important to note that while the clearance is being set, the tappet of the valve being operated on is on the back of its cam, i.e. opposite to its peak. As this cannot be accurately observed, the rocker adjustment is more easily carried out in the following order. This also obviates turning the crankshaft over more than is necessary.

Adjust No. 1 rocker with No. 8 valve fully open.
Adjust No. 3 rocker with No. 6 valve fully open.
Adjust No. 5 rocker with No. 4 valve fully open.
Adjust No. 2 rocker with No. 7 valve fully open.
Adjust No. 8 rocker with No. 1 valve fully open.
Adjust No. 6 rocker with No. 3 valve fully open.
Adjust No. 4 rocker with No. 5 valve fully open.
Adjust No. 7 rocker with No. 2 valve fully open.

It is helpful to remember that each of the above sequences totals nine.

1:17 Fault diagnosis

(a) Engine will not start

1 Defective coil
2 Faulty distributor capacitor (condenser)
3 Dirty, pitted or incorrectly set contact breaker points
4 Ignition wires loose or insulation faulty
5 Water on sparking plug leads
6 Corrosion of battery terminals or battery discharged
7 Faulty or jammed starter
8 Sparking plug leads wrongly connected
9 Vapour lock in fuel lines
10 Defective fuel pump
11 Overchoking
12 Underchoking
13 Blocked petrol filter or carburetter jets
14 Leaking valves
15 Sticking valves
16 Valve timing incorrect
17 Ignition timing incorrect

(b) Engine stalls

Check 1, 2, 3, 4, 10, 11, 12, 13, 14 and 15 in (a)
1 Sparking plugs defective or gaps incorrect
2 Retarded ignition
3 Mixture too weak
4 Water in the fuel system
5 Petrol tank vent blocked
6 Incorrect valve clearance

(c) Engine idles badly

Check 1 and 6 in (b)
1 Air leak at manifold joints
2 Slow-running jet blocked or out of adjustment
3 Air leak in carburetter
4 Over-rich mixture
5 Worn piston rings
6 Worn valve stems or guides
7 Weak exhaust valve springs

(d) Engine misfires

Check 1, 2, 3, 4, 5, 8, 10, 13, 14, 15, 16, 17 in (a); 1, 2, 3 and 6 in (b)
1 Weak or broken valve springs

(e) Engine overheats (see Chapter 4)

(f) Compression low

Check 14 and 15 in (a), 5 and 6 in (c) and 1 in (d)
1 Worn piston ring grooves
2 Scored or worn cylinder bores

(g) Engine lacks power

Check 3, 10, 11, 13, 14, 15, 16 and 17 in (a); 1, 2, 3 and 6 in (b); 5 and 6 in (c) and 1 in (d). Also check (e) and (f)
1 Leaking joint washers
2 Fouled sparking plugs
3 Automatic advance not operating

(h) Burnt valves or seats

Check 14 and 15 in (a); 6 in (b) and 1 in (d). Also check (e)
1 Excessive carbon around valve seat and head

(j) Sticking valves

Check 1 in (d)
1 Bent valve stem
2 Scored valve stem or guide
3 Incorrect valve clearance

(k) Excessive cylinder wear

Check 11 in (a) and see Chapter 4
1 Lack of oil
2 Dirty oil
3 Piston rings gummed up or broken
4 Badly fitting piston rings
5 Connecting rods bent

(l) Excessive oil consumption

Check 5 and 6 in (c) and check (k)
1 Ring gaps too wide
2 Oil return holes in piston choked with carbon
3 Scored cylinders
4 Oil level too high
5 External oil leaks
6 Ineffective valve stem oil seals

(m) Crankshaft and connecting rod bearing failure

Check 1 in (k)
1 Restricted oilways
2 Worn journals or crankpin
3 Loose bearing caps
4 Extremely low oil pressure
5 Bent connecting rod

(n) Internal water leakage (see Chapter 4)

(o) Poor water circulation (see Chapter 4)

(p) Internal corrosion (see Chapter 4)

(q) High fuel consumption (see Chapter 2)

(r) Engine vibration

1 Loose generator bolts
2 Fan blades out of balance
3 Incorrect clearance for front engine mounting rubbers
4 Exhaust pipe mountings too tight

CHAPTER 2

THE DIESEL ENGINE

2:1 Description

The BMC 1.5 litre diesel engine is offered as an alternative to the petrol engines described in **Chapter 1**. It is of the indirect injection type, using CAV Pintaux type injectors, with a bore of 2.875 inch (73 mm) and stroke of 3.5 inch (88.9 mm), and gives a maximum torque of 64 lb ft at 1900 rev/min on a compression ratio of 23:1.

The pistons are aluminium with three compression and two oil control rings, the crown being specially shaped to suit the characteristics of the Ricardo Comet V combustion chambers.

The camshaft is side mounted and driven by a double roller chain with a slipper-type tensioner. Valve gear is conventionally operated by pushrods and transverse rockers.

The CAV fuel injection pump is driven by the camshaft through a shaft and gear mounted transversely in the crankcase. The AC fuel lift pump is also driven by the camshaft through a rocker and supplies the injection pump through an external paper filter.

Lubrication follows conventional lines with an eccentric rotor oil pump driven by the camshaft and a fullflow externally mounted oil filter.

To meet the heavy demands of the diesel engine a Lucas pre-engaged type of starter is fitted, and to assist starting in cold weather, heater plugs are fitted to each cylinder. Cut-away and exploded views of the engine are given in **FIGS 2:1** and **2:2**.

2:2 Removing and replacing the engine

A number of maintenance and servicing operations which will be described can be carried out with the engine still in the car, but they may also be part of an extensive overhaul for which engine removal is necessary, so it may be convenient to describe the procedure for removing the engine first.

Fasten the sliding doors in the fully open position and remove the seats and the under-seat inspection plates. Lift off the engine cowling.

Disconnect the battery cables and remove the battery. Disconnect the stop control cable and outer casing from the fuel injection pump. Release the battery cable from the starter and from its clips on the bulkhead.

Remove the engine cowling floor base. Drain the cooling system. On later vehicles with an expansion tank, disconnect the pipe from the radiator neck. Remove the fan blades and pulley. Disconnect the radiator upper tie bars. Remove the radiator lower support brackets or disconnect the radiator from the former. Release the hose clips and remove the radiator.

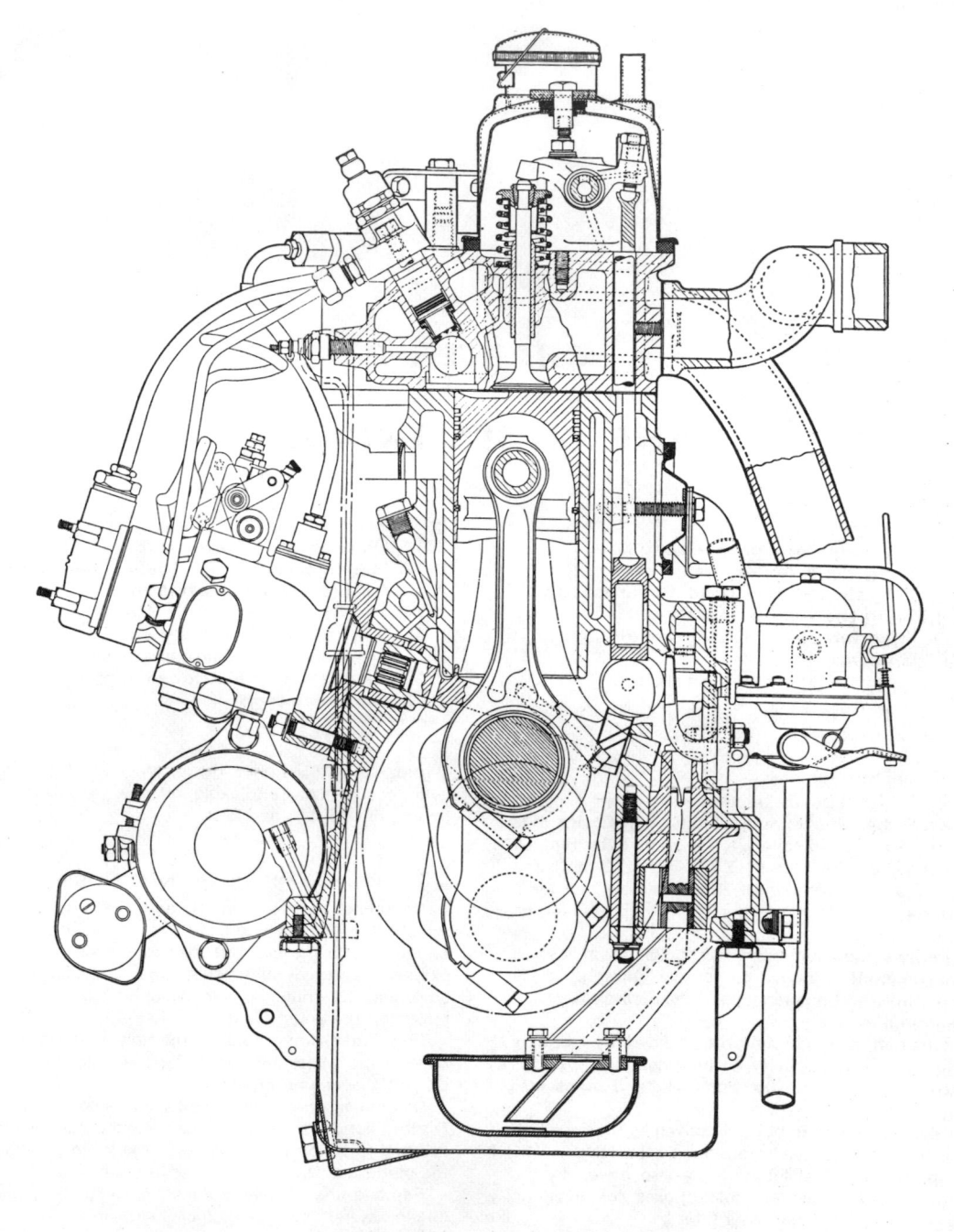

FIG 2:1 The diesel engine. Transverse section

Release the breather pipe from the rocker cover (early vehicles) or from the tappet side cover (later vehicles) and completely remove the air cleaner from the vehicle.

Disconnect the accelerator cable and heater connections (when fitted). Disconnect the fuel feed pipe to the lift pump and the leak-off pipe from the fuel filter.

Remove the wiring from the generator, starter, heater plugs, oil pressure and temperature gauge units.

Disconnect the exhaust down-pipe and remove the starter.

Support the gearbox on a jack and remove all the bell-housing bolts.

Preferably using a jib crane through the passengers doorway, attach sling brackets to the two lifting bolts on the rocker cover and take the weight of the engine. Remove the engine mounting bolts.

Swing the engine forward to remove the first motion shaft then withdraw the engine as shown in **FIG 1 : 4**.

The engine is refitted by reversing the above procedure but it may be made easier if more room to manoeuvre is obtained by removing the fuel filter, fuel lift pump and gearchange remote control shaft.

2 : 3 Removing the cylinder head

Manifolds:

Support the inlet manifold and unscrew the four manifold securing nuts. Remove the plain and large clamp washers from the manifold securing studs and withdraw the inlet manifold. Note that the exhaust manifold must be released to free the large washer on the foremost stud.

The exhaust manifold and gasket can be lifted off after the two remaining nuts with plain washers have been removed.

When refitting, make sure that all traces of the old jointing are removed, and use a new gasket. Do not forget to fit the foremost manifold clamp washer at the same time as the exhaust manifold is fitted.

Rocker shaft assembly:

Unscrew the two nuts securing the rocker cover withdraw the engine lifting brackets, cup washers and sealing bushes. Lift off the cover, taking care not to damage the cork gasket.

Support the main fuel filter and remove two bolts and nuts, and two set bolts securing the filter to the bracket and the bracket to the cylinder head nuts.

Slacken the fourteen cylinder head nuts a turn at a time in the order shown in **FIG 2 : 3**, noting that a special spanner 18G.694 is available to use on the three nuts located under the rocker shaft. This is necessary as four of the shaft retaining nuts also serve to retain the cylinder head and will prevent distortion of the head due to uneven retention.

Remove these four nuts and also the remaining four nuts securing the rocker shaft brackets, noting the rocker shaft retaining screw lock plate under the righthand nut on the rear bracket. Remove the rocker shaft complete with rockers and brackets.

Replacement of the rocker shaft is a reversal of the above procedure, tightening the cylinder head nuts to a torque of 71 lb ft. Do not omit to check and adjust rocker clearances before refitting the cover.

Withdraw the eight pushrods, storing them so that they may be replaced in their original positions.

Disconnect the fuel feed pipes from the injectors and the injection pump and remove the pipes complete with clamps and damper bushes. It is important to seal off the pump and injector unions to prevent the entry of foreign matter. Sealing caps 18G.216 are available for this purpose.

Remove the ten remaining cylinder head retaining nuts and lift the head vertically over the studs.

NOTE: The cylinder head joint face is machined with the combustion chamber inserts installed. As they were a loose fit in the head, they should be removed and clearly labelled to ensure replacement in their original positions.

When reassembling, which is a reversal of the above, ensure that the surface of both cylinder head and block are clean. A new gasket should be used and if it is the copper asbestos type both sides should be coated with Hylomar SQ32 jointing compound. The later, compound type, gasket is fitted dry. Note also that the gasket is marked FRONT and TOP.

On completion, start up the engine and run until it is thoroughly warm for a few minutes, then stop and retighten the cylinder head nuts (71 lb ft). This will probably necessitate a further adjustment of the rocker clearances.

2 : 4 Servicing the cylinder head. Decarbonizing

Valve rocker shaft assembly:

Remove the rocker shaft locating screw from the rear mounting bracket.

Withdraw the splitpin and washers from each end of the rocker shaft and slide off the rockers, brackets and spacing springs, carefully noting their position on the shaft. Unscrew the plug from the front end of the shaft.

Thoroughly clean all components with paraffin and dry. Clear all oilways in brackets, shaft and rockers with compressed air.

To reassemble, commence with the rear bracket and secure the shaft in position, ensuring that the dowel end of the locating screw properly engages the locating hole in the shaft. Although the rockers and brackets are interchangeable, used parts should always be returned to their original position.

Valves removal and replacement:

Detach the circlips from the valve spring cap retainers (see **FIG 2 : 4**). Compress the valve springs as shown and detach the two valve cap retainers (split collets). Release the spring compressor and remove the valve spring cap, valve guide shroud, valve oil seal, inner and outer valve springs and valve spring lower collar.

On removal from the head, it is important to store the valves in such a way that they will be replaced in their original position. This may conveniently be achieved by using a sheet of cardboard with small holes numbered from 1 to 8 through which to insert the valve stems.

Replacing a valve is a reversal of the removal procedure but do not omit to fit a new oil seal to the valve stem in the bottom of the spring cap retainer groove. The seal will be easier to install if well soaked in engine oil.

Due to the limited clearance between the crowns of the pistons and the cylinder head joint face when the pistons

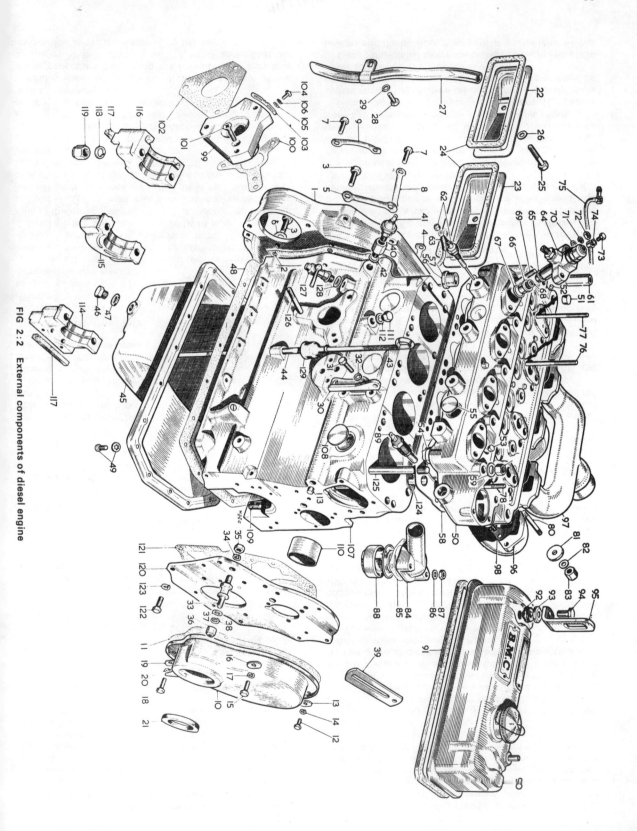

FIG 2:2 External components of diesel engine

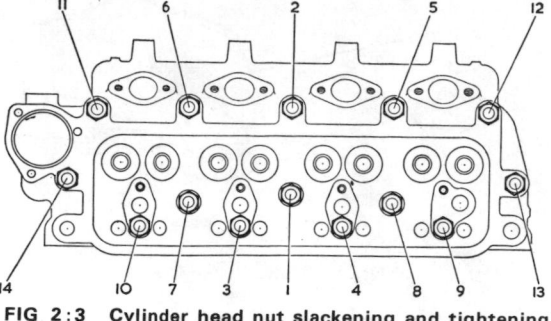

FIG 2:3 Cylinder head nut slackening and tightening sequence

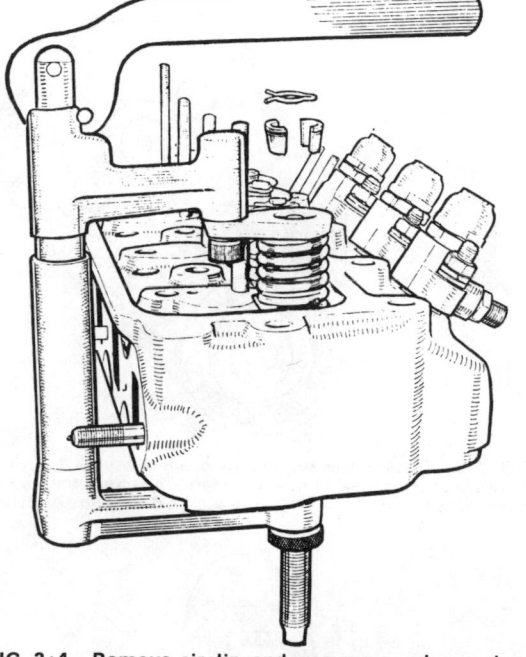

FIG 2:4 Remove circlip and compress valve springs with tool 18G.45

are at TDC it is essential that the top faces of the valve heads 'stand down' .018 to .038 inch (.46 to .96 mm) as indicated in **FIG 2:5**. A 'stand down' clearance greater than that specified may affect engine performances and the valve should be renewed.

When fitting new valves, the requisite 'stand down' is obtained by refacing or grinding-in the valves.

Decarbonizing:

Having withdrawn the valves, plug the waterways in the cylinder head and the block with clean rag to prevent the entry of foreign matter, then scrape the carbon deposits from the piston crown and the cylinder head. A blunt screwdriver which will not scratch the metal will be suitable.

By inserting an old piston ring into the bore and resting on the top of the piston, a ring of carbon can be

Key to Fig 2:2   1 Gearbox distance piece   2 Joint washer for distance piece   3 Screw for distance piece   4 Locking washer for distance piece   5 Locking washer for screw   6 Locking washer for screw   7 Screw for distance piece   8 Locking washer for screw   9 Locking washer for screw   10 Crankcase front cover   11 Joint washer for front cover   12 Screw for front cover to front plate   13 Washer plate for screw   14 Spring washer for screw   15 Screw for front cover and washer plate to crankcase   16 Washer plate for screw   17 Spring washer for screw   18 Screw for front cover to bearing cap   19 Washer plate for screw   20 Spring washer for screw   21 Crankshaft oil seal   22 Crankcase side cover   23 Cylinder side cover—front   24 Joint washer for side cover   25 Screw for side cover   26 Washer for screw   27 Crankcase vent pipe   28 Screw for vent pipe clip   29 Plain washer for screw   30 Dynamo rear bracket   31 Screw for dynamo bracket   32 Spring washer for screw   33 Pillar for dynamo adjusting link   34 Spring washer for pillar   35 Nut for pillar   36 Nut for link to pillar   37 Plain washer for nut   38 Spring washer for nut   39 Dynamo adjusting link   40 Oil pressure switch adaptor   41 Oil pressure switch   42 Washer for switch adaptor   43 Oil level indicator   44 Guide tube for oil level indicator   45 Sump   46 Drain plug for sump   47 Washer for drain plug   48 Joint washer for core support hole   49 Screw assembly for sump   50 Cylinder head   51 Plug for water jet boss and air vent   52 Plug for oil hole   53 Plug for core support hole   54 Plug for core support hole   55 Welch plug   56 Combustion chamber insert   57 Ball for insert   58 Joint washer for cylinder head   59 Washer for cylinder head stud   60 Nut for cylinder head stud   61 Pillar for fuel filter bracket   62 Heater plug   63 Connection for heater plug   64 Fuel injector assembly   65 Joint washer for injector nozzle holder   66 Heat shield for injector nozzle   67 Washer for heat shield   68 Seal washer for injector atomizer   69 Stud for injector nozzle holder   70 Plain washer for stud   71 Spring washer for stud   72 Nut for stud   73 Banjo bolt for injector leak-off pipe   74 Washer for banjo bolt   75 Fuel leak-off pipe for injectors   76 Short stud for rocker bracket   77 Long stud for rocker bracket   78 Stud for water outlet elbow   79 Stud for air and exhaust manifold   80 Stud for air and exhaust manifold   81 Clamp washer for air and exhaust manifold   82 Plain washer for air and exhaust manifold   83 Nut for air and exhaust manifold   84 Water outlet elbow   85 Joint washer for water outlet elbow   86 Plain washer for stud   87 Nut for stud   88 Thermostat   89 Thermal transmitter   90 Valve rocker cover   91 Joint washer for valve rocker cover   92 Rubber bush for valve rocker cover   93 Cup washer for valve rocker cover   94 Cap nut for valve rocker cover   95 Engine sling bracket   96 Exhaust manifold   97 Air inlet manifold   98 Joint washer for air and exhaust manifold   99 Hub for fuel injection pump   100 Joint washer for injection pump hub   101 Screw for injection pump hub   102 Joint washer for fuel injection pump   103 Timing indicator   104 Screw for injection pump   105 Plain washer for screw   106 Spring washer for screw   107 Cylinder and crankcase assembly   108 Welch plug   109 Main bearing stud   110 Camshaft front bearing liner   111 Joint washer for plug   112 Washer for plug   113 Plug for oil gallery   114 Cap for rear main bearing   115 Cap for centre main bearing   116 Cap for rear main bearing   117 Joint for front and rear main bearing cap   118 Spring washer for main bearing cap stud   119 Nut for main bearing cap stud   120 Engine front mounting plate   121 Joint washer for mounting plate   122 Screw for front mounting plate   123 Spring washer for screw   124 Long stud for cylinder head   125 Short stud for cylinder head   126 Stud for injection pump   127 Water drain tap   128 Washer for drain tap   129 Dust cap for oil level indicator

FIG 2:5 Checking valve 'stand-down' from cylinder head face

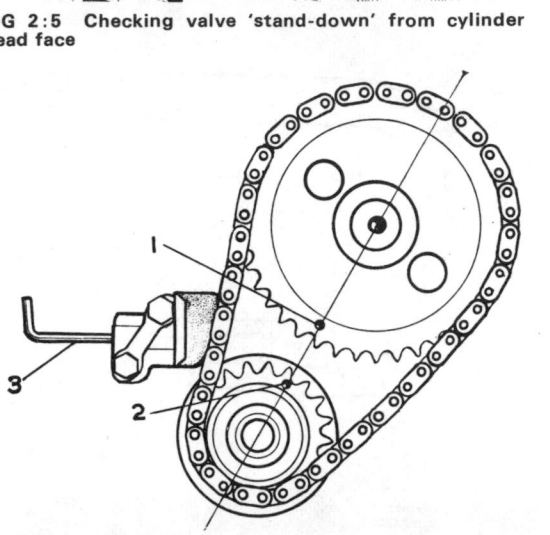

FIG 2:6 Rotate the engine to bring dimples **1** and **2** in line before removing chain wheels. The chain tensioner is retracted by turning Allen key **3** in a clockwise direction

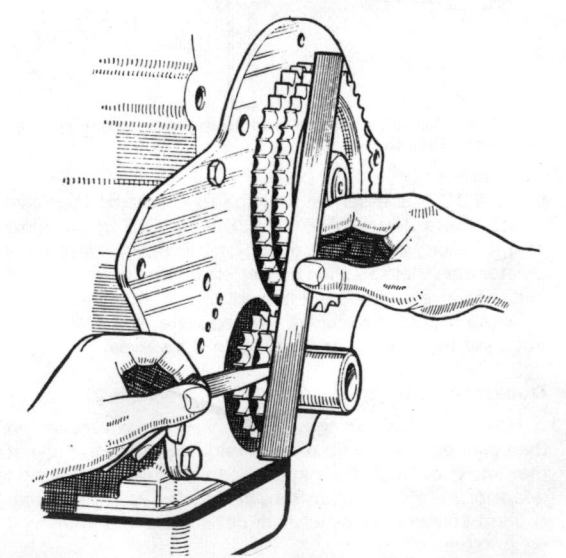

FIG 2:7 Checking chainwheel alignment with straight-edge

left round the piston crown. The rim of carbon round the top of each bore should also be left untouched.

Remove the carbon deposit from the valves, guides, ports and cylinder head. It should not be necessary to clean the spherical combustion chambers as the heat of combustion will prevent any build-up on the walls.

Valve grinding:

Accurate valve seating is of paramount importance in a compression ignition engine if good compression, and therefore performance, is to be maintained.

Clean the valves thoroughly and examine the face for signs of pitting. Any badly pitted valve should be either renewed or replaced by a service station if a suitable tool is not available. Badly worn valve seats should also be trued up with suitable cutting tools.

Normal wear on valves and seats can be made good by grinding with carborundum paste as described in the previous chapter, **Section 1:5**.

Adjusting valve rocker clearances:

This is carried out in the same way as on the petrol engine and is described in **Chapter 1, Section 1:16**. The correct clearance for both inlet and exhaust valves is .015 inch (.381 mm) with the engine cold.

2:5 Removing the timing gear

Remove the fan and generator drive belt. Press back the locking washer for the starting handle dog and unscrew it from the crankshaft. Using a suitable puller, withdraw the crankshaft pulley.

Remove the nine setscrews and washers securing the front cover and lift it off together with the joint washer. Put the oil thrower from the end of the crankshaft on one side for safety.

Remove the oil seal from the front cover and remove all traces of jointing from the joint faces.

Press back the lockwasher and unscrew the plug from the base of the chain tensioner body, insert a $\frac{1}{8}$ inch Allen key and turn it in a clockwise direction to retract the slipper. Remove two set bolts and withdraw the tensioner assembly with backplate and washer.

Check the tensioner body for ovality and if more than .003 inch (.076 mm) the complete unit must be replaced. If only the slipper head is worn a new head and cylinder assembly can be fitted to the body.

Before removing the timing chain, turn the engine until the timing marks on the chainwheels are in the positions shown in **FIG 2:6**. This will permit reassembly without rotating either the camshaft or crankshaft.

It must be noted that valves and pistons may foul each other if either shaft is turned after the timing chain has been removed. If rotation of the crankshaft or camshaft is necessary, the rocker shaft assembly should be removed.

Knock back the lockwasher and unscrew the nut securing the camshaft chainwheel. Remove the lockwasher noting that its locating tag fits into the camshaft chainwheel keyway.

The camshaft and crankshaft chainwheels, together with the chain, may now be levered forward a little at a time and removed. If it should be required to remove the packing washers located on the crankshaft behind the chainwheel, the two half-moon keys must first be withdrawn.

If new camshaft or crankshaft components are fitted it will be necessary to re-align the wheels. To determine the thickness of packing washers required, assemble and secure the two chainwheels to their respective shafts. Press them both to the rear to take up any end float and place a straightedge across the camshaft wheel teeth and measure with a feeler gauge the gap between the straightedge and the crankshaft chainwheel teeth (see **FIG 2:7**). Subtract .005 inch (.13 mm) from the feeler gauge reading and add the resultant thickness of crankshaft gear packing washer.

Refitting:

When refitting the timing chain and wheels, ensure first that the keys in the crankshaft and camshaft are in the 12 o'clock and 1 o'clock positions respectively as seen from the front. Assemble the wheels into the chain and then on to the shafts with the two dimples positioned as shown in **FIG 2:6**. A slight rotation of the camshaft is permissible to secure correct alignment of the camshaft key and chainwheel keyway. Secure the camshaft chainwheel with its nut and lockwasher.

Before refitting the chain tensioner, make sure that the oilways through the spigot and slipper are clear by blowing through with compressed air.

After fitting, check the slipper head for freedom of movement then release the tensioner by turning the Allen key in a clockwise direction until the head moves forward under spring pressure against the chain. Do not attempt to turn the key anticlockwise or force the head into the chain. Secure the bolts with the locking plate, replace the plug and lock with the tabwasher.

Insert a new seal into the crankcase front cover with the lip of the seal facing inwards, packing the inner groove of the seal with grease to provide initial lubrication. Fit the oil thrower on the crankshaft with its concave side facing away from the engine.

Fit a new joint washer and place the front cover in position and at this stage tighten the securing screws with the fingers only. Centralise the cover using tool 18G.3 for early engines and 18G.1046 for later engines, and then tighten the front cover screws (see **FIG 2:8**).

Remove the centralizing tool, fit the crankshaft pulley and the remainder of the parts in reverse order from dismantling.

2:6 Fuel injection pump driving spindle

Remove the fuel injection pump as described in **Chapter 4**, then unscrew the countersunk securing screw and withdraw the fuel injection pump hub and joint washer from the crankcase.

The driving spindle is withdrawn from the crankcase turning it in a clockwise direction to disengage it from the skew gear on the camshaft.

Before refitting the drive spindle the engine must be turned to bring No. 1 piston to a point 22 deg. BTDC on its compression stroke. This is done by means of the timing disc, or mark, on the crankshaft pulley and the pointer, or degree plate, on the under side of the front cover (see **FIG 2:9**).

Note that the timing disc has two sets of marks graduated in 5 deg. divisions and it is the set with the zero point identified by 1.4 which is used for this operation.

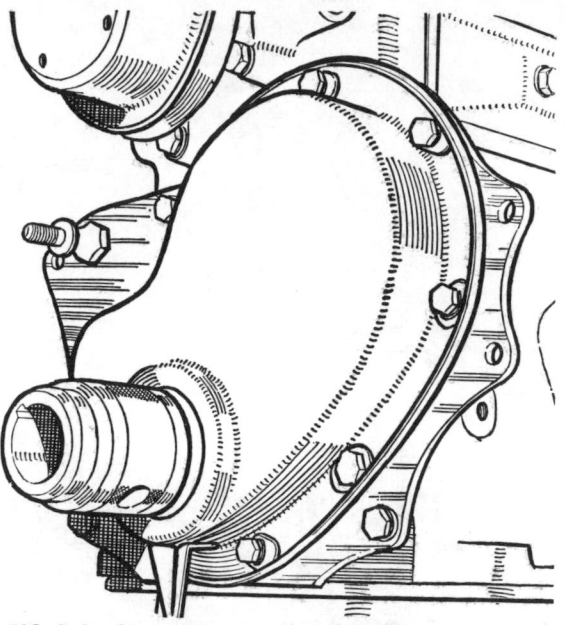

FIG 2:8 Centralizing front cover using tool 18G.3 for early engines and tool 18G.1046 for later engines

Turn the engine until the inlet valve of No. 1 cylinder is closed, which indicates the commencement of the compression stroke and then continue slowly until 22 deg. BTDC is shown on the scale as in the illustration. Insert the fuel injection pump driving spindle into the crankcase with the master spline of the spindle in the 7 o'clock position. As it engages the skewgear the spindle will turn slightly anticlockwise until the master spline is at 5 o'clock.

Refit the fuel injection pump hub using a new joint washer and replace the pump.

FIG 2:9 Timing mark and timing plate. Inset shows timing disc and pointer fitted to early engines

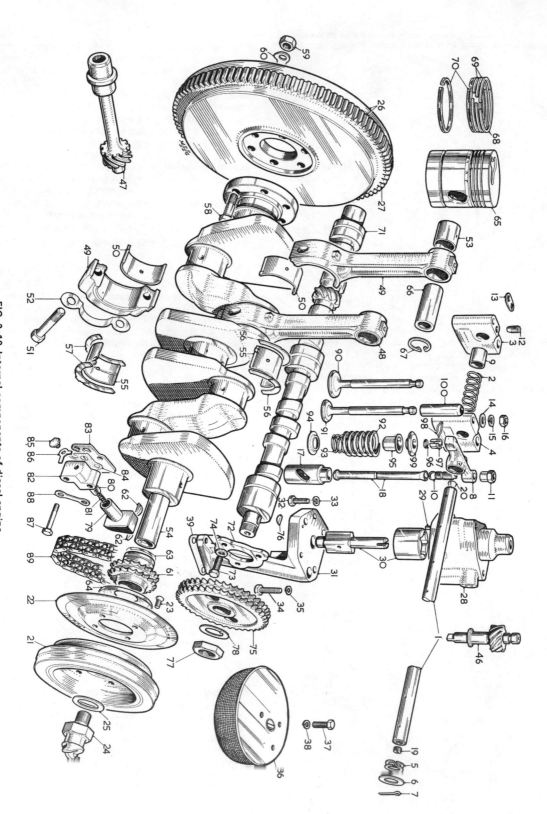

FIG 2:10 Internal components of diesel engine

Key to Fig 2:10
1 Valve rocker shaft
2 Rocker spacing spring
3 Rocker bush
4 Rocker bracket—plain
5 Spring washer—double-coil
6 Rocker shaft washer
7 Split cotterpin
8 Valve rocker
9 Valve rocker bush
10 Tappet adjusting screw
11 Adjusting screw locknut
12 Rocker shaft
13 Locking plate for locating screw
14 Plain washer for rocker bracket stud
15 Spring washer for rocker bracket stud
16 Nut for rocker bracket stud
17 Tappet
18 Pushrod
19 Screwed plug for locating screw
20 Plain plug for rocker shaft
21 Crankshaft pulley and vibration damper
22 Timing disc
23 Screw for timing disc
24 Starting nut
25 Lockwasher for starting nut
26 Plain plug for rocker shaft
27 Starter ring
28 Oil pump body
29 Dowel
30 Oil pump rotor assembly
31 Oil pump cover
32 Setscrew—short
33 Spring washer
34 Setscrew—long
35 Spring washer
36 Oil strainer
37 Setscrew
38 Spring washer
39 Joint washer for oil strainer
46 Oil pump driving spindle
47 Fuel injection pump driving spindle
48 Connecting rod assembly—Nos. 1 and 3
49 Connecting rod and cap—Nos. 2 and 4
50 Connecting rod bearing
51 Bolt for connecting rod cap
52 Lockwasher for bolt
53 Bush for connecting rod little-end
54 Crankshaft
55 Crankshaft main bearing
56 Crankshaft thrust washer—upper
57 Crankshaft thrust washer—lower
58 Bolt for flywheel
59 Nut for flywheel bolt
60 Lockwasher for nut
61 Crankshaft gear
62 Crankshaft gear and pulley key
63 Crankshaft gear packing washer
64 Crankshaft oil thrower—front
65 Piston
66 Gudgeon pin
67 Circlip for gudgeon pin
68 Piston ring—No. 1—compression
69 Piston ring—No.s 2 and 3—compression
70 Piston ring—Nos. 4 and 5—oil control
71 Camshaft
72 Camshaft locating plate
73 Screw for locking plate
74 Shakeproof washer for screw
75 Camshaft gear
76 Key for camshaft gear
77 Nut for camshaft gear
78 Lockwasher for nut
79 Timing chain tensioner slipper head
80 Cylinder for chain tensioner
81 Spring for chain tensioner
82 Body for chain tensioner
83 Tensioner backplate
84 Joint washer for tensioner body
85 Plug for tensioner body
86 Lockwasher for plug
87 Bolt for tensioner
88 Lockwasher for bolt
89 Timing chain
90 Inlet valve
91 Exhaust valve
92 Outer valve spring
93 Inner valve spring
94 Valve spring bottom collar
95 Valve guide shroud
96 Valve packing ring
97 Valve cotter
98 Circlip for valve cotter
99 Valve spring cap
100 Valve guide

2:7 The camshaft

To remove the camshaft it is first necessary to remove the fuel injection pump and drive, the sump, oil pump and driving spindle, the valve rocker shaft assembly, pushrods and tappets, the fuel lift pump, the crankcase front cover and the timing gear. Instructions for these operations will be found under the appropriate headings (see **FIG 2:10**).

Unscrew the three screws and shakeproof washers to release the camshaft retaining plate and then carefully withdraw the camshaft from the front.

Before reassembly, which is a reverse of the dismantling procedure, fit the retaining plate and chainwheel to the camshaft and measure the end float between the retaining plate and the thrust face of the camshaft front journal. This should be between .003 and .007 inch (.76 to .178 mm) and if it is excessive the retaining plate should be renewed.

2:8 Removing the sump and oil strainer

Remove the plug on the righthand side of the sump and drain off the oil into a suitable container. Remove the nineteen securing bolts and washers and detach the sump. Clean with paraffin and allow to dry.

The oil strainer is secured to the base of the oil pump by three setscrews and spring washers. Remove and clean it in paraffin using a stiff brush to remove the sludge from the gauze.

When refitting the strainer, use a new joint washer.

Before refitting the sump inspect the front and rear main bearing cap cork sides and the sump to crankcase joint washer. If they are in good condition they may be used again, but it is advisable always to use a new sump, washer. After cleaning off all traces of old jointing, smear the crankcase joint face with grease and place the joint washer in position. Fit the sump, tightening the screws in sequence, starting at the centre and working outwards.

2:9 The oil pump

After removing the sump and oil strainer as described in **Section 2:8**, remove the three securing nuts and washers and withdraw the pump and its joint washer.

The oil pump driving spindle cannot be extracted until the fuel injection pump and its driving spindle have been removed as described in **Section 2:6**.

The cover of the oil pump, which is located on the base by two dowels, can be removed after taking out the two securing screws, and then the rotors are removed and all the parts washed in paraffin and checked for wear.

1 Fit the rotors in the body and measure the distance between their top face and the underside of a straight edge laid across the joint face of the pump body. This should not exceed .005 inch (.127 mm). In some cases an excees may be remedied by removing the dowels and lapping the joint face of the pump body.

2 Check the diametrical clearance between the outer rotor and the rotor pocket in the pump body. If this exceeds .01 inch (.254 mm) and cannot be remedied by fitting a new body or rotors, a complete new pump assembly must be fitted.

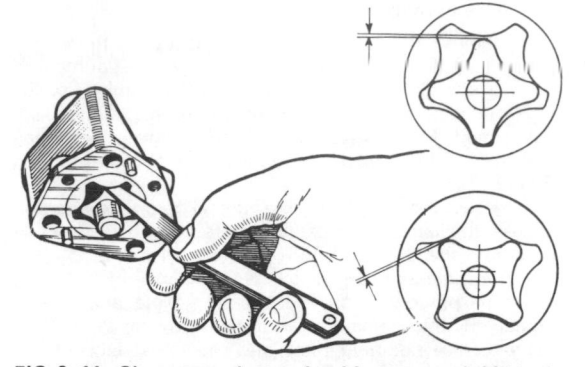

FIG 2:11 Clearances shown should not exceed .006 inch (.152 mm)

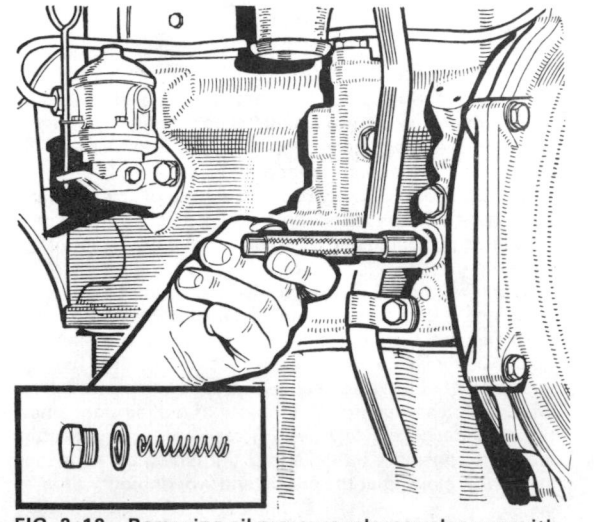

FIG 2:12   Removing oil pressure release valve cup with tool 18G.69

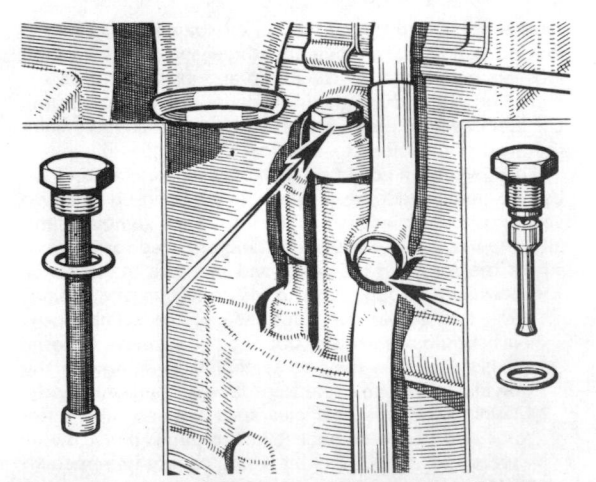

FIG 2:13 Showing location of lubricator and filter for fuel injection pump driving gear on left side of crankcase

3 With the rotors installed, measure the clearances shown in **FIG 2:11** and renew the rotors if the distance is more than .006 inch (.152 mm).

Reassembly is a reverse of the above, noting that all parts should first be dipped in clean engine oil and that the outer rotor is fitted with its chamfered end at the driving end in the pump body.

2:10 External oil filter

This is of the fullflow type with a star shaped felt element. Oil is fed to the filter from the pump at a pressure controlled at 50 lb/sq in by the oil pressure release valve, but this pressure will decrease as the filter element becomes progressively contaminated with foreign matter removed from the oil.

Should the filter become completely choked, a balance valve is provided which will open at a pressure difference of 15 to 20 lb/sq in and bypass the filter allowing the oil to flow unfiltered to the oilways in the engine.

The filter element should be renewed at every engine oil change. To do this, unscrew the centre bolt and withdraw the bowl complete with element. Remove the circlip from the central bolt and dismantle the bowl and its components which should be washed in petrol and allowed to dry.

Reassemble the bowl ensuring that the felt washer fitted between the pressure plate and the spring washer is in good condition.

Fit a new filter element, see that the bowl sealing washer is positioned correctly in the filter head, prime the filter with clean engine oil and refit.

2:11 Oil pressure release valve

This is non-adjustable and is situated at the rear, left-hand side of the crankcase as shown in **FIG 2:12**.

During major overhauls, or if oil pressure is low and all else is known to be in good condition, the release valve should be removed and examined to see that the cup is seating correctly and the spring has not lost its tension. If the valve cup is scored or worn it should be renewed.

The spring is checked by measuring its length. This should be 2.859 inch (72.64 mm) when free and 2.156 inch (54.77 mm) at $31\frac{1}{2}$ lb (6.12 kg) load.

The valve seating should be checked and if necessary lapped in using Tool 18G.69.

2:12 Fuel injection pump driving gear lubricator

The fuel injection pump driving gear is pressure lubricated through a lubricator and filter gauze, both of which are screwed into tappings in the main feed passage from the oil pump on the lefthand side of the engine (see **FIG 2:13**).

The lubricator and filter should be taken out and cleaned in petrol at every other engine oil change. A stiff brush should be used to clear the sludge from the gauze and the lubricator blown clear with compressed air.

It will be necessary first to detach the crankcase vent pipe. This is done by unscrewing the setscrew securing the lower end of the vent pipe and then, with a twisting movement, pulling the pipe downwards to detach it from the elbow on the engine rear side cover.

When replacing, make sure that the copper joint washers are in good condition and make an oil tight seal.

2:13 Pistons and connecting rods

These can only be withdrawn from the top of the cylinder block, so it is necessary first to remove the cylinder head and the sump as described earlier in **Section 2:3** and **2:8**. Remove the big-end bearing cap bolts and lift off the cap. Push the connecting rod and piston upwards and pull out of the bore. In order not to misplace the cap, this should be refitted to the rod.

It will be noted that the big-end bearings are offset in the connecting rods: Nos. 1 and 3 are offset towards the rear, Nos. 2 and 4 towards the front.

It will also be seen that in order to ensure that these assemblies are always returned to their original positions, each rod and cap is marked with its cylinder number as shown in **FIG 2:14**.

Gudgeon pins:

Remove the two circlips and press the pin out, after marking both pin and piston for refitting. Check both the gudgeon pin and the little end bush for wear and renew if necessary.

New gudgeon pins should be fitted by selective assembly. At a room temperature of 68°F (20°C) it should be a hard hand push fit. Note that the combustion cavity in the piston crown is on the same side of the connecting rod as the oil jet hole in the big-end bearing.

Piston rings:

These may be removed by means of an old feeler gauge by levering up one end and resting the raised portion on the land above the ring groove while sliding the blade around the piston.

Carefully clean any carbon deposit from the grooves without removing any metal before refitting the rings.

No. 1 compression ring is chrome plated and Nos. 2 and 3 are tapered but carry the word TOP to indicate the upper surface.

When refitting new rings they should be checked first for the correct gap by pushing them squarely down the bore on top of a piston into an unworn part of the bore where the gap is measured with a feeler gauge. If necessary the gap can be opened by careful use of a file. See **Technical Data** for the correct ring gaps.

Pistons:

New pistons are fitted by selective assembly and identification figures are stamped on the piston crowns. Oversize pistons are marked with the actual oversize dimensions, and a piston marked .020 is suitable only for a bore .020 inch larger than standard.

After a rebore or if pistons differing in size from those removed from the engine are fitted do not omit to stamp on the top face of the block the size of the piston fitted in each bore.

A standard piston is suitable for a bore of 2.8757 to 2.8760 inch (73.043 to 73.050 mm). The following oversizes are available: + .010, .020, .030, .040 inch (.254, .508, .762, 1.016 mm).

As mentioned earlier it is essential to refit an original piston in its original bore and also that all pistons are fitted the same way round, i.e. the combustion cavity in the piston crown and the oil jet hole in the big-end bearing must be on that side of the engine opposite to the camshaft.

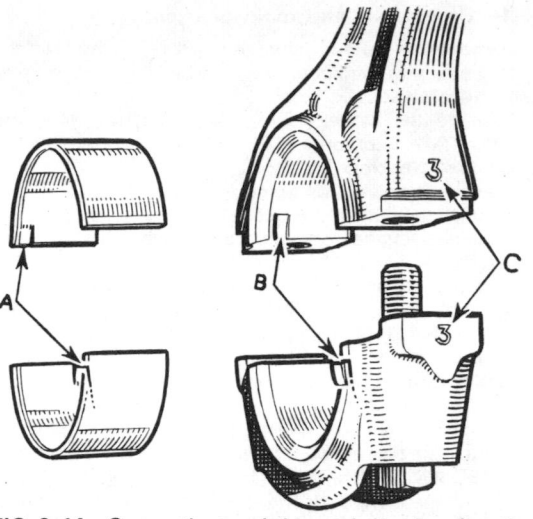

FIG 2:14 Connecting rod big-end bearing locating tags **A** and grooves **B**. Cylinder number is shown at **C**

It is also important when installing a piston in its bore that the piston ring gaps are set at 180 deg. to each other and, in the absence of a ring compressor, that great care is taken not to break a ring during the operation.

New lockwashers should always be used and the big-end bearing bolts tightened to a torque of 35 lb ft.

2:14 The flywheel

To remove the flywheel it is necessary first to remove the starter motor then unlock and remove the six nuts securing the flywheel to the crankshaft.

The flywheel may now be driven off the crankshaft flange and the six bolts using a hammer with a piece of hardwood to take the blow on the front face of the flywheel. As the front face of the flywheel is accessible only through the starter motor aperture in the engine rear distance piece, it is necessary to turn the flywheel through 90 deg. after each blow to keep the flywheel square with the securing bolts.

To remove the flywheel bolts the sump must be removed and the rear main bearing cap withdrawn.

When reassembling, crank the engine until the 1/4 zero mark on the timing disc mounted on the crankshaft pulley is in line on the pointer located under the crankcase front cover. Nos. 1 and 4 are now at TDC and the flywheel should be fitted with the TDC 1/4 mark at the top. Tighten the securing nuts to a torque of 37 lb ft.

2:15 The gearbox distance piece

Remove the starter and the flywheel, then press back the locking plate tabs and unscrew the securing bolts, noting the positions of the lockplates to assist when reassembling. The use of a hide mallet may be necessary to ease the distance piece off the two locating dowels.

Clean all joint faces and examine the distance piece, particularly around the dowel holes, for burrs which should be carefully removed with a scraper.

Refitting is a reversal of the removal procedure, tightening the bolts to a torque of 20 lb ft for the $\frac{5}{16}$ inch and 30 lb ft for the $\frac{3}{8}$ inch bolts.

2:16 Crankshaft and main bearings

Remove the fan and generator belt (see **Chapter 6**).

Remove the crankcase front cover and timing gear (see **Section 2:5**).

Remove the starter motor (see **Chapter 14**), the flywheel (see **Section 2:14**) and the gearbox distance piece (see **Section 2:15**).

Remove the sump, oil pump and strainer.

Slacken the nuts securing the fuel injectors sufficiently to release engine compression when rotating the crankshaft.

Remove the rocker shaft assembly (see **Section 2:3**) to prevent fouling of valves and pistons. Take out the pushrods and store them as mentioned in **Section 2:3**.

Disconnect the connecting rods from the crankshaft (see **Section 2:13**) and push each rod and piston up to the top of its bore as soon as it is disconnected.

Remove the six self-locking nuts and spring washers from the main bearing cap studs. Withdraw the caps using tool 18G.42A with adaptor 18G.42B noting the lower halves of the crankshaft thrust washers on each side of the centre main bearing cap. This cap is stamped FRONT to assist on reassembling.

Lift the crankshaft out of the crankcase and remove the upper halves of the crankshaft thrust washers.

Remove the bearing liners from the bearing caps and housings in the crankcase, marking them for later replacement. Do not use a punch for this purpose.

The bearing liners are located in their housings by a small tag on one side of the liner engaging a corresponding groove in the bearing housing and cap.

If a bearing is found to have run, it is most important to ensure that any traces of the run metal are removed from the oilways and filters by cleaning thoroughly with petrol or paraffin and blowing through with compressed air.

Thoroughly clean the thrust faces of the crankshaft centre main journal, the bearings and thrust washers and fit them in the crankcase. Mount a dial gauge on the front end of the crankcase and by pressing the crankshaft backwards and forwards measure the shaft end float. This should be between .002 and .003 inch (.051 to .076 mm).

Crankshaft end float is taken on thrust washers at the centre main bearing and adjustment is made by fitting new thrust washers at this point for which an oversize of .003 inch (.076 mm) is available. Note that the oil grooves on the washers must face outwards towards the crankshaft webs.

When installing new bearings no scraping is necessary as they are machined to give the correct clearance.

Reassembly is a reversal of the dismantling procedure with particular reference to the following:

The two timing wheels must be lined up if any crankshaft components have been changed, as described in **Section 2:5**.

The rear main bearing cap joint should be treated with Hylomar SQ32 jointing compound.

The correct torque for the main bearing cap nuts is 70 lb ft and for big-end bolts 35 lb ft.

Remove the fuel injection pump and check, and adjust if necessary, the timing of the injection pump as described in **Chapter 4**.

2:17 Reassembling a stripped engine

All dismantling and reassembly operations have been covered in earlier Sections, so this is simply a matter of carrying out the various operations in the correct sequence. Before commencing, a complete set of gaskets should be obtained together with a supply of special washers, circlips, splitpins, etc., which should always be renewed after dismantling. Make sure that all oilways are clear and that all running surfaces are lubricated with clean engine oil as assembly proceeds.

Start by installing the crankshaft, pistons, connecting rods and flywheel. Insert the camshaft, fit the oil pump and bolt on the sump. Now turn the engine right way up and fit the tappets and then the cylinder head and valve gear. Fit the timing wheels and chain and replace the front cover. Fit the crankshaft pulley and starting dog.

The engine can now be replaced in the vehicle and all the external components added such as starter, generator and carburetter (if not fitted with the cylinder head) and the associated piping and wiring.

2:18 Fault diagnosis

(a) Engine will not start
1 Incorrect starting procedure
2 Starter motor defective
3 Battery discharged
4 Heater plug circuit broken
5 Foreign matter in fuel system
6 Fuel supply restricted
7 Loss of compression
8 Injector settings incorrect
9 Injector spray hole blocked

(b) Engine stalls
1 Slow-running wrongly adjusted
2 Injector setting incorrect
3 Injectors blocked
4 Loss of compression

(c) Lack of power, rough running
1 Broken valve spring
2 Tappet clearances incorrect
3 Burnt valve
4 Broken piston rings
5 Uneven compression
6 Injectors burnt, nozzle valve not seating
7 Fuel injection pump wrongly timed
8 Fuel supply restricted
9 Injectors loose
10 Lift pump defective

(d) Engine overheats
1 Cooling system defective
2 Lubrication system defective
3 Injectors defective
4 Incorrect injection timing
5 Restricted fuel supply

(e) Low oil pressure
1 Pump defective
2 Release valve not seating
3 Worn bearings
4 Incorrect or insufficient oil

CHAPTER 3

THE PETROL FUEL SYSTEM

3:1 Fuel Pump

The fuel pump, which may be referred to as the lift pump to distinguish it from the fuel injection pump, is bolted to the lefthand side of the cylinder block and is operated mechanically from an eccentric on the camshaft as will be seen from the sectioned drawing in **FIG 3:1.**

A hand priming lever is included for use if the system has been emptied for any reason.

An alternative type may be fitted, but the following instructions for the AC-Delco pump will be basically suitable for both types.

Removal and dismantling:

Remove the lefthand seat and the inspection plate beneath it. Disconnect the two fuel pipes from the pump. Unscrew the two bolts securing the pump and lift off.

Unscrew the centre bolt and lift off the filter bowl cover. Remove the filter gauze 2 and the cork gasket then remove the six screws securing the upper and lower portions of the pump body and separate them after marking for later assembly.

Remove the screw and take out the valve plate and the two valves 1 and 4 not forgetting the gasket.

To remove the diaphragm 14 and pullrod assembly 11, rotate the diaphragm clockwise through 90 deg. and lift it out. This also releases the diaphragm spring 13.

Remove the two rocker pin clips and push out the rocker arm pivot pin 9 and so release the pin washers, the rocker arm 7 and the spring 6.

Remove the springs and rod from the priming lever 12 and body assembly.

Further dismantling is not advised unless parts are to be renewed.

Clean all parts thoroughly and inspect for wear or damage, renewing as required. All gaskets should be renewed and so should the diaphragm assembly unless it is seen to be in entirely sound condition.

Reassembly:

This is a reversal of the dismantling procedure, noting the following points:

The rocker arm pin should be a tap fit in the body, but if wear has loosened it a little, the ends of the holes should be burred over slightly.

When installing the diaphragm assembly, first place the diaphragm with the locating tab at 11 o'clock as shown in

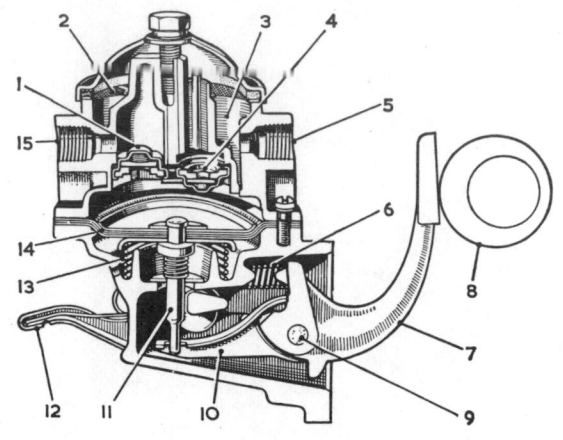

FIG 3:1   Fuel lift pump components, AC-Delco

Key to Fig 3:1   1 Delivery valve   2 Filter gauze
3 Sediment chamber   4 Suction valve   5 Inlet
6 Rocker arm spring   7 Rocker arm   8 Camshaft eccentric
9 Pivot pin   10 Link   11 Pullrod   12 Hand priming lever
13 Diaphragm spring   14 Diaphragm   15 Outlet

FIG 3:2. Press down and turn the diaphragm through 90 deg. as shown by the dotted lines. This action will allow the pullrod to engage the fork in the link and will line up the fixing holes with the body flanges.

Make sure that the two body halves are in the same position as before and tighten the securing screws in rotation while holding the diaphragm at the top of its stroke by pushing the rocker arm away from the pump.

Lubricate the moving parts and rocker arm end before fitting and do not omit to use a new pump to block gasket.

Testing:

The operation of the pump can be checked by disconnecting the outlet pipe and turning the engine. There should be a good squirt of petrol at every other revolution.

3:2 Fuel tank

This is mounted towards the rear of the floor assembly. A dome type air vent is fitted on top of the tank and a combined drain plug and filter is fitted underneath.

Removal:

Place a suitable receptacle in position and remove the drain plug and filter. Disconnect the electric cable from the fuel gauge tank unit.

Remove the tank filter neck and hose by releasing the two hose clips. Remove the rubber seal from the neck. Disconnect the fuel supply pipe from the tank union.

Support the tank while taking out the four bolts securing it to the floor. Then withdraw the tank downwards.

The tank should be cleared of any sediment by flushing out with petrol and then checked for rusting. If rust is present in any quantity it is best to renew the tank.

Always use new gaskets when refitting—which is a reversal of the above—and also a rubber sealing ring when installing the filler neck extension.

3:3 Solex carburetter type B26 HN

This carburetter, which is fitted to 1489 cc engines is a compact horizontal type with the choke tube above the float chamber which it is claimed makes it suitable for operation at high tilt angles. A semi-automatic strangler is provided for cold starting.

Starting—refer to FIG 3:3:

The strangler is operated by a lever connected by a flexible cable to the cab control knob. To start from cold the knob is pulled fully out, thus closing the strangler valve 1 and at the same time, by means of the fast idle cam, opening the throttle 6 a predetermined amount for a satisfactory fast idle.

As soon as the engine starts and runs the rise in the manifold depression causes the poppet valve 16 to open and so admit a quantity of air for the purpose of securing a suitably rich mixture to prevent the engine stalling whilst warming up.

As the engine warms up the strangler control should be progressively pushed in until at operating temperature it is fully home and the enrichment system out of use.

Removal and dismantling:

Take out the lefthand seat and the inspection plate underneath. Remove the air cleaner.

Disconnect the accelerator control rod from the throttle lever, and the cable from the strangler lever.

Disconnect the fuel feed pipe from behind the air cleaner base plate and remove the vacuum pipe from the body of the choke tube.

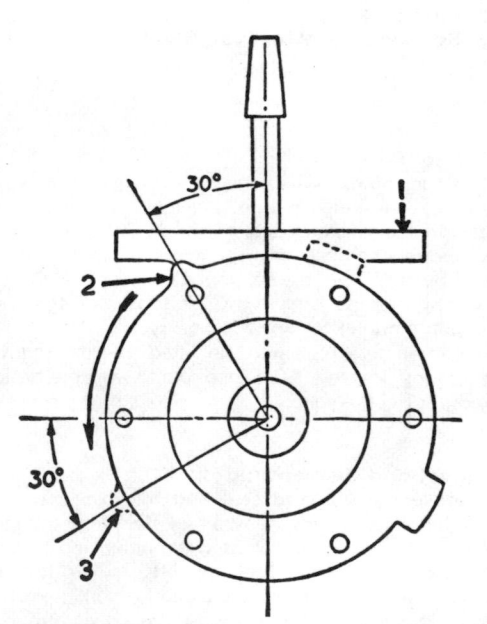

FIG 3:2   Fuel pump—fitting the diaphragm

Key to Fig 3:2   1 Pump mounting flange   2 Initial position of diaphragm locating tab   3 Final position of diaphragm locating tab

Remove the two nuts securing the carburetter to the inlet manifold and lift it off together with the joint gasket.

Observe absolute cleanliness in handling the carburetter components and if reference is made to **FIG 3:3** no difficulty should be experienced in dismantling the instrument.

Clean all parts thoroughly in petrol and examine for wear or damage, particularly the float assembly and the butterfly throttle parts. Wear or distortion here can cause starting problems and poor idling. Replacement of the faulty parts is the best cure.

Check on all air passages and jets. Clean them by blowing compressed air through. **NEVER** use a wire, pin or similar instrument as the soft metal is easily scratched and the delicate calibration may be upset.

Reassembly:

This is a reversal of dismantling, remembering to renew all joint washers and seals and being careful not to use excessive force in tightening up jets or nuts and bolts.

Idling adjustment:

This must be carried out with the engine at normal operating temperature.

Reference to **FIG 3:4** will show the two screws by which the adjustment is made. Set the slow-running screw so that the engine speed is about 500 rev/min, noting that clockwise rotation of the screw increases the engine speed and vice versa. Then adjust the volume control screw to obtain the most even running of the engine, noting that this may alter the engine speed to necessitate a resetting of the slow-running screw.

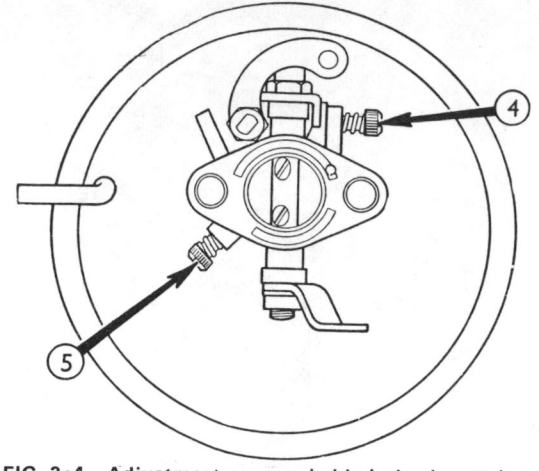

FIG 3:4 Adjustment screws behind air cleaner baseplate, type B26.HN

Key to Fig 3:4   4 Slow-running screw   5 Volume control screw

If, after making this adjustment, the engine is speeded up and the throttle closed quickly resulting in a stall, the cure is usually a slight increase in the engine speed setting or the mixture strength. Note that unscrewing the volume control screw has the effect of richening the mixture.

3:4 Solex carburetter type 30 AHG

This type of carburetter is fitted as standard to 1622 cc engines and is shown broken open in **FIG 3:5**. It is a conventional horizontal type, but has a different method of mixture enrichment from that described earlier in **Section 3:3**.

The so-called bi-starter device is a disc valve controlled chamber operated by a lever which rotates a spring-loaded disc with holes which register with petrol ducts through which fuel enters and passes into the air-way below the throttle butterfly.

This device has three positions: shut, open and an intermediate position obtained by moving the control knob halfway where a suitably rich mixture is provided for warming up or driving away without stalling or overchoking.

The construction of this simple carburetter is shown in the illustration and a reference to that together with the following details should be sufficient to enable part replacement or maintenance to be carried out.

Removal:

Remove the lefthand seat box cover and the engine top cowl. Remove the air cleaner.

Disconnect the accelerator control rod from the throttle lever and the cable from the bi-starter lever. Disconnect the fuel feed pipe and the vacuum ignition control pipe.

Remove the two securing nuts and lift off the carburetter and gasket.

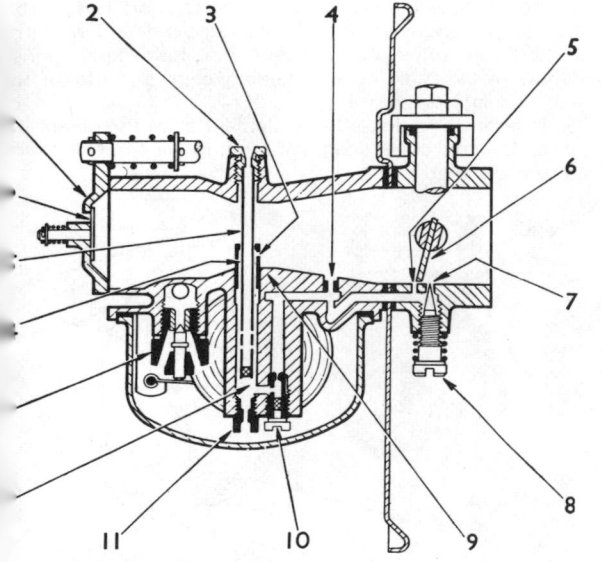

FIG 3:3   Solex carburetter type B26.HN

Key to Fig 3:3   1 Strangler valve   2 Correction jet   3 Orifices   4 Pilot jet air bleed   5 Bypass   6 Throttle   7 Orifice   8 Volume control screw   9 Choke tube   10 Pilot jet   11 Main jet   12 Pressure well   13 Needle valve   14 Main spraying well   15 Emulsion tube   16 Poppet valve

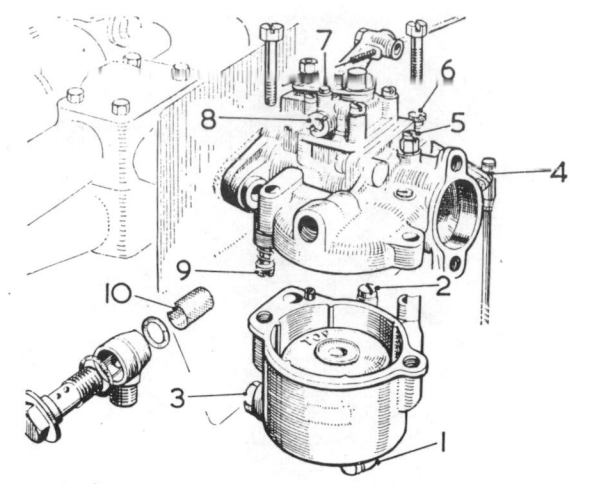

FIG 3:5   Solex carburetter type 30.AHG

Key to Fig 3:5   1 Main jet carrier   2 Auxiliary jet
3 Starter fuel jet   4 Throttle lever   5 Air correction jet
6 Slow-running adjustment screw   7 Bi-starter   8 Starter
air jet   9 Volume adjustment screw   10 Filter gauze

Dismantling:

Very little dismantling should be necessary beyond that required for occasionally cleaning the carburetter.

All jets apart from the auxiliary jet, are fitted externally and are easily reached. The emulsion tube is held in position by the air correction jet and should not be removed as it is carefully set in production.

Access to the float and needle valve is obtained by removing the screws in the float chamber cover and dropping the float chamber as shown. Lift out the float for cleaning. The needle valve assembly is screwed in the float chamber cover and is removed as a complete assembly. It should not be dismantled.

The throttle butterfly assembly is mounted in the throttle chamber and should not require attention other than at long intervals when wear may indicate a renewal.

All the component parts should be cleaned in petrol and examined for wear or damage and all passages and jets blown through with compressed air. Do not omit to clean the gauze filter in the inlet banjo union.

Reassembly:

Reverse the dismantling procedure, renewing all fibre washers and joints. Do not use excessive force when screwing up the jets, reasonable tightness is all that is required.

Slow-running:

This must be adjusted after the engine has been allowed to warm up to working temperature.

The slow-running screw 6 limits the closing of the throttle and so the idling speed of the engine. Turning the screw in a clockwise direction increases the engine speed and vice versa.

The volume control screw 9 is provided to vary the mixture strength. Screwing it in weakens the mixture and unscrewing will richen it.

Set the slow-running screw to give an engine speed of about 500 rev/min and then adjust the volume control screw to give the smoothest possible running. If this changes the engine speed, reset the slow-running screw as necessary to keep the idling speed at the required figure. The ideal setting is when the engine is turning at the slowest speed, consistent with smooth running.

3:5 Air cleaners

Oil-wetted:

Air cleaners and silencers of this type are fitted to 1489 cc engines and should be removed for cleaning at intervals as recommended in the Owners Handbook, although more frequent attention is desirable when the car is operating under very dusty conditions.

Access is obtained by taking out the lefthand seat and the inspection plate underneath. Detach the breather pipe from the rocker cover on early vehicles, on later vehicles from the tappet side cover, undo the centre screw of the element retaining plate and withdraw the element. Release the spring clips from the carburetter backplate and withdraw the cleaner body.

The interior of the body should be wiped clear of any deposits and the wire gauze element washed in petrol and dried before dipping in clean engine oil, drained and reinstalled.

Dry element:

This type of cleaner, shown in **FIG 3:6** is fitted on 1622 cc engines, and a new element should be fitted at the mileages recommended in the Owners Handbook.

The passengers seat must be removed and also the battery on some models and the inspection panel. Unfasten the three cover retaining clips and lift off the cover complete with element.

Take out, and discard, the element from the cover and clean both the cover and the mounting plate before fitting a new element.

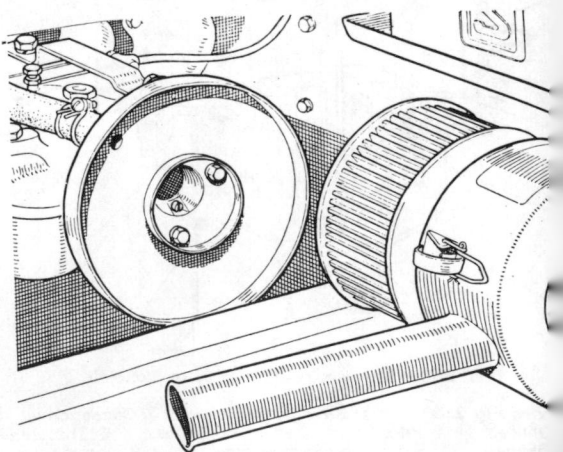

FIG 3:6   Dry element air cleaner, showing one of three cover retaining clips

3:6 Fault diagnosis

(a) Leakage or insufficient fuel delivered

1 Air vent in tank restricted
2 Petrol pipes blocked
3 Air leaks at pipe connections
4 Pump or carburetter filters blocked
5 Pump gaskets faulty
6 Pump diaphragm defective
7 Pump valves sticking or seating badly
8 Fuel vaporizing in pipelines due to heat

(b) Excessive fuel consumption

1 Carburetter needs adjusting
2 Fuel leakage
3 Sticking controls or choke device
4 Dirty air cleaner
5 Excessive engine temperature
6 Brakes binding
7 Tyres under-inflated
8 Idling speed too high
9 Car overloaded

(c) Idling speed too high

1 Rich fuel mixture
2 Carburetter control sticking
3 Slow-running screws incorrectly adjusted
4 Worn carburetter throttle valve

(d) Noisy fuel pump

1 Air leaks on suction side and at diaphragm
2 Obstruction in fuel pipe
3 Clogged pump filter

(e) No fuel delivery

1 Float needle stuck
2 Electric pump connections faulty
3 Electric pump contacts dirty
4 Pipeline obstructed
5 Vent in tank blocked
6 Pump diaphragm stiff or damaged
7 Inlet valve in pump stuck open
8 Bad air leak on suction side of pump

NOTES

CHAPTER 4

THE DIESEL FUEL SYSTEM

4 : 1 Description

The fuel is drawn from the supply tank by a mechanical lift pump driven by an eccentric on the camshaft and delivered to the fuel injection pump, which is of the CAV distributor type.

Since it is imperative that the fuel delivered to the injectors is absolutely free from any foreign matter, the filtration of the fuel is performed by no less than three separate filters. These are gauze type elements in both the fuel lift and injection pumps and a paper element type in the feed line between the two pumps.

The injectors which are of the pintle type include an auxiliary hole to provide a fine spray into the hottest area of the combustion chamber to ensure good starting under the coldest conditions, especially when used with the heater plugs which are fitted.

The accelerator pedal operates the control lever on the injection pump, which also includes a governor and automatic advance unit, both of which are hydraulically operated.

4 : 2 The fuel lift pump

This pump, which is similar to the conventional camshaft driven petrol pump, is mounted on the lefthand side of the crankcase and includes a hand priming lever to permit pumping of fuel to vent the system of air whenever necessary. The fuel enters from the supply tank into a sediment chamber before passing through a gauze filter and the suction valve into the pumping chamber when it is forced on to the main filter and the injection pump.

Later vehicles have a slightly different pump, but the following instructions will be found basically satisfactory for the later type.

Removing and dismantling (see FIG 4:1):

Unscrew the two fuel pipe unions and remove the two nuts securing the pump to the crankcase. Lift off the pump and its gasket.

Before commencing to strip the pump clean it thoroughly and mark the upper and lower body flanges as a guide when reassembling.

Remove the central bolt with its fibre washer and lift off the domed cover and its sealing ring 2. Remove the filter gauze 1.

Unscrew the six setscrews and separate the two halves of the pump body.

Remove the screws to release the valve retaining plate from the upper half of the body and lift out the inlet and outlet valves 18 and 4. Carefully remove the valve gasket.

Press down lightly on the centre of the diaphragm 5 and turn it clockwise through 90 deg. to release the pull-rod 14 from the operating link fork 12 and withdraw the diaphragm assembly and return spring 6.

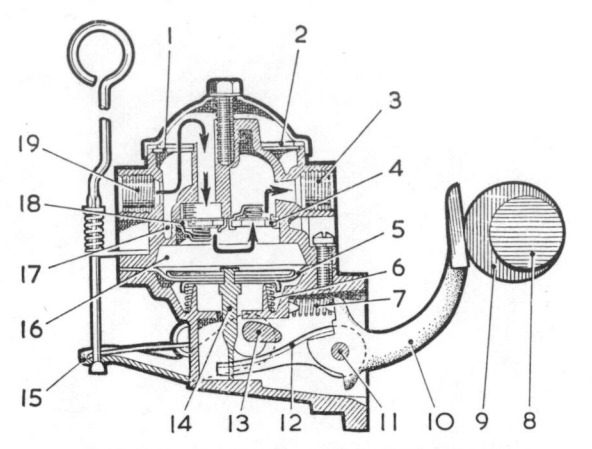

FIG 4:1 Section through fuel lift pump

Key to Fig 4:1   1 Filter gauze   2 Sealing ring
3 Outlet port   4 Delivery valve   5 Diaphragm
6 Diaphragm spring   7 Rocker arm spring   8 Engine
camshaft   9 Camshaft eccentric   10 Rocker arm
11 Pivot pin   12 Link   13 Priming cam   14 Pullrod
15 Hand priming lever   16 Pumping chamber   17 Sediment
chamber   18 Inlet valve   19 Inlet port

Remove the retaining clips from the ends of the rocker arm pivot pin 11 and press the pin out to release the rocker arm 10, washers, rocker arm spring 7 and link 12. Detach the spring from the priming lever and body assembly.

Further dismantling is not recommended.

Clean all parts and examine for wear or damage, particularly the valve assemblies and the rocker linkage where only a very slight amount of wear can be permitted.

Reassembly:

To install the valves, first place a new gasket in position and then insert the outlet valve 4, spring end first, into its port. The inlet valve can only be fitted in the correct manner.

The pivot pin for the rocker arm should be a tap fit in the body and if it is looser than this, the holes in the body may be closed by peening to restore the fit.

When fitting the diaphragm assembly ensure that the upper end of the diaphragm return spring is correctly centred in the lower protector washer and place the diaphragm in the pump body with its locating tab in the 11 o'clock position as shown in **FIG 4:2**. Press downwards and turn the diaphragm anticlockwise through 90 deg. to engage the slots in the pullrod with the link fork. This will put the pullrod in the correct working position and also align the holes in the diaphragm with those in the flange of the pump body.

When mating up the two body sections, push the rocker arm towards the pump body until the diaphragm is level with the joint flange. Fit the securing screws finger tight and press the rocker arm right in to position the diaphragm at the bottom of its stroke. Tighten the screws fully in a diagonal sequence.

Before refitting the pump its action may be checked while held in a bath of clean paraffin. Always use a new joint washer and see that the rocker arm movement is well lubricated. It will assist the installation if the engine is turned so as to bring the camshaft with the small side of the eccentric in contact with the rocker arm.

4:3 Main fuel filter

This is mounted at the rear of the cylinder head and consists basically of a paper element in a thin metal canister clamped between the filter head and the base casting (see **FIG 4:3**). Synthetic rubber rings are used to provide seals between the various components.

The head casting is provided with two inlet, two outlet and one vent connections. One outlet connection is not used and is fitted with a blanking plug, while the second inlet connection allows fuel surplus to the injection pump requirements to return to the dirty side of the filter. This connection has a non-return valve to ensure that no unfiltered oil is passed to the injection pump.

An auxiliary pipe joins the vent connection to the injector leak-off pipe to provide continuous air venting of the filter.

The paper element cannot be cleaned in any way. It is intended to be renewed at the recommended intervals.

Removal:

Thoroughly clean the outside of the filter then disconnect the fuel inlet and outlet pipes and the leak-off pipe from the filter head, being careful not to misplace the sealing washers on each side of the banjo union.

Unscrew the two securing bolts and lift away the filter from its bracket.

Make sure that all washers are in good condition when refitting and bleed the system as described in **Section 4:5.**

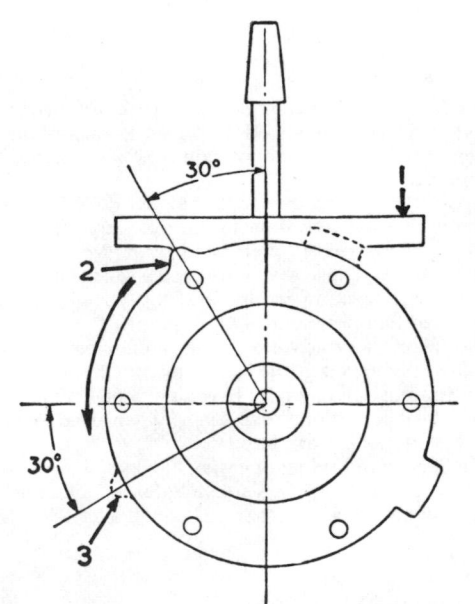

FIG 4:2 Fitting the diaphragm

Key to Fig 4:2   1 Pump mounting flange   2 Initia
position of diaphragm locating tab   3 Final position o
diaphragm locating tab

4:4 Servicing the filter

Unscrew the central retaining bolt and detach the base casting. Remove the element and sealing rings which should be renewed as normal procedure.

Clean the head and base castings in petrol and either allow to dry, or use compressed air for this purpose. Do not use cloth for drying. Check the operation of the non-return valve.

Refit the sealing plug 10 and the non-return valve 4. Fit new sealing rings to the head casting and see that they are properly located in their grooves. Place the new element in position, strengthened rim uppermost, using a twisting movement to seat it on the seals.

Place the base casting in position with a new sealing ring 8 and fit the central retaining bolt and washer.

4:5 Bleeding the fuel system

The following procedure should be used to vent (bleed) any air from the system after first ensuring that there is an adequate supply in the fuel tank.

1 Slacken off the union nut at the filter end of the fuel feed pipe to the injection pump. Operate the lift pump and as soon as air bubbles cease to appear tighten the nut.
2 Unscrew the blanking plug on the filter head. Operate the lift pump and when no more air bubbles appear, tighten the plug.
3 Slacken the two air bleed valves on the injection pump. One of these is on the governor housing, the other is incorporated in the hydraulic head locking screw immediately above the nameplate. Operate lift pump until no more air bubbles are seen then tighten the bleed valves.
4 Slacken the union nut at the injector end of any two high-pressure pipes. Make sure that the stop control is in the RUN position and set the accelerator in the fully open position then crank the engine until the fuel flowing from both pipes is free from air bubbles and tighten the union nuts.
5 Start the engine and run it until all four cylinders are firing.

Bleeding after renewing the filter element, provided the engine has not been turned, is only necessary as in 1 and 2 above.

4:6 The fuel injection pump

No servicing of this unit is possible. In the event of failure it must be taken to a qualified service station for attention or replacement.

Removing:

Remove either the external oil filter or the starter motor to provide access to the underside of the pump. Thoroughly clean the outside of the body and then disconnect the accelerator and shut-off controls, also the fuel feed and return pipes from the pump.

Disconnect the high-pressure pipes from the pump and the injectors and withdraw the pipes complete with clamp and damper bushes from the engine. Seal the pump outlets with sealing caps 18G.216 to prevent the entry of any foreign matter.

Unscrew the three securing nuts and lift off the pump.

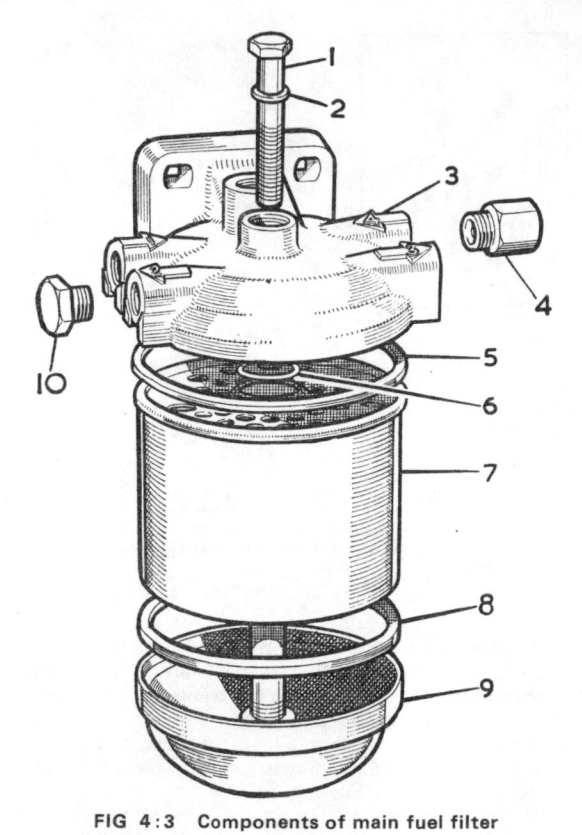

FIG 4:3 Components of main fuel filter

Key to Fig 4:3   1 Retaining bolt   2 Washer
3 Head casting   4 Non-return valve   5 Sealing washer
6 O-ring   7 Element   8 Sealing ring   9 Base casting
10 Blanking plug

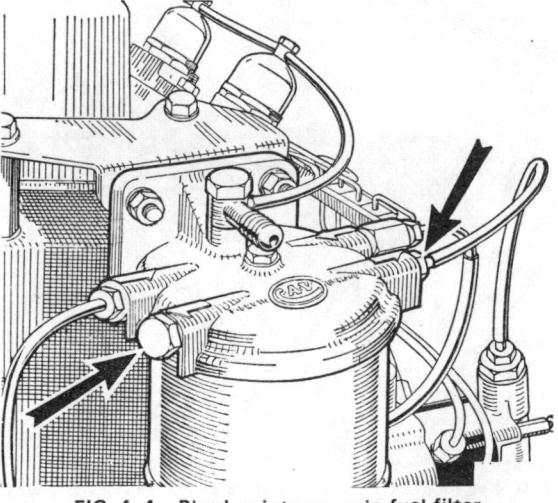

FIG 4:4 Bleed points on main fuel filter

FIG 4:5 Fuel injection pump air bleed points. The location of the bleed point on the later type governor is shown inset

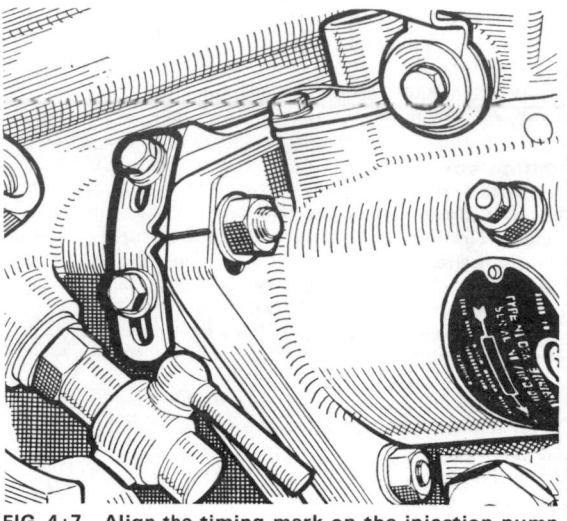

FIG 4:7 Align the timing mark on the injection pump mounting flange with the pointer on the drive hub

Refitting and timing the injection pump:

To ensure correct timing relationship between the injection pump and the engine, the pump drive shaft and the drive coupling on the engine are provided with master splines. There is also a timing mark scribed on the pump mounting flange and a pointer secured to the pump hub in the crankcase.

Crank the engine in the normal direction until the master spline in the drive coupling is at 4 o'clock: No. 1 piston is now on its compression stroke. Continue turning the engine slowly until No. 1 piston is at 22 deg. BTDC as indicated on the timing disc (see **FIG 2:9**). The master spline in the drive coupling should now be at 5 o'clock.

Insert timing gauge 18G.629 into the pump drive hub engaging the splined end of the gauge with the internal

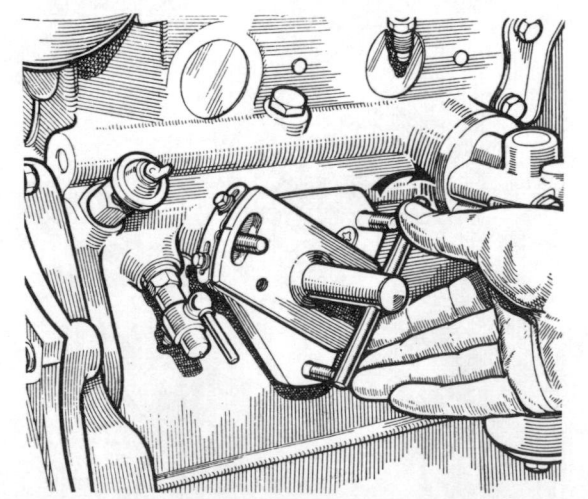

FIG 4:6 Checking the position of the injection pump timing pointer with gauge 18G.629

splines of the drive coupling. This can occur in one position only. Gently turn the gauge in a clockwise direction to take up any backlash in the pump drive (see **FIG 4:6**) hold the gauge in this position and check that the timing pointer on the drive hub is in line with the mark on the edge of the gauge. If necessary slacken the two setscrews and move the pointer to line it up with the mark on the gauge. Tighten the setscrews to secure the pointer in the correct position and remove the timing gauge.

Note: After every occasion of injection pump removal or attention to crankshaft, camshaft or timing gear the position of the timing pointer on the injection pump drive hub must be checked as described above.

Rotate the drive shaft of the injection pump until the master spline is at 7 o'clock, when looking on the drive end of the pump and the hydraulic governor housing uppermost. This is to facilitate the entry of the drive shaft into the drive coupling.

Position a new joint washer on the pump mounting studs and place the pump in position on the engine engaging the drive and fitting the lower securing nut and washer finger tight as the pump is pushed on to the mounting studs. Loosely fit the remaining two securing nuts and rotate the body of the pump about its axis to align the timing mark on the pump flange with the pointer (see **FIG 4:7**). Tighten the three securing nuts.

Connect the fuel feed, return and high-pressure pipes to their respective unions on pump and injectors. Reconnect the accelerator and stop controls making sure that both levers on the injection pump governor housing have a full range of movement when their respective control is operated.

Bleed the fuel system and start the engine.

Maximum speed adjustment:

Warm up the engine, then slacken the locknut and unscrew the idling damper on top of the governor housing two complete turns. Tighten the locknut.

Using a tachometer adjust the maximum speed stop screw to give a maximum light running speed of 4400 rev/min. Fit the rubber plug, plug retaining plate and set-screw (early pumps) or locking sleeve (later pumps) and seal with wire and lead seal.

Idling speed adjustment:

With the engine stopped, unscrew the idling damper until it is known to be out of contact with the metering valve. Tighten the locknut in this position.

Start the engine and adjust the idling stop screw to give 500 to 600 rev/min.

Screw in the idling damper until the idle speed is increased slightly, then unscrew the damper one-third of a turn and lock.

Run the engine at about 3000 rev/min and release the accelerator to test for stalling and rate of deceleration.

If the engine stalls screw the idling damper in slightly and retest.

If deceleration is slow unscrew the damper slightly and retest.

Check the operation of the shut-off control.

4:7 The fuel injectors

These items cannot be serviced satisfactorily by the private operator as specialised equipment is necessary. It is possible, however, to make a check on the vehicle and isolate a defective unit.

Run the engine at idling speed and loosen the fuel feed pipe union on each injector in turn and listen to the engine performance on the other three cylinders.

If the injector has been working satisfactorily there will be a reduction in engine speed and a worsening in the rough running. If the faulty injector is loosened it will make little or no difference to the engine performance.

4:8 Accelerator pedal stop

If the accelerator controls are disconnected or setting disturbed, the pedal stop must be readjusted to ensure that the throttle lever stop on the injection pump is not subjected to undue strain at full throttle.

Slacken the locknut and unscrew the adjusting screw until the end of the screw is flush with the face of the locknut. Press down the pedal until the lever on the pump is in the fully open position. Hold the pedal in this position without imposing any strain on the control lever, and screw in the adjuster until the pedal starts to move upwards and takes the control lever just off the maximum open position. Tighten the locknut and check that the control lever is still just short of its maximum travel when the pedal is firmly against the adjusting screw.

4:9 Fault diagnosis

(a) Engine will not idle

1 Slow-running control wrongly adjusted
2 Injector nozzle faulty

(b) Loss of power, rough running

1 Fuel starvation. Check at each nozzle by loosening union
2 Faulty injector or not firmly seated
3 Injector overheated
4 Injection pump timing incorrect

(c) Engine overheats

1 Check 1 in (b)
2 Faulty injector
3 Injection pump timing incorrect

(d) Black smoke from exhaust

1 Faulty injector
2 Injector pump timing incorrect

CHAPTER 5

THE IGNITION SYSTEM

5:1 Description

The ignition system fitted to petrol engines is a conventional 12-volt coil and distributor arrangement and using a Lucas type 25D.4 distributor with automatic ignition timing control. An exploded view of the distributor is given in **FIG 5:1** in which can be seen the centrifugal weight assembly by means of which the ignition point is advanced with increasing engine revolutions.

A vacuum operated timing control is also fitted designed to give additional advance under part throttle conditions. The combined effects of the centrifugal and vacuum operated timing controls give added efficiency over the full operating range of the engine, with a corresponding economy in fuel consumption. A micrometer adjustment is fitted by which fine alterations to the timing can be made to allow for changes in running conditions as a result of carbonization or change of fuel grade.

A completely sealed, metalized paper capacitor is fitted to the distributor. This has the property of being 'self healing' in the event of a breakdown, so that trouble arising from this source should be very infrequent.

The high-tension pick-up brush in the distributor cover is of composite construction, the top portion consisting of a resistive compound, and the lower of softer carbon to prevent wear taking place on the rotor electrode.

The resistive portion of the brush is in circuit between the coil and distributor and gives a measure of radio interference suppression. Under no circumstances must a short non-resistive brush be used as a replacement for one of the longer, resistive type.

5:2 Uneven firing, fault finding

Start the engine and set it to run at a fairly fast idling speed.

Shortcircuit each plug in turn by pulling the insulator sleeve up the cable and placing a hammer head or screwdriver blade with a wooden or insulated handle between the terminal and the cylinder head. No difference in the engine performance will be noted when shortcircuiting the plug in the defective cylinder. Shorting the other plugs will make the uneven running more pronounced.

Having located the cylinder which is at fault, stop the engine and remove the cable from the terminal of the sparking plug. Restart the engine and hold the end of the cable about $\frac{1}{4}$ inch from the cylinder head.

If the sparking is strong and regular, the fault probably lies in the sparking plug. Remove the plug, clean it and adjust the gap to the correct setting, or alternatively fit a new plug.

If there is no spark, or if it is weak and irregular, examine the cable from the sparking plug to the distributor. After a long period of service, the insulation may be cracked or perished, in which case the cable should be renewed.

Finally, examine the distributor moulded cap. Wipe the inside and outside with a clean dry cloth, see that the carbon brush moves freely in its holder, and examine the moulding closely for signs of breakdown. After long service it may become tracked, that is, a conducting path may have formed between two or more of the electrodes and some part of the distributor in contact with the cap. Evidence of a tracked cap is shown by the presence of a thin black line. A replacement distributor cap must be fitted in place of one that has become tracked.

5:3 Testing the LT circuit

Spring back the securing clips on the distributor and remove the moulded cap and rotor. If the rotor is a tight fit it may be levered off carefully with a screwdriver.

Check that the contacts are clean and free from pits, burns, oil or grease. Turn the engine and check that the contacts are opening and closing correctly and that the clearance is correct when the contacts are fully open.

Disconnect the cable at the contact breaker terminal of the coil and at the low-tension terminal of the distributor. Connect a test lamp between these terminals. If the lamp lights when the contacts close and goes out when the contacts open, the low-tension circuit is in order. Should the lamp fail to light, the contacts are dirty or there is a broken or loose connection in the low-tension wiring. To isolate the fault follow the following procedure:

Switch on the ignition and turn the engine until the contact breaker points are fully open. Refer to the wiring diagram and check the circuit with a 0 to 20 volt voltmeter as follows:

Noting that if a circuit is in order the voltmeter should read approximately 12 volts.

1 **Cable—battery to starter solenoid.** Connect the voltmeter between the supply terminal on the solenoid and earth. No reading indicates a faulty cable or loose connection.
2 **Cable (brown)—solenoid to ammeter.** Connect the voltmeter between ammeter terminal and earth. No reading indicates faulty cable or loose connection.
3 **Ammeter.** Connect the voltmeter between ammeter (brown and white cable terminal) and earth. No reading indicates a faulty ammeter.
4 **Cable (brown and white)—ammeter to control box.** Connect the voltmeter between control box terminal **A** and earth. No reading indicates faulty cable or loose connection.
5 **Control box.** Connect the voltmeter between control box terminal **A1** and earth. No reading indicates a faulty control box.

6 **Cable (brown with blue)—control box to ignition/master switch.** Connect voltmeter between switch terminal 1 and earth. No reading indicated faulty cable or connection.
7 **Ignition/master switch.** Connect voltmeter between switch terminal 2 and earth. No reading indicates a faulty switch.
8 **Cables (white and white with blue)—ignition/master switch to coil.** Connect voltmeter between coil terminal **SW** and earth. No reading indicates faulty cable or connections.
9 **Ignition coil.** Connect voltmeter between coil terminal **CB** and earth. No reading indicates a faulty coil.
10 **Cable (white with black)—coil to distributor.** Connect voltmeter between distributor terminal and earth. No reading indicates faulty cable or connection.
11 **Distributor.** Connect voltmeter across distributor contacts. If no reading, remove capacitor and retest. If there is now a reading, the capacitor is faulty.

5:4 Capacitor and coil

Capacitor (condenser):

This is of a .2 microfarad capacity and it will be seen that the eyelet on the cable connected to the contact breaker terminal post is squared and slotted to prevent it twisting round and shortcircuiting against the distributor.

The best method of checking on a suspect capacitor is by substitution. Disconnect the original unit and connect a new one between the low-tension terminal of the distributor and earth.

Coil:

The coil does not require any attention beyond seeing that the terminal connections and the mounting bolts are tight, and that the exterior is kept clean and dry, particularly between the terminals.

5:5 Distributor maintenance

Lift the rotor off the top of the spindle by pulling it squarely, and add a few drops of oil to the cam bearing (see **FIG 5:2**). Do not remove the screw which is exposed. There is a clearance between the screw and the inner face of the spindle for oil to pass.

Replace the rotor with its drive lug correctly engaged in the spindle slot, and push it into the shaft as far as it will go.

Lightly smear the cam with a very small amount of grease or, if this is not available, oil can be used.

Add an occasional drop of oil to the moving contact pivot pin.

Contact breaker:

Check the contact breaker action and setting as follows:

Turn the engine until the contact breaker points are fully opened and check the gap with a feeler gauge of .014 to .016 inch (.36 to .40 mm).

To adjust the setting, keep the engine in the position which gives maximum opening of the points and then slacken the fixed contact plate securing screw and move the plate as necessary to obtain the required gap clearance. Tighten the screws.

If the contacts are dirty or pitted, they should be cleaned by polishing with a fine carborundum stone and wiping with a petrol moistened cloth. If desired the moving contact can be removed to assist cleaning. Adjust the contact breaker gap after cleaning.

Check that the moving arm turns freely on its pivot. If necessary remove the arm and polish the pivot pin with fine emerycloth. After polishing wipe carefully and apply a drop of clean engine oil.

5:6 Removing and refitting the distributor

The distributor can be removed and replaced without interfering with the ignition timing, provided the clamp plate pinch bolt is not disturbed (see FIG 5:3).

To facilitate the replacement of the distributor, turn the engine over until the rotor arm is pointing to the segment in the cover for No. 1 cylinder plug lead. This will provide a datum for replacement.

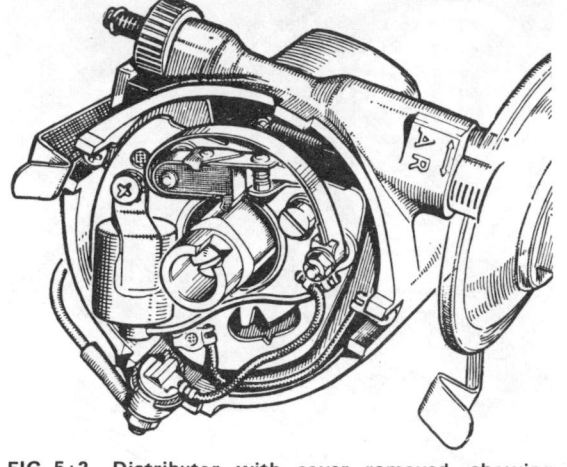

FIG 5:2 Distributor with cover removed, showing contact breaker mechanism

Removal:

1 Remove the distributor cover and disconnect the low-tension lead from the terminal on the distributor.
2 Disconnect the suction advance pipe at the union on the distributor.
3 Extract the two bolts securing the distributor clamp plate to the distributor housing and withdraw the distributor.

Replacement:

1 Insert the distributor into the distributor housing until the driving dog rests on the distributor drive shaft.
2 The rotor arm should then be rotated slowly until the driving dog lugs engage with the drive shaft slots, both of which are offset to ensure correct replacement.
3 Turn the distributor body to align the clamping plate holes with those in the housing. The remainder of the assembly is now in the reverse order to that of removal.
4 Provided that the engine has not been turned the rotor arm will be opposite the segment for No. 1 plug lead. The high-tension leads can then be replaced on their respective plug terminals in the order of firing, i.e. 1–3–4–2. Remember that the distributor rotation is anticlockwise when viewed from above.
5 Apply some silicone grease to the lip of the distributor cap and where the high-tension leads enter the distributor head.

5:7 Dismantling and reassembling the distributor

Remove the distributor from the engine as detailed in Section 5:6. The contact breaker plate may be removed as an assembly to give access to the centrifugal weights without completely dismantling the distributor. To do this, first remove the rotor arm and then withdraw the slotted nylon low-tension terminal post from the distributor body.

Take out the two screws which secure the plate assembly to the distributor body, ease up the plate and unhook the flexible actuating link connected to the contact breaker plate.

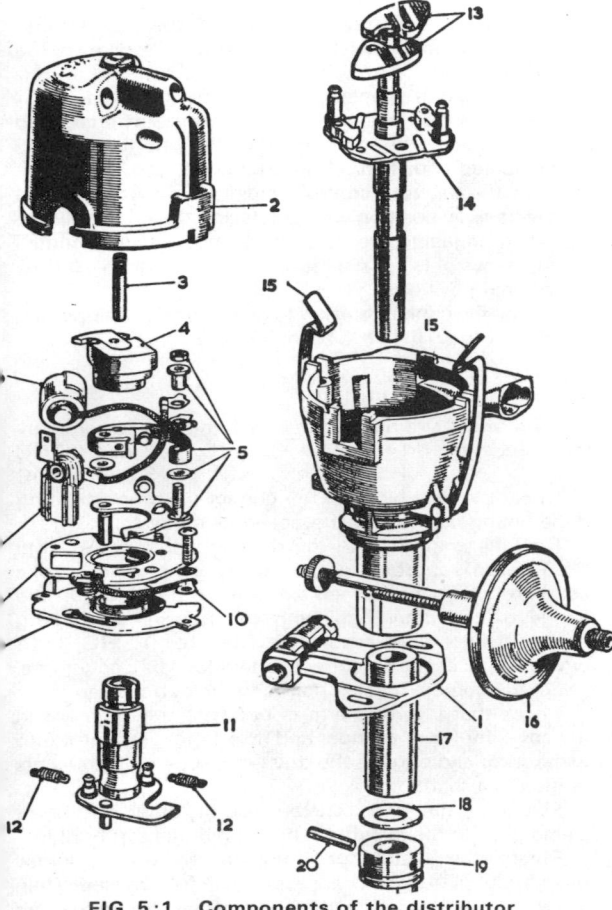

FIG 5:1 Components of the distributor

Key to Fig 5:1   1 Clamping plate   2 Moulded cap
3 Brush and spring   4 Rotor arm   5 Contacts (set)
6 Capacitor.   7 Terminal and lead (low-tension)   8 Moving contact breaker plate   9 Contact breaker base plate
10 Earth lead   11 Cam   12 Automatic advance spring
13 Weight assembly   14 Shaft and action plate   15 Cap retaining clips   16 Vacuum unit   17 Bush   18 Thrust washer   19 Driving dog   20 Parallel pin

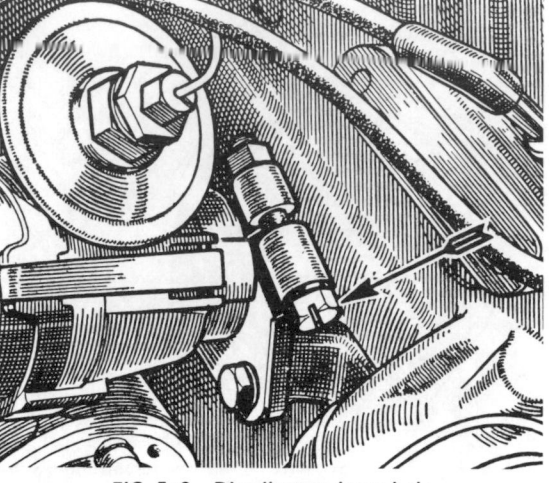

FIG 5:3   Distributor clamp bolt

The following procedure is necessary if the distributor is to be completely stripped. Before dismantling, make a careful note of the positions in which the various components are fitted in order that they may be replaced correctly.

1 Spring back the clips and remove the moulded cap.
2 Lift the rotor off the top of the spindle. If it is a tight fit it must be levered off carefully with a screwdriver.
3 Remove the nut and washer from the moving contact anchor pin. Withdraw the insulating sleeve from the capacitor lead and low-tension lead connectors, noting the order in which they are fitted. Lift the moving contact from the pivot pin and remove the large insulating washer from the anchor pin.
4 Take out the screw, spring washer, and flat washer securing the fixed contact plate and remove the plate.
5 Take out the securing screw and removed the capacitor
6 Extract the two screws securing the base plate to the distributor body, noting that one also secures the earthing lead, and lift out the base plate. Unhook the

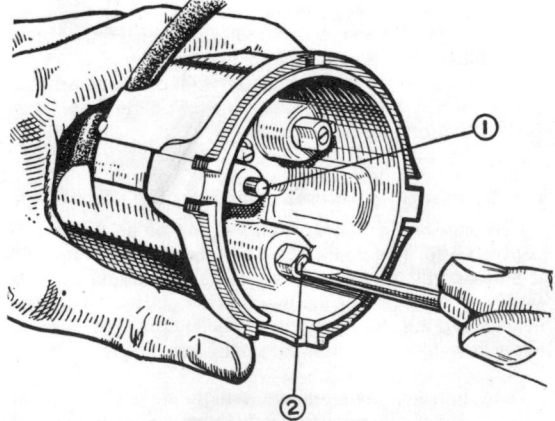

FIG 5:4   Method of connecting HT leads

Key to Fig 5:4   1 Carbon brush   2 Screw securing cable

flexible actuating link connecting the diaphragm in the vacuum unit with the moving contact breaker plate.

7 Note the relative position of the rotor arm drive slot in the cam spindle and the offset drive dog at the driving end of the spindle. This will ensure that the timing is not 180 deg. out when the cam spindle is engaged with the centrifugal weights during assembly. Take out the cam retaining screw and remove the cam spindle. On later type distributors the advance springs must be removed before the cam is withdrawn.
8 Take out the centrifugal weights. These may be lifted out as two assemblies, each complete with a spring and toggle.
9 To release the suction advance unit remove the circlip, adjusting nut and spring. Withdraw the unit, taking care not to lose the adjusting nut lock spring clip.
10 To release the spindle from the body, drive out the parallel driving pin passing through the collar of the driving tongue member at the lower end of the spindle.

Reassembly is a direct reversal of the dismantling instructions although careful attention must be given to the following points:

1 As they are assembled the components of the automatic advance mechanism, the distributor shaft and the portion of the shaft on which the cam fits must be lubricated with thin, clean engine oil.
2 Turn the vacuum control adjusting nut until it is in the halfway position when replacing the control unit.
3 When engaging the cam driving pin with the centrifugal weights, make sure that they are in their original positions.
4 Adjust the contact breaker to give a maximum opening of .014 to .016 inch (.36 to .40 mm).

5:8 Timing the ignition

The correct settings for the two engines covered by this manual are: 1489 cc   ..   .. $7\frac{1}{2}$ deg. BTDC
                                      1622 cc   ..   ..   5 deg. BTDC

To set the distributor in the correct position for firing if the timing has been lost proceed as follows:

Turn the crankshaft in the direction of rotation until No. 1 piston is approaching TDC on its compression stroke i.e. with both valves closed and line up the notch in the flange of the crankshaft with the appropriate timing pointer on the front cover. See **Chapter 1, FIG 1:14** where the inset shows correct setting for 1622 cc engine.

Set the contact breaker points to the correct gap.

Check that the rotor arm is opposite the segment in the cover for No. 1 cylinder and insert the distributor into its housing and engage the drive dog lugs with the slots in the drive shaft.

Screw in the two screws securing the distributor clamp plate to the distributor housing finger tight only.

Rotate the distributor body in an anticlockwise direction until the points are seen to be fully closed. Then slowly turn it clockwise until the points just begin to open and secure the distributor in this position by tightening up the clamp bolt and the two clamp plate screws.

A more accurate method of determining the actual moment when the points break is to connect a 12-volt bulb between the LT terminal on the distributor body and earth. With the ignition switched on, the bulb will light up immediately the points break.

5:9 HT cables

The high-tension cables must be examined carefully and any which have the insulation cracked, perished or damaged in any way must be renewed.

To fit the cables to the terminal of the ignition coil, thread the knurled moulded terminal nut over the lead, bare the end of the cable for about $\frac{1}{4}$ inch, thread the wite through the brass washer removed from the original cable, and bend back the strands over the washer. Finally, screw the terminal into the coil.

To make the connections to the terminals in the distributor moulded cap (see **FIG 5:4**); first remove the cap and slacken the screws on the inside of the moulding till they are clear of the cables. Fill the holes in the distributor cap with Silicone grease, then cut the new cables off to the required length. Push them completely home then tighten the securing screws.

The cables from the distributor to the sparking plugs must be connected up in the correct firing order, which is 1–3–4–2. Secure them firmly to the connectors.

5:10 Sparking plugs

Inspect, clean and adjust the sparking plugs regularly. The inspection of the deposits on the electrodes is particularly useful because the type and colour of the deposit gives a clue to conditions inside the combustion chamber, and is therefore most helpful when tuning.

Remove the sparking plugs by loosening them a couple of turns and then blowing away loose dirt from the plug recesses with compressed air or a tyre pump. Store them in the order of removal.

Examine for signs of oil fouling. This will be indicated by a wet shiny, black deposit on the insulator. This is caused by oil pumping due to worn cylinders and pistons or gummed up or broken rings. Under such conditions, oil from the cylinder wall is forced up past the rings on the suction stroke of the piston and is eventually deposited on the plugs. A permanent remedy for this cannot be effected, the only cure being the fitting of a new piston and rings, or in extreme cases, a rebore may be necessary.

Next examine the plugs for signs of petrol fouling. This is indicated by a dry, fluffy black deposit which is usually caused by overrich carburation, although ignition system defects such as a run-down battery, faulty distributor, coil or condenser defects, or a broken or worn out cable may be additional causes. If the plugs appear to be suitable for further use, proceed to clean and test them.

First remove the plug gaskets and examine them for condition. A large proportion of the heat from the plug is normally dissipated to the cylinder head through the steel gasket between the plug and head. Plugs not screwed down tightly can thus easily become overheated so that they operate out of their proper heat range, producing pre-ignition, short plug life, and 'pinking'. On the other hand, it is unnecessary to tighten up the plugs too much. A reasonably good seal is required between the plug and cylinder head and the use of a torque wrench is recommended to tighten them to 30 lb ft (4.15 kg m).

If the plugs require cleaning it is only possible to do the job properly by using a plug cleaner and any service station can do this for you.

FIG 5:5 An overheated plug, showing severely eroded electrodes and white, blistered insulator

Occasionally a blistered insulator or a badly burnt electrode may be noticed when examining the plugs. An example of this is shown in **FIG 5:5**.

If the plug is of the type recommended for the engine and it was correctly installed, this condition may have been brought about by a very lean mixture or an overheated engine. There is, however, a possibility that a plug of another type is required, but as a rule the recommended plug should be adhered to.

Have the sparking plugs cleaned on an abrasive blasting machine and tested under pressure after attention to the electrodes. File these until they are clean, bright and parallel. Set the electrode gap to .024 to .026 inch (.62 to .66 mm). Do not try to bend the centre electrode.

Before replacing the plugs, clean the threads with a wire brush. Do not use a wire brush on the electrodes. If it is found that the plugs cannot be screwed in by hand, run a tap down the threads in the cylinder head. Failing a tap, use an old sparking plug with crosscuts down the threads. If a torque wrench is not available, screw the plugs down by hand to the end of the thread, then tighten with a box spanner through half a turn.

5:11 Fault diagnosis

(a) Engine will not fire

1 Battery discharged
2 Distributor points dirty, or out of adjustment
3 Distributor cap wet, dirty, or cracked
4 Carbon brush not contacting rotor
5 Faulty cable or connection in LT circuit
6 Rotor arm cracked
7 Faulty coil
8 Broken contact breaker spring
9 Points stuck open

(b) Engine misfires

1 Check 2, 3, 5 and 7 in (a)
2 Weak contact breaker spring
3 HT leads faulty
4 Sparking plugs insulation cracked
5 Sparking plug gap incorrect
6 Ignition timing too far advanced

NOTES

CHAPTER 6

THE COOLING SYSTEM

6:1 Description

The cooling system is pressurized and the water circulation is assisted by a pump attached to the front of the engine. The pump is driven by a belt from the crankshaft pulley.

A relief valve is incorporated in the radiator filler cap. This controls the pressure at approximately 4 lb/sq inch.

The water circulates from the base of the radiator and passes round the cylinders and cylinder head, reaching the header tank of the radiator via the thermostat and top hose. From the header tank it passes down the radiator core to the base tank of the radiator. Air is drawn through the radiator by a fan attached to the water pump pulley.

6:2 The thermostat

For maximum efficiency, the engine operating temperature is maintained within certain limits by a bellows type thermostat fitted in the water outlet at the front of the cylinder head.

When the engine is cold this valve is closed, and when the engine is started the flow of water to the radiator is temporarily restricted. Due to this, the temperature of the water in the cylinder head and cylinder jackets will quickly rise, thus ensuring rapid warm up. The heat generated will gradually expand the bellows, so opening the valve and ultimately permitting fullflow of water to the radiator.

The thermostat is detachable.

A small hole drilled in the head of the valve provides a bypass to cope with any expansion of the cooling water. When the system has been completely drained it is essential, when refilling, to allow sufficient time for any trapped air to escape through the bypass hole in the valve before finally topping up.

The thermostat opening is set by the manufacturer and cannot be altered. It opens at the temperature marked on the body of the thermostat.

During decarbonizing it is policy to test this opening by immersing the thermostat in water raised to the requisite temperature. The valve should open under these conditions, but if it does not a new unit must be fitted as no repairs can be effected.

6:3 Maintenance, flushing, belt tension, antifreeze

There is a plug in the water pump casing of early types which requires periodical lubrication. The location of the plug can be seen in **FIG 6:1**. Remove the plug and introduce some recommended lubricant. Do not force the

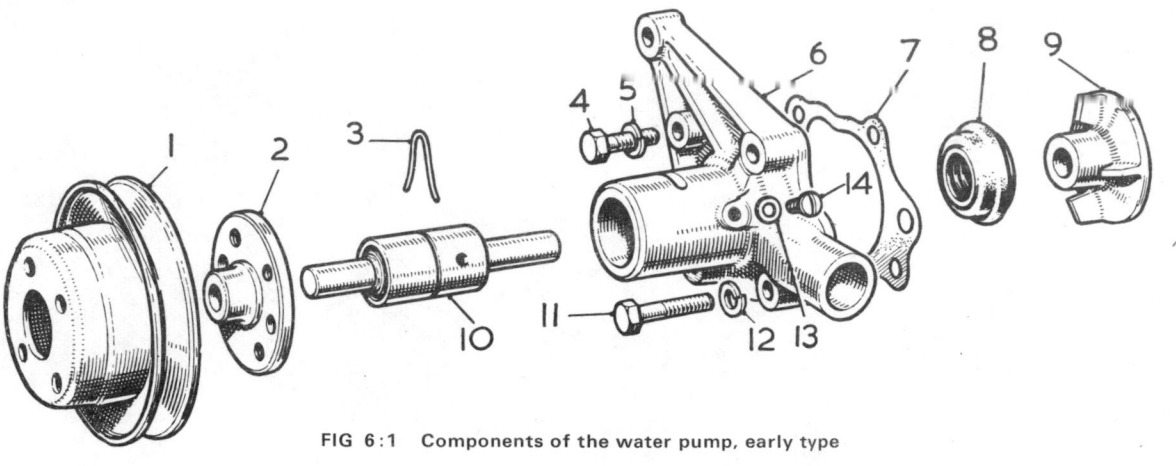

FIG 6:1   Components of the water pump, early type

Key to Fig 6:1   1 Pulley   2 Hub for pulley   3 Bearing locating wire   4 Set bolt   5 Spring washer   6 Water pump body   7 Joint washer   8 Water seal   9 Water pump vane   10 Spindle and bearing assembly   11 Set bolt   12 Spring washer   13 Fibre washer   14 Lubricating plug

lubricant in under pressure or it may pass through the bearings and get onto the pump seal, impairing the efficiency.

The cooling system should be drained, flushed through and refilled at regular intervals. Antifreeze may be used for two years, so it may be collected for re-use during that period.

The cooling system is under pressure while the engine is hot, and the radiator filler cap must be removed very carefully, or left in position until the water has cooled.

If it is necessary to remove the filler cap when the engine is hot, it is absolutely essential to release the cap gradually, and the filler spout is provided with a specially shaped cam to enable this to be done easily.

Unscrew the cap slowly until the retaining tongues are felt to engage the small lobes on the end of the filler spout cam, and wait until the pressure in the radiator is fully released before finally removing the cap. It is advisable to protect the hand against escaping steam while removing the cap.

Draining:

1 Remove the radiator header tank filler cap.
2 Open the two drain taps or remove the drain plugs, whichever is applicable. One is fitted at the rear of the cylinder block on the righthand side and the other at the base of the radiator. If antifreeze mixture is being used it should be drained into a suitable container and preserved for future use.

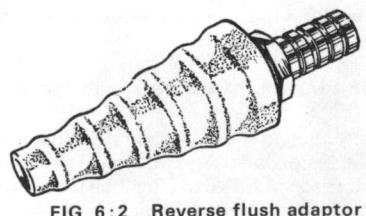

FIG 6:2   Reverse flush adaptor

3 In the event of a drain tap becoming clogged, it is advisable to completely remove the tap from the cylinder block or radiator and then remove any foreign matter. The use of stiff wire to dislodge any obstruction would prove ineffective as the construction of the taps is such as to prevent complete penetration behind them.
4 When the system is completely drained, and refilling is to be deferred until some later date, a suitable notice should be fixed to the front of the radiator, indicating that the coolant has been drained. Alternatively, place the filler cap on the drivers seat or leave the bonnet propped open as a reminder to fill the cooling system before starting the engine again.
5 If a heater is fitted, under no circumstances should draining of the cooling system be resorted to as an alternative to the use of antifreeze, due to the fact that complete draining of the heater unit by means of the cooling system drain taps is not possible.

Flushing the system:

To ensure efficient circulation of the coolant and to reduce the formation of scale and sediment in the radiator, the system should be periodically flushed out with clear running water. This should preferably be done before putting in antifreeze and again when taking it out.

The water should be allowed to run through until it comes out of the taps clean.

This method is adequate under normal circumstances, but in extreme cases where excessive 'furring up' is experienced, a more efficient method is to completely remove the radiator and flush in the reverse way to the flow, i.e. turn the radiator upside down and let the water flow in through the bottom and out of the top connection. Adaptors are available to assist in the flushing operation (see **FIG 6:2**). These adaptors should be used in pairs, one for the radiator inlet hose and one for the outlet hose. The brass inlet pipe is 1 inch diameter. This is the size of the water mains supply hose generally used but if there is any variation a reducing sleeve can be used.

Filling the system:

1 Close the radiator and cylinder block drain taps or refit the drain plugs, whichever is applicable.
2 Ensure that all hose connections are tight.
3 Fill up the system through the filler in the radiator header tank until the level of the water can just be seen. Run the engine until hot and then add sufficient water to raise the level to within 1 inch of the bottom of the filler neck.
4 When possible, soft water, such as clean rain water should be used to fill the system.
5 When using the antifreeze avoid overfilling and prevent loss due to expansion. Screw the filler cap firmly into position.

Antifreeze:

As the cooling system is sealed, relatively high temperatures are developed in the radiator upper tank. For this reason, antifreeze solutions having an alcohol base are unsuitable owing to their high evaporation rate producing rapid loss of coolant and a consequent interruption of circulation.

Only antifreeze of the ethylene glycol-type incorporating the correct type of corrosion inhibitor is suitable for use in the cooling system and Bluecol, or any antifreeze that conforms to the specification BS.3151 or BS.3152 is recommended.

Before introducing antifreeze mixture to the radiator it is advisable to clean out the cooling system thoroughly by flushing out the passages with a hose inserted in the filler cap, keeping the drain taps open.

Make sure that the cooling system is watertight and examine all joints, replacing any defective hoses with new items.

Antifreeze can remain in the system for two years provided that the specific gravity of the coolant is checked periodically and antifreeze added as necessary. Only top up the system when the cooling system is at its normal running temperature, in order to avoid losing antifreeze due to expansion.

The correct quantities of antifreeze for different degrees of frost resistance are given in the table below:

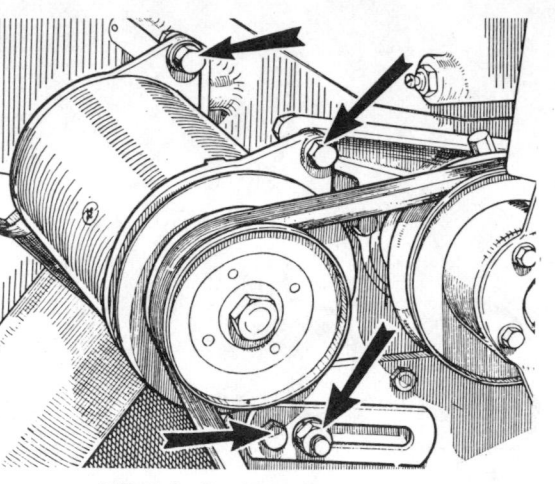

FIG 6:3 Fan belt adjusting bolts

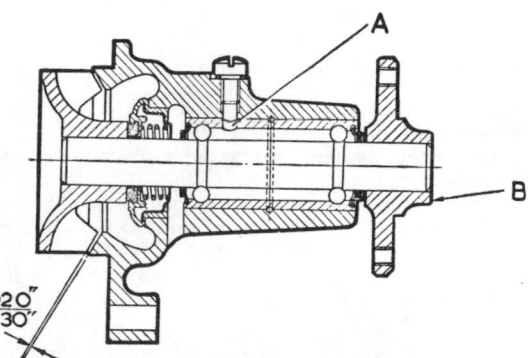

FIG 6:4 Section through water pump, early type

Key to Fig 6:4 **A** Hole in bearing coinciding with hole in pump body **B** Face of hub flush with end of spindle

Solution (%)	Commences Freezing °C	°F	Frozen Solid °C	°F	Petrol Models with Heater Pints	US Pints	Litres	Diesel Models with Heater Pints	US Pints	Litres
25	—13	9	—26	—15	3	3¾	1.7	3¼	4	1.8
33⅓	—19	—2	—36	—33	4	5	2.3	4½	5½	2.6
50	—36	—33	—48	—53	6	7¼	3.4	6½	8	3.6

Fan belt replacement and adjustment:

To fit a new fan belt, slacken slightly the two bolts (see **FIG 6:3**) on which the generator pivots, and release the bolt securing it to the slotted link and the nut securing it to the slotted link to the engine. Move the generator to the engine as far as it will go. Slide the belt over the fan and onto the fan pulley; ease the belt onto the crankshaft pulley and generator pulley. It may be found helpful to turn the engine with the starting handle whilst easing the belt over the generator pulley.

To adjust the tension of the belt, raise the generator upwards away from the engine. A gentle hand pressure only must be used, or the belt tension will be excessive and undue strain will be thrown onto the generator bearings.

Tighten up the bolts with the generator in this position.

The belt should be sufficiently tight to prevent slip, yet it should be possible to move the belt laterally 1 inch in the centre of its longest run.

6:4 Removing and refitting the radiator

Drain the cooling system as described earlier in **Section 6:3**. Remove the seats, battery and engine cowling floor base.

Remove the fan blades and pulley. Release the clips from top and bottom water hoses and pull off the hoses.

Disconnect the radiator upper tie-bars. Remove the radiator lower support brackets or disconnect the radiator from them. Lift out the radiator.

Refitting is the reverse of the above. Close the drain taps, refill the system and check for leaks.

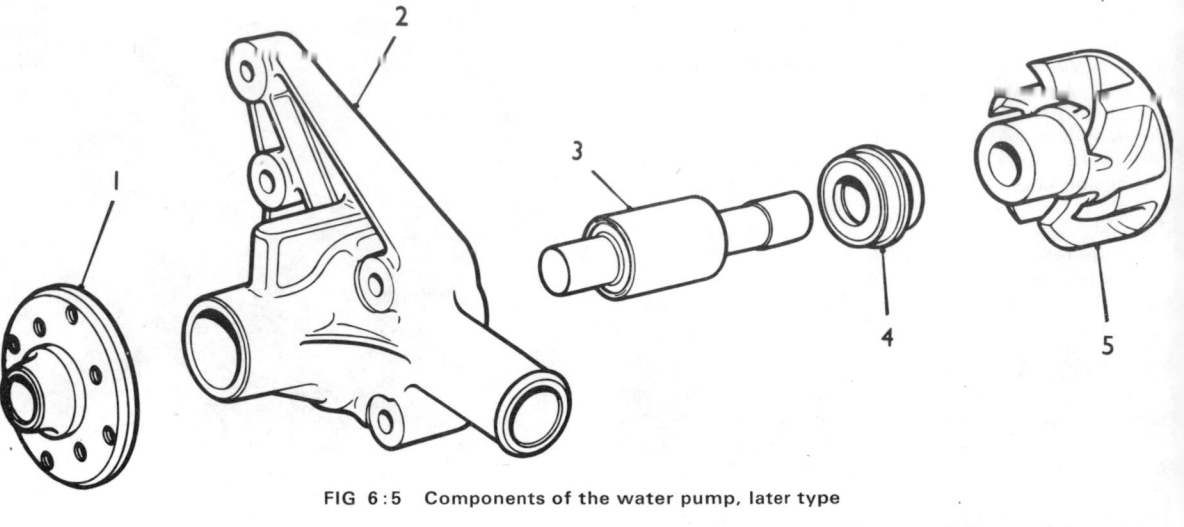

FIG 6:5 Components of the water pump, later type

Key to Fig 6:5   1 Pulley hub   2 Pump body   3 Spindle and bearing assembly   4 Pressure balanced seal
5 Impeller

6:5 Water pump removal and refitting

Drain the cooling system and remove the seats, battery and engine cowling floor base.

Disconnect the leads to the generator and remove it from the engine.

Unscrew four bolts attaching the pump assembly to the front of the cylinder block and remove the fan and pump together.

Replacement is a reversal of the removal procedure, but do not omit to fit a new gasket.

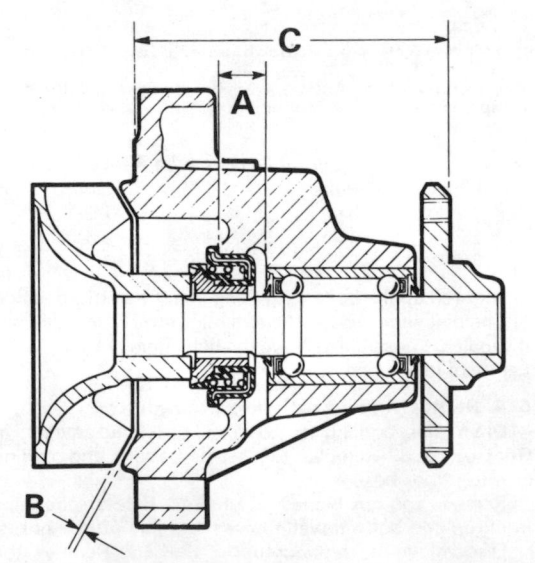

FIG 6:6 Water pump assembly dimensions, later type

Key to Fig 6:6   A .527 to .537 inch   B .020 to .030 inch
C 3.244 to 3.264 inch for Petrol engines
  3.730 to 3.750 inch for Diesel engines

6:6 Pump dismantling and reassembly, early type

Unscrew the four bolts attaching the fan and belt pulley to the hub and remove (see **FIG 6:1**).

Remove the fan hub with a suitable extractor.

Pull the bearing locating wire 3 through the hole in the top of the pump body.

Gently tap the bearing assembly out of the pump body to the rear. This releases the combined bearing and spindle assembly 10 together with the seal 8 and vane 9.

Remove the vane from the bearing assembly with a suitable extractor and remove the pump seal assembly.

Before reassembly, which is the reverse of the above, make sure that the seal assembly is in good condition. At any sign of damage or excess wear fit a new seal.

Refer to **FIG 6:4**. When the bearing assembly is fitted into the pump the hole A in the bearing must coincide with the lubricating hole in the pump body, and a clearance of .020 to .030 inch (.5 to .8 mm) must be maintained between the vanes and the pump body. Note also that the face of the hub B must be flush with the end of the spindle.

Should the interference fit of the fan hub have been impaired during withdrawal, a new hub should be fitted.

6:7 Pump dismantling and reassembly, later type

Remove the fan and pulley, and press the bearing spindle out of the hub. Press the spindle assembly out of the pump body. Press the spindle out of the impeller, and remove the seal (see **FIG 6:5**).

Inspect all parts for wear or damage, and reassemble in the reverse order to the dimensions given in **FIG 6:6**.

6:8 Sealed cooling system, later vehicles

The radiator on these vehicles has a plain cap which is only used for filling after the system has been drained. The radiator remains full at all times, and any overflow passes to an expansion tank mounted on the lefthand wheel arch below the radiator level.

The expansion tank is fitted with a pressure release cap and the usual precautions should be observed. When the radiator cools, coolant is drawn back from the expansion tank to keep the radiator full. The correct depth of coolant in the expansion tank when cold is $2\frac{1}{2}$ inch. Regular topping up is unnecessary, but an inspection should be made every 3000 miles or 3 months and the expansion tank topped up if necessary.

Filling:

If the radiator has been drained refill as follows:
1 Fill the radiator right up and refit the cap.
2 Check the level in the expansion tank, it is important that this level is correct, and refit the cap.
3 Run the engine for half a minute and check the radiator, top up if necessary and replace the cap.

When antifreeze is being used, add $\frac{1}{4}$ pint of undiluted antifreeze to the coolant in the expansion tank.

6:9 Fault diagnosis

(a) Internal leakage

1 Cracked cylinder wall
2 Loose cylinder head nuts
3 Cracked cylinder head
4 Faulty head gasket
5 Cracked tappet chest wall

(b) Poor circulation

1 Radiator core blocked
2 Engine water passages restricted
3 Low water level
4 Loose fan belt
5 Defective thermostat
6 Perished or collapsed radiator hoses

(c) Corrosion

1 Impurities in the water
2 Infrequent draining and flushing

(d) Overheating

1 Check (b)
2 Sludge in crankcase
3 Faulty ignition timing
4 Low oil level in sump
5 Tight engine
6 Choked exhaust system
7 Binding brakes
8 Slipping clutch
9 Incorrect valve timing
10 Retarded ignition
11 Mixture too weak

NOTES

CHAPTER 7

THE CLUTCH

7:1 Description

An exploded view of the clutch is shown in **FIG 7:1**. It is of the single-plate dry-disc type operated hydraulically. No adjustment for wear is provided in the clutch itself but individual adjustment is provided for locating each lever during initial assembly. The adjusting nuts are locked in position and must never be disturbed unless the clutch is dismantled.

The driven plate assembly, which can be seen in cross-section in **FIG 7:2**, consists of a splined hub and flexible steel driven plate, to the outer diameter of which are fixed the annular friction facings. This plate is attached to the splined hub by a spring mounting which provides a torsional cushion.

The withdrawal bearing assembly comprises the graphite release bearing mounted in a cup attached to the throw-out form, and a release plate attached to the inner ends of the release levers by means of the retainer springs. Release is accomplished by moving the release bearing forward and thus applying pressure to the release levers.

Each release lever is pivoted on a floating pin which remains stationary in the lever and rolls across a short flat portion of the enlarged holes in the eyebolts. The outer ends of the eyebolts extend through the holes in the clutch cover and are fitted with adjusting nuts by means of which each lever is located in its correct position. The outer or shorter ends of the release levers engage the pressure plate lugs by means of struts which provide knife-edge contact between the outer ends of the levers and the pressure plate lugs, eliminating friction at this point. Thus the pressure plate is pulled away from the driven plate, compressing the six thrust coil springs which are assembled between the pressure plate and the clutch cover.

When the foot pressure is removed from the clutch pedal, the clutch springs force the pressure plate forward against the driven plate, gradually and smoothly applying the power of the engine to the rear wheels.

The hydraulic master cylinder is mounted on the bulkhead and is operated directly by the clutch pedal. Fluid pressure is transmitted to the slave cylinder, moving the piston, pushrod and clutch lever to disengage the clutch.

The clutch master cylinder is similar to that of the brake master cylinder, the inner assembly consisting of a pushrod, dished washer, circlip, plunger, seal, spring thimble, plunger return spring, valve spacer, spring washer valve stem and valve seal. A rubber dust cover protects the opend end of the cylinder.

The clutch slave cylinder is bolted to the clutch housing and normally requires no maintenance. If the system is drained of fluid it will be necessary to bleed the cylinder after reassembly and refilling.

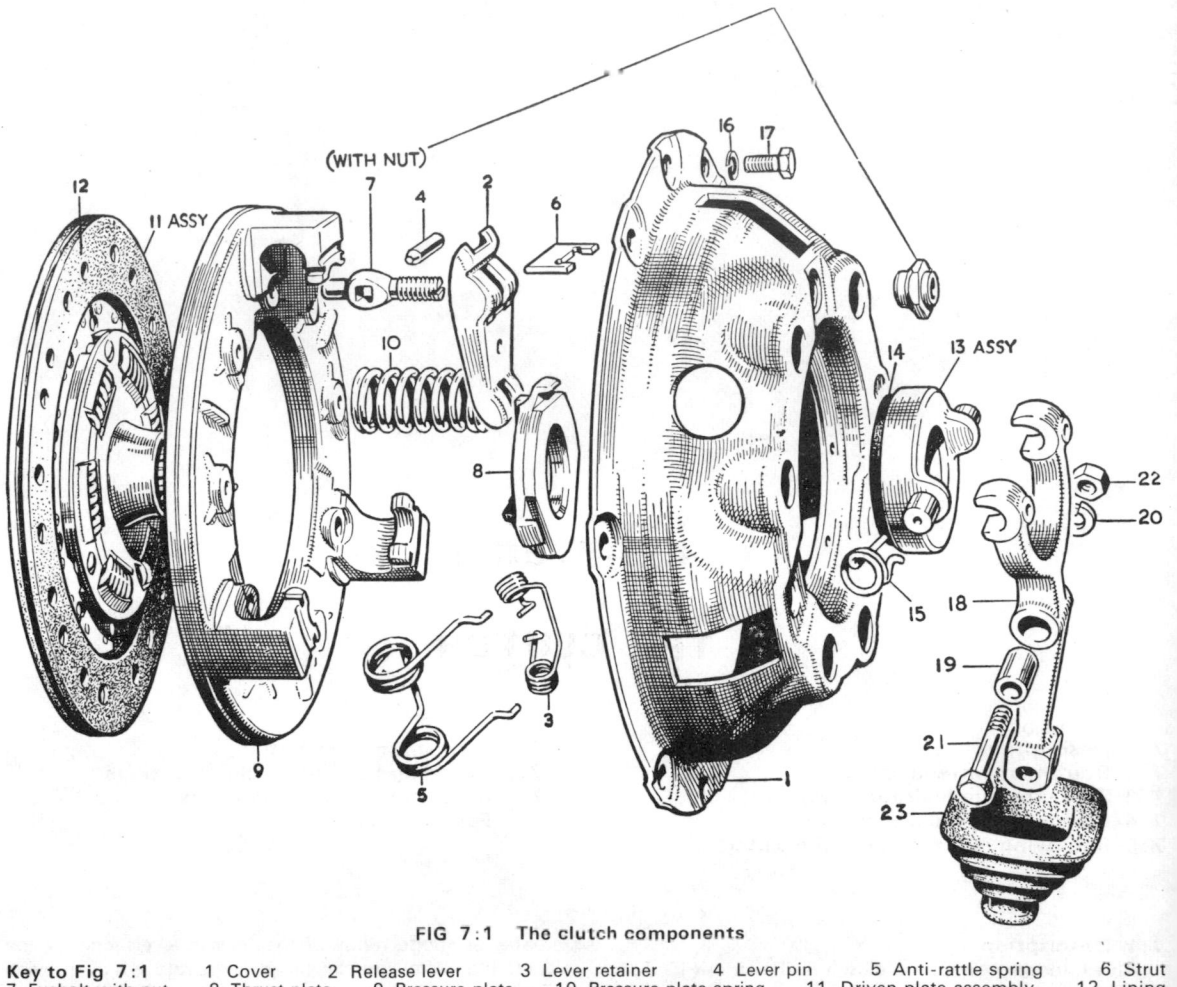

FIG 7:1 The clutch components

Key to Fig 7:1   1 Cover   2 Release lever   3 Lever retainer   4 Lever pin   5 Anti-rattle spring   6 Strut
7 Eyebolt with nut   8 Thrust plate   9 Pressure plate   10 Pressure plate spring   11 Driven plate assembly   12 Lining
13 Release bearing assembly   14 Release bearing   15 Bearing retainer   16 Spring washer   17 Set bolt   18 Withdrawal lever
19 Bush   20 Spring washer   21 Pivot bolt   22 Nut   23 Rubber boot

7:2 Routine maintenance

Check the level of fluid in the master cylinder reservoir and maintain it at the level indicated on the outside of the cylinder. Use Castrol Girling Brake and Clutch Fluid Crimson, or a fluid conforming to specification SAE.70.R3. The necessity for frequent topping up is an indication of a leak in the system which should be traced immediately and rectified.

7:3 Servicing the hydraulic system

Master cylinder, removal:

Extract the splitpin and withdraw the clevis pin from the pushrod yoke. Disconnect the pressure pipe union from the cylinder and remove the two screws and washers from the master cylinder mounting flange. The master cylinder may now be withdrawn from the bulkhead.

Dismantling:

1 Refer to **FIG 7:3** and remove the retaining circlip with a pair of long-nosed pliers.
2 Extract the dished washer and pushrod.
3 When the pushrod has been removed, the plunger with its seal(s) attached will be exposed. Remove the plunger assembly complete.
4 Separate the assembly by lifting the thimble leaf over the shouldered end of the plunger. Depress the plunger return spring, allowing the valve stem to slide through the elongated hole in the thimble, thus releasing the tension on the spring. Remove the thimble, spring and valve complete.
5 Detach the valve spacer, taking care of the spacer spring washer which is located under the valve head, and remove the seal from the valve head.
6 Examine all parts, especially the seals, for wear or distortion, and fit new parts where necessary. Any

imperfections on the plunger or cylinder bore may provide a track for fluid leaks under pressure, and any damaged parts must be discarded. All hydraulic components must be handled very carefully to avoid any possibility of accidental scoring.

Assembly:

1 Replace the valve seal so that the flat side is correctly seated on the valve head.
2 Locate the spring washer with the domed side against the under side of the valve head. Hold in position with the valve spacer, the legs of which face towards the valve seal.
3 Replace the plunger return spring centrally on the spacer, insert the thimble into the spring, and depress until the valve stem engages through the elongated hole of the thimble. Ensure that the stem is correctly located in the centre of the thimble. Check also that the spring is still central on the spacer.
4 Fit a new plunger seal with the flat face of the seal against the face of the plunger.
5 Insert the reduced end of the plunger into the thimble until the thimble leaf engages under the shoulder of the plunger. Press home the thimble leaf.
6 Smear the plunger assembly with the recommended hydraulic fluid and insert the assembly into the cylinder bore, valve end first, carefully easing the plunger seal lips into the bore.
7 Replace the pushrod, with the dished side of the washer under the spherical head, into the cylinder followed by the circlip, which engages in the groove machined in the cylinder body.

Refitting:

Locate the master cylinder on the mounting bracket on the bulkhead and fit the bolts, washers and self-locking nuts.

Replace the rubber dust cover. Line up the pushrod fork with the hole in the clutch pedal lever, insert the clevis pin and secure it with a new splitpin.

Bleed the clutch hydraulic system.

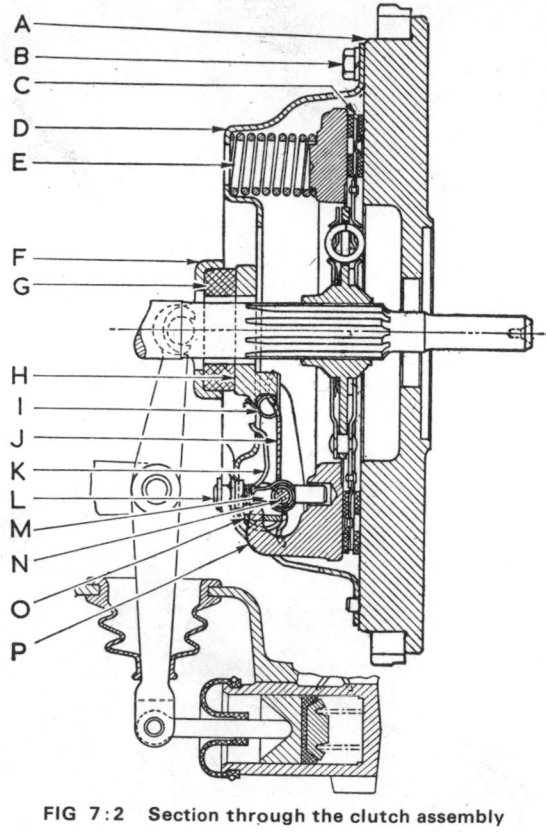

FIG 7:2 Section through the clutch assembly

Key to Fig 7:2   A Flywheel   B Securing bolts
C Driven plate   D Clutch cover   E Thrust coil springs
F Release bearing cup   G Graphite release bearing
H Release plate   I Lever retainer springs   J Release levers
K Anti-rattle springs   L Adjusting nuts   M Eyebolts
N Floating pins   O Struts   P Pressure plate

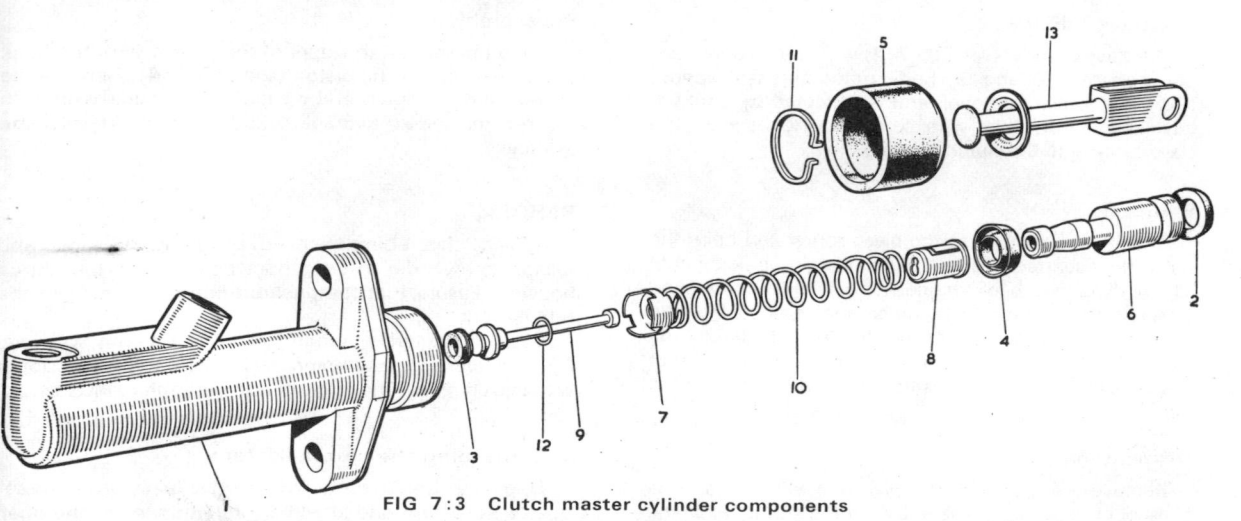

FIG 7:3 Clutch master cylinder components

Key to Fig 7:3   1 Master cylinder body   2 End seal   3 Valve seal   4 Plunger seal   5 Dust cover   6 Plunger
7 Valve spacer   8 Thimble   9 Valve stem   10 Plunger return spring   11 Circlip   12 Washer   13 Pushrod

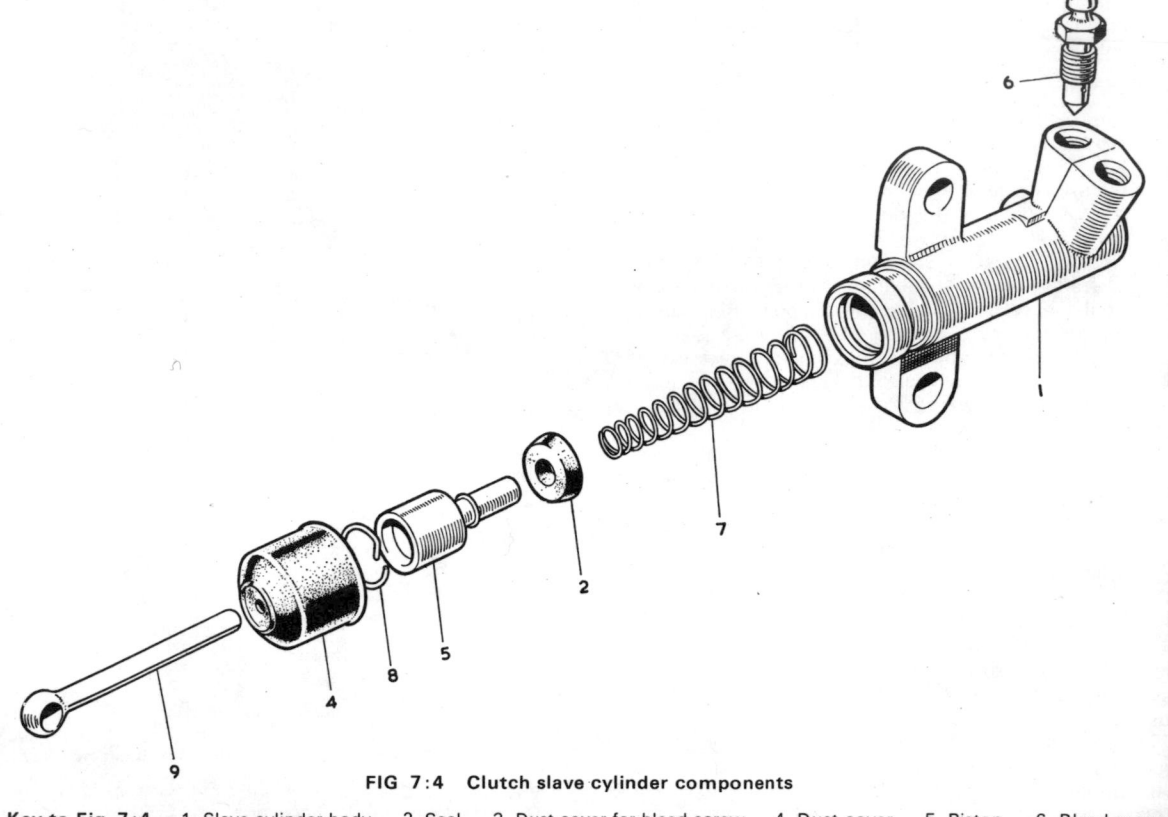

FIG 7:4 Clutch slave cylinder components

Key to Fig 7:4 1 Slave cylinder body   2 Seal   3 Dust cover for bleed screw   4 Dust cover   5 Piston   6 Bleed screw
7 Spring   8 Circlip   9 Pushrod

The slave cylinder:

The slave cylinder (see **FIG 7:4**) is of simple construction, consisting of an alloy body, piston and seal, spring, and bleed screw. The open end is protected by a rubber dust cover. Two bolts with spring washers secure the slave cylinder to the clutch housing.

Removal:

Attach a rubber tube to the bleed screw and open the screw threequarters of a turn. Pump the clutch pedal until all the fluid has been drained into a clean container. Unscrew the pressure pipe union and remove the two bolts and spring washers securing the cylinder to the clutch housing. The cylinder may now be removed from the vehicle, leaving the pushrod attached to the clutch fork.

Dismantling:

Remove the rubber dust cover, and with an air-line blow out the piston and seal. Extract the spring. Examine all parts, especially the seal, and renew if worn or damaged.

Reassembly:

Place the seal on the stem of the piston with the back of the seal against the piston (see **FIG 7:4**). Replace the spring with the small-end on the stem, smear well with the recommended hydraulic fluid, and insert into the cylinder.

Refitting:

Replace the rubber dust cover on the cylinder and locate the cylinder in its correct position on the clutch housing. Ensure that the pushrod enters the hole in the rubber boot.

Replace the two mounting bolts and spring washers. Refit the pressure pipe union, taking care to fit the copper washers correctly. Bleed the clutch hydraulic system.

7:4 Bleeding the clutch system

Open the bleed screw on the slave cylinder threequarters of a turn and attach a tube, immersing the open end in a clean receptacle containing a small quantity of recommended hydraulic fluid. Fill the master cylinde

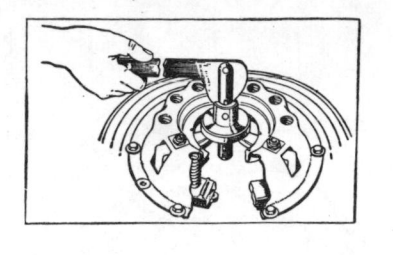

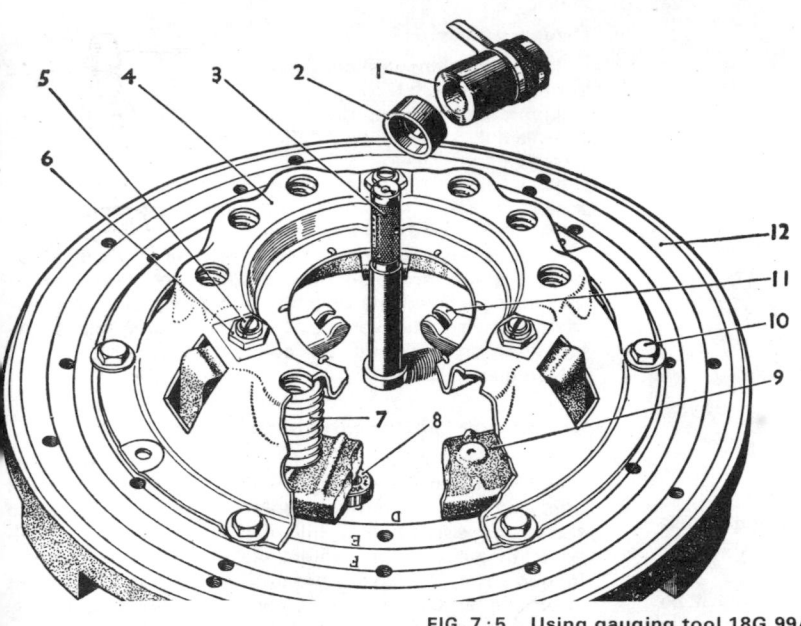

FIG 7:5   Using gauging tool 18G.99A

Key to Fig 7:5   1 Height finger   2 Distance piece   3 Centre pillar   4 Clutch cover   5 Eyebolt   6 Eyebolt locknut
7 Pressure spring   8 Spacing washer   9 Pressure plate   10 Set bolt   11 Release lever   12 Baseplate

reservoir, with Unipart 410 or 550 Brake Fluid, or if not available, a fluid to specification SAE J1703C. **Do not use any other type.**

Using full, slow strokes, pump the clutch pedal until the fluid entering the container is completely free from air bubbles. It is essential to keep the level of the fluid in the master cylinder topped up during the bleeding process. When the fluid is completely free from all air bubbles, tighten the bleed screw on a down stroke of the pedal. Tighten up the bleed screw completely and remove the bleed tube.

7:5 Removing and replacing the clutch

Remove the gearbox as detailed in **Chapter 8.** Remove the clutch housing bolts and withdraw the gearbox from the engine, being very careful to support it until the first motion shaft is clear of the driven plate and the release lever plate.

Loosen each of the hexagon bolts securing the clutch to the flywheel a turn at a time until spring pressure is released. The clutch cover can now be disengaged from the dowels on the flywheel and the whole assembly lifted off.

When refitting the clutch, place the driven plate assembly on the flywheel with the larger chamfered spline end of the driven plate hub away from the flywheel.

Centralize the driven plate with tool 18G.39 for petrol engines or 18G.628 for diesel, fitted into the splined bore of the hub and the pilot bearing in the flywheel. If this tool is not available a spare first motion shaft makes a good substitute. Then locate the cover assembly on the flywheel dowels and tighten the bolts diagonally a turn at a time.

Remove the clutch centralizing tool when all the bolts are fully tightened and refit the gearbox, again being most careful to support the weight in order to avoid any strain on the shaft and damage to the driven plate assembly.

7:6 Dismantling the clutch

Two methods are possible in dismantling the clutch, using the clutch assembly gauging fixture 18G.99A or by using a press and blocks of wood.

Using the clutch assembly gauging fixture:

The gauging fixture in use for dismantling the clutch can be seen in **FIG 7:5.** Consult the code card to determine the correct spacers for the particular clutch. Place the spacers on the base plate in the positions indicated on the code card and place the clutch on the spacer. Screw the actuator into the central hole in the base plate and press the handle to clamp the clutch. Screw the set bolts firmly into the base plate. The clutch can now be compressed or released as required.

Compress the clutch with the actuator and remove the adjusting nuts gradually to relieve the load of the thrust springs. Lift the cover off the clutch and carry out whatever additional dismantling may be necessary.

Using a press and wood blocks:

Place the cover on the bed of a press with the pressure plate resting on wood blocks so arranged that the cover is left free to move downwards. Place a block or bar across the top of the cover, resting it on the spring bosses (see **FIG 7:6**).

Apply pressure to the cover with the spindle of a press and, holding it under compression, remove the three

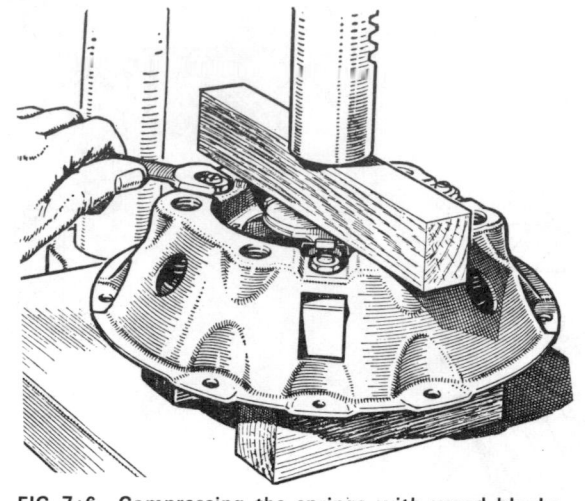

FIG 7:6 Compressing the springs with wood blocks and press

adjusting nuts. The pressure from the press may now be released gradually until the clutch springs are fully extended.

While stripping down the coverplate assembly, the parts should be marked so that they may be reassembled in the same relative position to each other to ensure that the correct balance is maintained. When a new pressure plate is fitted it is essential that the complete cover and pressure plate assembly be accurately balanced, and it is not a practical proposition to fit new pressure plates unless balancing facilities are available.

All parts are available for inspection when the cover is lifted off.

To remove the release levers, grasp the lever and eyebolt between the thumb and fingers so that the inner end of the lever and the threaded end of the eyebolt are as near together as possible, keeping the eyebolt pin seated in its socket in the lever. The strut can then be lifted over the ridge on the end of the lever, making it possible to lift the eyebolt off the pressure plate. It is advisable to renew any parts which show any signs of wear.

7:7 Servicing the clutch, clutch facings

Spring pressure:

A tolerance of not more than 10 to 15 lb (4.5 to 6.8 kg) pressure is allowable on the compression load of the operating springs when at their assembled height and all clutch springs are tested for this before assembly.

The clutch operating springs are not affected by high clutch temperatures, as the pressure plate absorbs heat rapidly, the springs have only line contact, and a draught is continually passing under them when the engine is running.

Tolerances:

Wear on the working faces of the driven plate is about .001 inch (.02 mm) per 1000 miles (1600 km) under normal running conditions. The accuracy of the alignment of the face of the driven plate must be within .015 inch (.38 mm).

Driven plates:

It is most important that neither oil or grease should contact the clutch facings.

Lubrication of the splines of the driven plate is provided at assembly only, when CS881 graphite grease or zinc based Keenol is used.

It is essential to install a complete driven plate assembly when renewal of the friction surfaces is required. If the facings have worn to such an extent as to warrant renewal, then slight wear will have taken place on the splines and also on the torque reaction springs and their seatings. The question of balance and concentricity is also involved. Under no circumstances are repairs to be carried out, or faults rectified, in the clutch driven plate centres.

Condition of clutch facings in service:

It is natural to assume that a rough surface will give a higher frictional value against slipping than a polished one, but this is not necessarily correct. A roughened surface consists of small hills and dales, only the 'high spots' of which make contact. As the amount of useful friction for the purpose of taking up drive is dependent upon the area in actual contact, it is obvious that a perfectly smooth face is required to transmit the maximum amount of power for a given surface area.

Since non-metallic facings of the moulded asbestos type have been introduced in service the polished surface is common, but it must not be confused with the glazed surface which is sometimes encountered due to other conditions. The ideally smooth or polished condition will therefore provide proper surface contact, but a glazed surface entirely alters the frictional value of the facing, and will result in excessive clutch slip. These two conditions might simply be illustrated by a comparison between a piece of smoothly finished wood and one with a varnished surface. In the former the contact is made directly by the original material, whereas in the latter instance a film of dry varnish is interposed between the contact surfaces and actual contact is made by the varnish.

If the clutch has been in service for some time under satisfactory conditions, the surface of the facing assumes a high polish through which the grain of the material can be clearly seen. The polished facing is of light colour when in perfect condition.

Should oil in small quantities gain access to the clutch and find its way onto the facings, it will be burnt off as a result of the heat generated by the slipping occurring under normal starting conditions. The burning of this small quantity of lubricant has the effect of gradually darkening the faces, but provided the polish of the facings remains so that the grain of the material can be distinguished clearly, it has little effect on clutch performance.

Should increased quantities of oil obtain access to the facing, then one of two conditions, or a combination of these, may arise, depending upon the nature of the oil:

1 The oil may burn off and leave a carbon deposit on the surface of the facings, which assume a high glaze producing further slip. There is a very definite, though very thin, deposit, and in general it hides the grain of the material.

2 The oil may partially burn and leave a resinous deposit on the facings. This has a tendency to produce

a fierce clutch, and may also cause excessive 'spinning' due to the tendency of the face of the linings to adhere to the surface of the flywheel or pressure plate.

3 There may be a combination of these two conditions which produce a tendency to 'judder' on engagement. Still greater quantities of oil produce a dark and soaked appearance of the facings, and the result will be further slip, accompanied by fierceness or 'juddering'.

If the conditions listed above are experienced, the clutch driven plate should be replaced by a new one. The cause of the presence of oil must be traced and removed. It is, of course, necessary for the clutch and flywheel to be cleaned out thoroughly before assembly.

Where the graphite release bearing ring is badly worn, either a complete replacement assembly or a new graphite ring should be fitted. These graphite rings are inserted into their metal cup by heating the metal cup to a cherry red, then forcing the graphite ring into position. Immediately the ring is forced into position, the whole should be quenched in oil. Alignment of the thrust pad in relation to the face and trunnions should be within .005 inch (.12 mm).

In almost every case of rapid wear on the splines of the clutch driven plate, misalignment is responsible.

Looseness of the driven plate on the splined shaft results in noticeable backlash in the clutch. Misalignment also puts undue stress on the driven member, and may result in the hub breaking loose from the plate, with consequent total failure of the clutch.

It may also be responsible for a fierce chattering or dragging of the clutch, which makes gear changing difficult. In cases of persistent difficulty, it is advisable to check the flywheel for truth with a dial indicator. The dial reading should not vary more than .003 inch (.07 mm) anywhere on the flywheel face.

7:8 Reassembly, adjusting release levers, refitting

Reassembly:

1 Lay the pressure plate on the wood block on the bed of the press (or on the base plate of the clutch assembly gauging fixtures), and place the springs on it in a vertical position, seating them on their small locating bosses.

2 Clean all parts and renew any which show signs of wear or damage.

3 Assemble the release levers, eyebolts and eyebolt pins, holding the threaded end of the eyebolt and the inner end of the lever as close together as possible. With the other hand insert the strut in the slots of the pressure plate lug just sufficiently to allow the plain end of the eyebolt to be inserted in the hole in the pressure plate.

4 Move the strut upwards into the slots in the pressure plate lugs, over the ridge on the short end of the lever, and drop it into the grooves formed in the lever.

5 Lay the cover over the parts, taking care that any anti-rattle springs are in position as shown in **FIG 7:2** and that the springs are directly under the seats in the cover. Also make sure, if using the original parts, that the eyebolts, eyebolt nuts, pressure plate lugs, and cover are fitted in their correct relative positions, as marked when dismantling, to ensure correct balance being maintained.

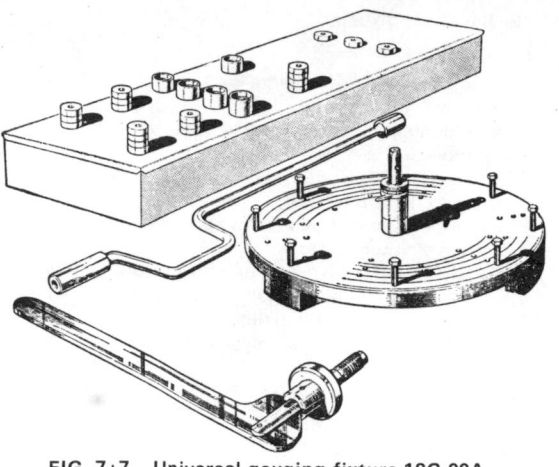

FIG 7:7   Universal gauging fixture 18G.99A

6 Compress the springs either by actuator if the gauging fixture is being used, or by the use of a wooden block across the cover and a press. Take care to guide the eyebolts and the pressure plate lugs through the correct holes in the cover. Check that the thrust springs remain correctly seated.

7 Replace the eyebolt nuts on the eyebolts and release the pressure compressing the cover assembly.

Adjusting the release levers:

Satisfactory operation of the clutch is dependent upon accurate adjustment of the release lever so that the pressure plate face is maintained parallel to the flywheel face.

This cannot be accomplished by setting the levers parallel to the face of the release bearings after the clutch has been assembled to the flywheel because of the variation in thickness of the driven plate.

For an accurate adjustment the universal gauging fixture must be used. This is shown in **FIG 7:7** and with the use of this tool a clutch assembly can be quickly dismantled, rebuild and finally adjusted with a high degree of accuracy.

After carrying out any necessary servicing, reassemble the parts of the clutch pressure plate, and place the cover on it and the whole assembly on the base plate of the gauging fixture. It is essential that the correct spacers are used, as indicated on the code card.

Bolt the cover to the base plate and screw the adjusting nuts onto the bolts until the tops of the nuts are flush with the tops of the bolts. Screw the actuator into the base plate and work the handle a dozen times to settle the mechanism. Remove the actuator. Screw the pillar firmly into the base plate and place the appropriate adaptor on the pillar with the recessed side downwards. Place the gauge finger in position.

Turn the adjusting nuts until the finger just touches each release lever, pressing downwards on the finger assembly to ensure that it is bearing squarely on the adaptor. Remove the finger and the pillar and replace the actuator, operate the actuator several times. Recheck with the finger assembly and make any necessary further adjustments. Lock the adjusting nuts.

7:9 Fault diagnosis

(a) Drag or spin

1 Oil or grease on driven plate linings
2 Bent engine backplate
3 Misalignment between the engine and the gearbox first motion shaft
4 Leaking master cylinder, slave cylinder or pipeline
5 Driven plate hub binding on first motion shaft splines
6 Binding of first motion shaft spigot bearing
7 Distorted clutch plate
8 Warped or damaged pressure plate or clutch cover
9 Broken driven plate linings
10 Dirt or foreign matter in clutch
11 Air in the clutch hydraulic system

(b) Fierceness or snatch

1 Check 1, 2, 3 and 4 in (a)
2 Worn clutch linings

(c) Slip

1 Check 1, 2 and 3 in (a)
2 Check 2 in (b)
3 Weak pressure springs
4 Seized piston in clutch slave cylinder

(d) Judder

1 Check 1, 2 and 3 in (a)
2 Pressure plate not parallel with flywheel face
3 Contact area of driven plate linings not evenly distributed

4 Bent first motion shaft
5 Buckled driven plate
6 Faulty engine or gearbox rubber mountings
7 Worn suspension shackles
8 Weak rear springs
9 Loose propeller shaft bolts
10 Loose rear spring clips

(e) Rattle

1 Check 3 in (c)
2 Broken springs in driven plate
3 Worn release mechanism
4 Excessive backlash in transmission
5 Wear in transmission bearings
6 Release bearing loose on fork

(f) Tick or knock

1 Worn first motion shaft spigot or bearing
2 Badly worn splines in driven plate hub
3 Release plate out of line
4 Faulty Bendix drive on starter
5 Loose flywheel

(g) Driven plate fracture

1 Check 2 and 3 in (a)
2 Drag or distortion due to hanging gearbox in plate hub

CHAPTER 8

THE GEARBOX

8:1 Description

The gearbox fitted to these vehicles has four forward speeds and a reverse, of which the three upper ratios have synchromesh engagement.

A combined dipstick and filler is on the top of the gearbox and a drain plug is situated underneath.

The bellhousing is integral with the gearbox and accommodates the clutch release mechanism. An extension bolted to the rear end of the gearbox contains the third motion shaft and the speedometer drive.

An exploded view of the gearbox components is given in **FIG 8:1**.

8:2 Removing and replacing the gearbox

The gearbox can be removed without disturbing the engine. The vehicle should be run over a pit or raised sufficiently to permit the gearbox to be lowered and withdrawn from underneath.

Disconnect the propeller shaft as described in **Chapter 10**. Without disconnecting the fluid pipe, release the slave cylinder from the clutch housing and secure the pushrod to prevent accidental ejection.

Disconnect the speedometer cable from the gearbox. Disconnect the remote control rod from the extension arm on the gearbox. Remove the starter and solenoid cables.

Detach the carburetter air cleaner and remove the exhaust down-pipe and silencer complete. Drain the gearbox oil.

Take the weight of the engine on a jack or suitable lifting tackle and remove the bolts securing the clutch housing to the engine and support the clutch housing.

Unscrew the bolts securing the gearbox crossmember to the body frame longitudinal members and carefully withdraw the gearbox to the rear without allowing its weight to rest on the clutch driven plate.

Replacement of the gearbox is the reverse of the removal procedure.

8:3 Dismantling the gearbox

Remove the gearbox mounting crossmember. Unscrew the speedometer drive, but do not withdraw the pinion from the bush or damage to the oil seal may result.

Undo the setscrews and remove the remote control extension casing (see **FIG 8:2**). Remove six bolts and take off the rear extension cover and joint washer. Remove the interlock arm and bracket from the aperture in the rear extension.

Unscrew three countersunk screws and seven setscrews and remove the gearbox cover.

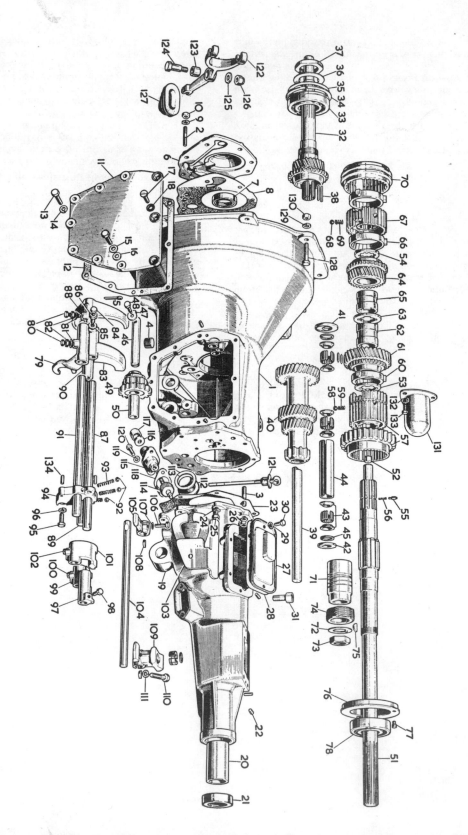

FIG 8:1 Components of gearbox

Remove two nuts and six setscrews and pull the extension from the gearbox, at the same time manoeuvring the remote control shaft selector lever down and out from the selectors.

Cut the locking wire and unscrew the three change-speed fork setscrews. Release the three locknuts and slacken the fork locating screws.

Unscrew the two setscrews and remove the shifter shaft locating block with shifter shaft, from the gearbox, noting the two dowels in the block. If the rods are withdrawn from the locating block take care to catch the three selector balls and springs.

Withdraw the forks from the box in the following order: reverse, top and third, first and second.

Unscrew the clutch lever pivot nut, take out the pivot bolt and remove the lever with the thrust bearing.

Unscrew the nuts and remove the gearbox front cover complete with oil seal, noting the bearing shims between the cover and the front bearing. Tap out the layshaft and allow the gear unit to rest in the bottom of the box.

Undo the retaining screw and remove the reverse shaft and gear.

Withdraw the third motion shaft (mainshaft) assembly to the rear. Withdraw the first motion shaft and drive gear not omitting to retrieve the 18 spigot needle rollers. Lift out the layshaft gear unit and the two thrust washers.

8:4 The third motion shaft (mainshaft)

Dismantling:

Remove the following items in this order: baulk ring, top and third synchromesh sleeve and hub, second baulk ring. Note the three locating balls and springs that will be released if the synchromesh sleeve is separated from the hub.

Press down the third-speed cone thrust washer locating plunger, rotate the thrust washer to align its splines with those on the shaft and remove the washer. Withdraw the third-speed gear and its splined bush (see **FIG 8:3**).

Withdraw the bush interlocking washer to free the second-speed gear with its bush and baulk ring.

Remove the rear thrust washer from the splines on the shaft and withdraw the first-speed gear and second-speed synchronizer taking care not to lose the three balls if the gear is separated from the synchronizer.

Tap up the locking washer and unscrew the rear retaining nut. Withdraw the washer, speedometer drive gear and key and the distance sleeve from the shaft.

Press the rear bearing and its housing from the shaft.

Assembly:

This part is carried out from the front end. Fit the rear thrust washer on the front end of the splines with its ground face to the front.

Push the longer phosphor-bronze bush up to the splines with the dogs to the front. This bush is a tight fit and heating in warm oil will assist the fitting. Note that the oil hole in the bush must register with the hole in the shaft.

Fit the second-speed baulk ring and gear on the bush with the plain side of the gear to the front.

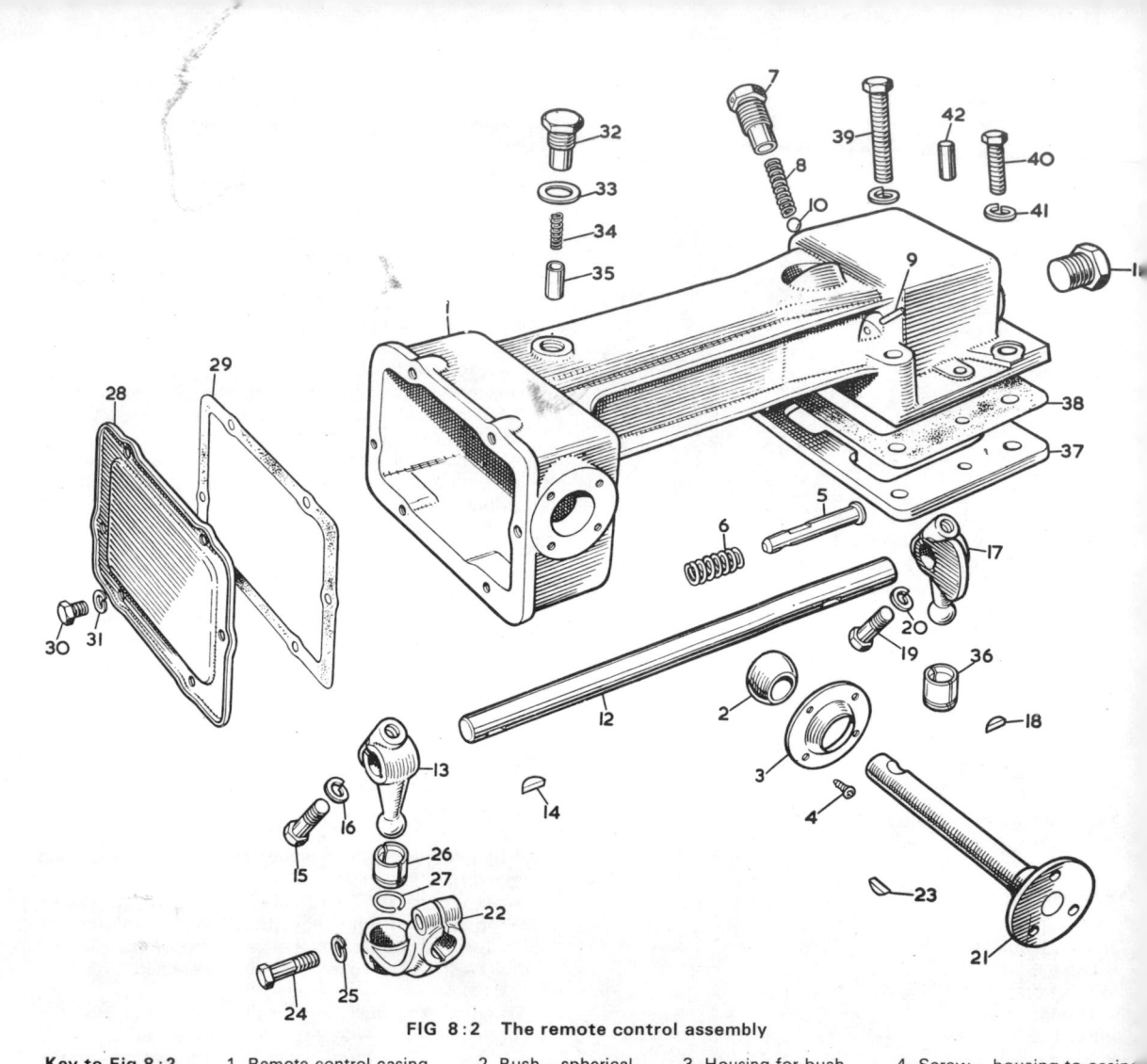

FIG 8:2   The remote control assembly

Key to Fig 8:2   1 Remote control casing   2 Bush—spherical   3 Housing for bush   4 Screw—housing to casing
5 Plunger—reverse   6 Spring—plunger   7 Plug for plunger detent   8 Spring—plunger detent   9 Dowel—selector plunger
10 Ball—plunger   11 Plug for casing   12 Cross-shaft   13 Lever (outer)   14 Key for lever   15 Setscrew for lever
16 Washer (spring)   17 Lever (inner)   18 Key for lever   19 Setscrew for lever   20 Washer (spring)   21 Coupling shaft
and flange   22 Gear change lever (outer)   23 Key for lever   24 Setscrew for lever   25 Washer (spring)   26 Bush—lever
27 Circlip for bush   28 Plate—cover   29 Gasket for plate   30 Setscrew   31 Washer (spring)   32 Plug—ball retaining
33 Banjo washer   34 Spring—selector lever   35 Plunger—control shaft   36 Bush—selector lever—inner   37 Plate—stop
38 Gasket   39 Setscrew to extension   40 Setscrew to extension   41 Washer   42 Dowel to extension

Slide on the bush interlocking washer and the shorter splined bush, locating the dogs of both bushes in the interlocking washer. Again, heating in warm oil will assist.

Insert the spring and plunger into the hole in the shaft (see **FIG 8:3**).

Fit the third-speed gear onto the bush with the cone towards the front.

Thread on the front thrust washer, machined face to the rear, while holding down the plunger by means of a thin punch through the hole in the gear cone, and push the washer over it (see **FIG 8:4**). Turn the washer to allow the plunger to engage in the splines.

Fit the three springs and balls to the third-speed synchronizer and, using tool 18G.223, push on the synchronizer sleeve (striking dog).

Push on the top and third gear synchromesh assembly hub with its two baulk rings, having the plain side of the hub facing the rear.

This part is assembled from the rear end.

Insert the three balls and springs in the second gear hub and, using tool 18G.222, push the synchronizer sleeve into position on the hub.

Fit the first-speed gear and synchromesh hub assembly and the baulk ring to the splines on the shaft.

Press the rear bearing into its housing and fit it to the shaft, the flange of the housing to the rear.

Push on the distance sleeve, speedometer drive gear and key and secure with the lockwasher and nut.

8:5 The layshaft gear

Extract one of the circlips from the layshaft gear and push out the bearing and distance tube assembly. Note that there are three needle races and one distance tube spaced in the layshaft gear which are retained by a circlip at each end, two races being fitted at the front end and one at the rear.

Assembly:

Fit a circlip to the innermost groove in the gear and then hold the shaft vertically in a vice. Assemble a roller bearing on the shaft against the vice jaws and then slide the gear over the shaft and the bearing with the large gear downwards.

Remove the shaft from the vice and push the bearing into the gear against the circlip. Fit a circlip, the end roller bearing assembly and the retaining circlip.

Slide the distance tube into the other end of the gear, followed by the other end bearing and circlip. Remove the gear from the shaft.

8:6 The first motion shaft

Unlock and remove the securing nut and withdraw the locking washer.

Press the bearing from the shaft and remove the circlip from the bearing.

The bearing is refitted to the shaft with the spring ring away from the gear. Replace the locking washer and tighten the retaining nut and secure with the locking tab.

8:7 Assembling the gearbox

Place the layshaft gear in the gearbox complete with the end thrust washer but do not fit the layshaft, use dummy layshaft tool 18G.471 to retain the thrust washers in position (see **FIG 8:5**).

Replace the first motion shaft and insert the 18 needle roller bearings. Insert the third motion shaft assembly from the rear of the gearbox entering the spigot in the needle rollers of the first motion shaft. Use the gasket fitted between the gearbox and the rear extension to position the dowel and bearing housing. Push the shaft right home.

Fit the layshaft, lining up the cutaway portion of the front end with the locating groove in the front cover.

Fit the reverse gear and shaft, tighten the setscrew and secure with the locking washer.

Refit the front end cover, replacing the bearing shims which were removed on dismantling. Correct fitting is most important, together with scrupulous cleanliness and condition of the mating components. Always use a new joint gasket and renew the cover if it is not in good condition.

Offer up the front cover, less oil seal, to the gearbox and push it fully onto the studs doing any polishing up necessary to ensure that it is free to float a little in all directions. Lift off the cover and fit a new oil seal with its inner lip facing towards the gearbox. Apply a thin coat of grease and fit the gasket to the gearbox front face.

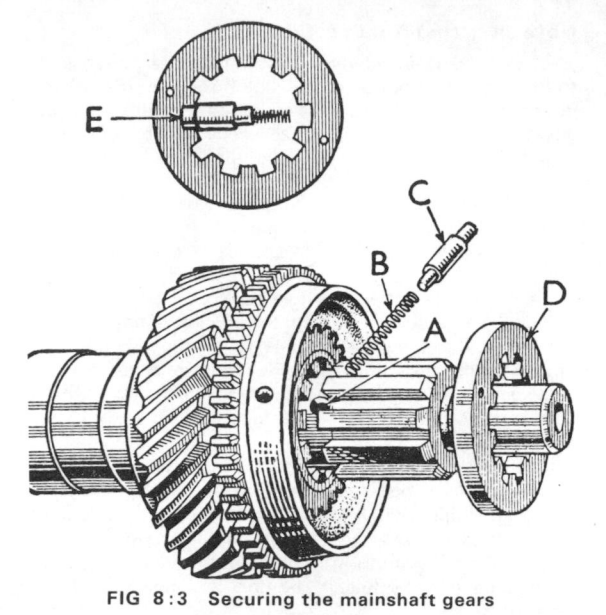

FIG 8:3 Securing the mainshaft gears

Key to Fig 8:3   **A** Hole for spring   **B** Spring
C Locating peg   **D** Locking washer   **E** Peg located in washer

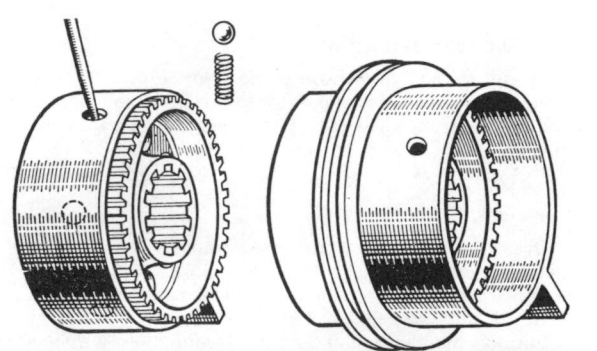

FIG 8:4 Using a thin punch as a guide when reassembling the balls and springs into the synchromesh unit

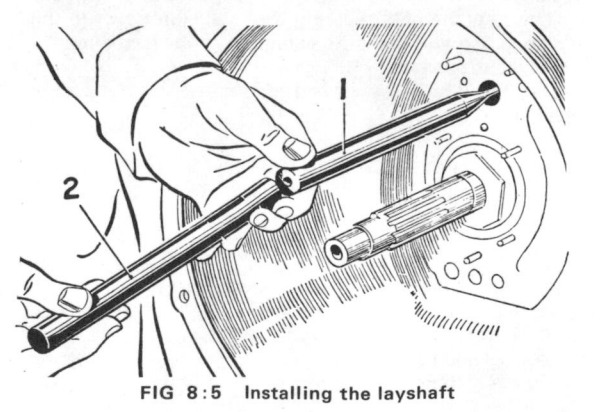

FIG 8:5   Installing the layshaft

Key to Fig 8:5   1 Pilot shaft 18G.471   2 Layshaft

Note on fitting front cover:

In the course of removal it may have been necessary to remove the pivot bolt of the clutch fork and the rubber dust seal and to withdraw the fork together with the front cover. In these cases, it is equally necessary to refit them together.

The centralizing tool 18G.630 must be fitted into the seal before offering it to the gearbox. Position the clutch fork loosely to the cover and manipulate the plate until the oil seal has safely passed the splines of the first motion shaft.

Remove the centralizer while the fork is positioned in the cover and clutch housing. Replace the centralizer in the oil seal and push the cover fully onto the gearbox studs. Fit the nuts and spring washers with the fingers only and keeping the centralizer firmly in position tighten them diagonally half a turn at a time until fully secured.

Position the gearchange forks in the gearbox in the following order: first and second, third and top, reverse.

Bolt the shifter shaft locating block to the rear face of the gearbox, replace the balls and springs and push the shifter shafts through the block into their respective changespeed forks. Insert, tighten and lock the three locating screws.

Position the selectors on the rear end of the shifter shafts. Insert, tighten and wire up the setscrews.

8 : 8 The rear extension

To obtain access to those components inside the rear extension such as the rear extension bush, joint washer and speedometer drive gear it is necessary to remove the gearbox.

Removal:

Drain the oil from the gearbox. Remove the speedometer drive and the breather assembly. Remove the propeller shaft. Remove the oil seal assembly using tools 18G.389 and 18G.389A or 18G.389B.

Support the gearbox and engine, preferably by means of a jib crane and a hook sling on the rear lifting stud bracket, and remove the bolts and nuts securing the gearbox crossmember to the floor longitudinal members.

Unscrew the nuts securing the extension cover to the gearbox and withdraw the extension cover to the rear to clear the mainshaft.

Tap back the lockwasher and unscrew the nut on the mainshaft.

Remove the key, speedometer drive and distance piece.

Clean all parts in paraffin and blow out the oil channels. Examine the bush for wear and renew if necessary.

Replacement:

This is a reversal of the above procedure, remembering to dip all parts in clean engine oil before assembly. Use a new gasket joint and fit a new oil seal assembly with tools 18G.123 and 18G.314M or 18G.134N.

Assembling:

Having fitted the new oil seal, locate the remote control rod in the rear extension.

Fit the front and rear selector levers to the remote control rod, making sure that these are secured and located by the setscrews and keys.

Fit the rear extension to the gearbox, locating the control rod selector arm in the shifter rod selectors. Fit the interlock arm to the rear extension and refit the cover.

Attach the stop plate and remote control cross assembly after locating the inner selector lever and bush in the rear extension.

Replace the side cover, using a new joint, fit the speedometer drive gear assembly, drain plug and breather. Refill with the recommended grade of oil.

8 : 9 Fault diagnosis

(a) Jumping out of gear

1 Broken spring behind locating ball for selector rod
2 Excessively worn groove in selector rod
3 Worn coupling dogs
4 Fork to selector rod securing screw loose

(b) Noisy gearbox

1 Insufficient oil
2 Excessive end float in layshaft
3 Worn or damaged bearings
4 Worn or damaged gear teeth

(c) Difficulty in engaging gear

1 Incorrect clutch pedal adjustment
2 Worn synchronizing cones
3 Wear in selectors

(d) Oil leaks

1 Damaged joint washers
2 Worn or damaged oil seals
3 One of the covers loose or damaged
4 Extension cover and shafts out of alignment

CHAPTER 9

THE AUTOMATIC TRANSMISSION

9:1 Description

The automatic transmission incorporates a fluid torque converter coupling in place of the usual flywheel and clutch. The converter is coupled to a hydraulically operated planetary gearbox which provides three forward ratios and reverse. All forward ratios are automatically engaged in accordance with accelerator position and speed of the car.

Over-riding control with appropriate engine braking is available for the first and second gear ratios by manual selection of 'L'. The automatic transmission is shown in section in **FIG 9:1**.

The use of a hydraulic torque converter (see **FIG 9:2**) in conjunction with a threespeed automatic gearbox provides a means of obtaining a smooth application of engine power to the driving wheels and additional engine torque multiplication to the first and second gears of the gearbox.

The converter also provides extreme low speed flexibility when the gearbox is in third gear and due to its ability to multiply engine torque, it provides good acceleration from very low road speeds without having to resort to a downshift in the gearbox.

Torque multiplication from the converter is infinitely variable between the ratios of 2:1 and 1:1. The speed range, during which torque multiplication can be achieved, is also variable, depending upon the accelerator position.

The hydraulic torque converter for use in conjunction with the automatic gearbox is $9\frac{1}{2}$ inches (241 mm) in diameter.

It is of the single phase, three element type, comprising an impeller connected to the engine crankshaft, a turbine connected to the input shaft of the gearbox, and a stator mounted on a sprag type, one-way clutch, supported on a fixed hub projecting from the gearbox case.

Gear set:

The planetary gear set (see **FIG 9:3**), consists of two sun gears, two sets of pinions, a pinion carrier and a ring gear. Helical involute tooth forms are used throughout. Power enters the gear set via the sun gears. In all forward gears power enters through the forward sun gear; in reverse gear power enters through the reverse sun gear. Power leaves the gear set by the ring gear. The pinions are used to transmit power from the sun gears to the ring gear.

In reverse a single set of pinions is used, which causes the ring gear to rotate in the opposite direction to the sun gear. In forward gears a double set of pinions is used to

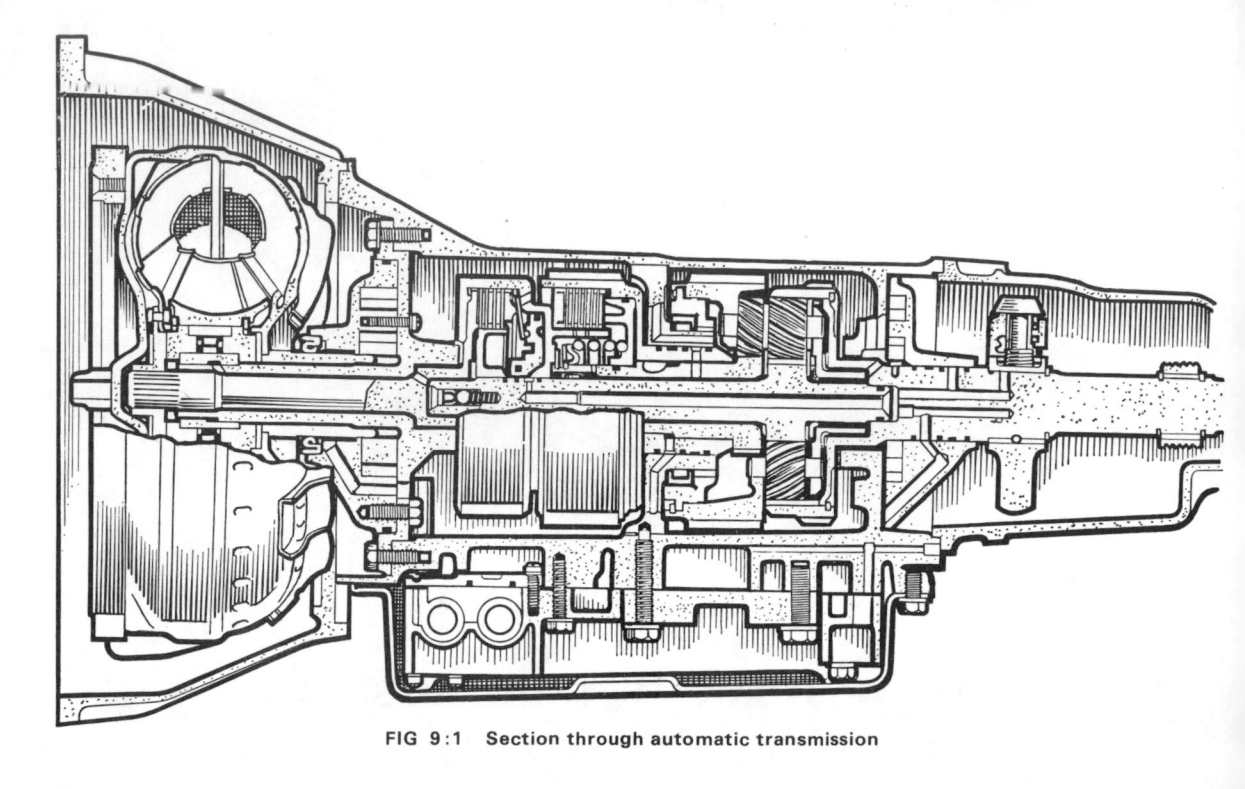

FIG 9:1   Section through automatic transmission

cause the ring to rotate in the same direction as the sun gear. The carrier locates the pinions in their correct positions relative to the sun gears and the ring gear, and also forms a reaction member for certain conditions. The various mechanical ratios of gear set are obtained by the engagement of hydraulically operated multi-disc clutches and brake bands.

Clutches:

Multi-disc clutches operated by hydraulic pistons connect the converter to the gear set. In all forward gears the front clutch connects the converter to the forward sun gear, for reverse the rear clutch connects the converter to the reverse sun gear.

Bands:

Brake bands, operated by hydraulic servos, hold elements of the gear set stationary to effect an output speed reduction and a torque increase. In first gear of lock-up the rear band holds the pinion carrier stationary and provides the first gear ratio of 2.39:1 and, in reverse, a ratio of 2.09:1. The front band holds the reverse sun gear stationary to provide the second gear ratio of 1.45:1.

One-way clutch:

In drive a one-way clutch is used in place of the rear band to prevent the pinion carrier from turning in the opposite direction to engine rotation, thus also providing a first gear ratio of 2.39:1. This one-way clutch, allowing the gear set to freewheel in first gear, provides smooth ratio changes from first to second, and vice versa.

Hydraulic system:

The hydraulic system contains a front and rear pump, both of the internal/external gear pattern, picking up fluid from the oil pan through separate strainers. Shift control is provided by a centrifugally operated hydraulic governor on the transmission output shaft. The governor works in conjunction with valves in the valve body assembly located in the base of the transmission. These valves regulate fluid pressure and direct it to appropriate transmission components.

Front pump:

The front pump, driven by the converter impeller, is in operation whenever the engine is running. This pump, through the primary and secondary regulator valves, supplies the hydraulic requirements of the transmission with the engine running when the vehicle is stationary, as well as at low vehicle speeds before the rear pump becomes effective. When the rear pump is effective the front pump check valve closes, but a bypass permits the pump to still supply the converter and lubrication requirements in conjunction with the rear pump. It then operates at reduced pressure, excess flow exhausting to inlet and thus minimizing pump losses.

Rear pump:

The rear pump is driven by the drive shaft of the transmission. It is fully effective at speeds above 20 mile/hr approximately, and then supplies the hydraulic requirements of the transmission.

If, due to a dead engine, the front pump is inoperative, the rear pump, above 20 mile/hr, can provide all hydraulic requirements, thus enabling the engine to be started through the transmission.

Control system:

The control system utilizes three basic types of valve, i.e. regulating valves, shuttle valves and a manual valve. A simplified diagram of the system is shown in **FIG 9:4.**

Pressure control is provided by primary and secondary regulator valves, the former operating in conjunction with throttle pressure acting upon the spring end, and modulated throttle pressure acting on the opposite end.

Shift control is provided by 1-2 and 2-3 shift valves operated by governor pressure acting upon one end, and throttle pressure acting upon the spring end, line pressure acting upon differential areas providing shift speed hysteresis.

Manual control is provided by the manual control valve, which, according to the position of the selector, directs fluid to or provides an exhaust for clutch and servo pistons.

9:2 Operation and driving procedure

Operation of the automatic transmission is controlled by a selector mounted beneath the steering wheel on early vehicles (see **FIG 9:5**). Later vehicles have the selector lever mounted on the ducting forward of the engine cover. The position of the lever is indicated by a pointer and a quadrant, the quadrant being marked with the following five positions, 'L', 'D', 'N', 'R' and 'P'. A stop plate is provided to prevent direct selection of 'P', 'R' or 'L' from either 'N' or 'D'. 'D' may be instantly engaged from 'N'.

On early vehicles before engaging 'L', 'R' or 'P', pull the hand lever knob outwards. Before disengaging 'P' pull the hand lever knob outwards. On later vehicles, lift the collar in the lever. Do not engage 'R' or 'P' while the car is in motion.

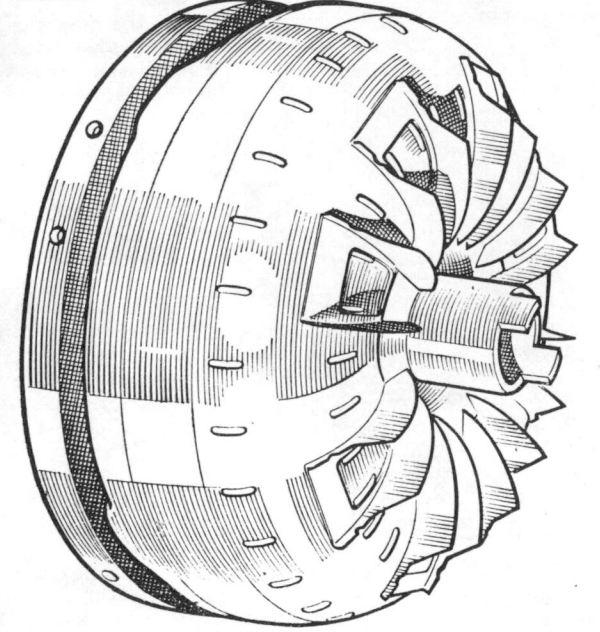

FIG 9:2 Hydraulic torque converter

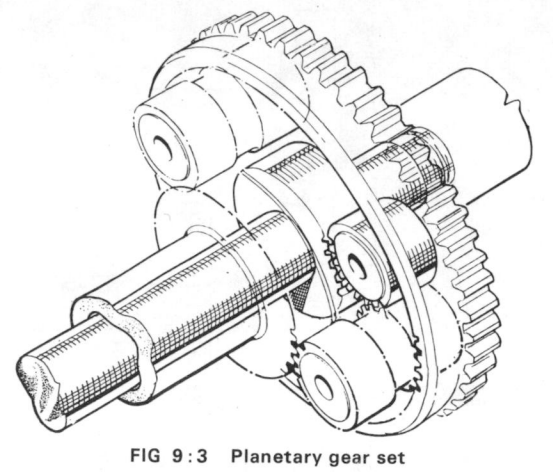

FIG 9:3 Planetary gear set

'P' (Park):

In the park position no engine power is transmitted to the rear wheels. The gearbox is mechanically locked by a parking pawl that engages with a gear on the driven shaft.

Use of the park position is recommended whenever the car is parked or when the engine is to be run for tuning or adjustment.

Do not select 'P' when the car is moving.

'R' (Reverse):

This position provides a reverse ratio with full engine braking.

Do not select 'R' when the car is moving forward.

'N' (Neutral):

In the neutral position no engine power is transmitted to the rear wheels. The handbrake must be applied when the selector is at 'N' and the car is at rest.

'D' (Drive):

The position for all normal driving. This position covers a range of three ratios, all of which are engaged automatically and progressively up and down according to the vehicle speed and the position of the accelerator. Provided the vehicle speed is below a preset maximum, down-changes may be effected by fully depressing the accelerator past a detent button mounted on the pedal (kick-down).

'L' (Lock up):

Provides over-riding control for the first or second gear ratios with appropriate engine braking.

When starting from rest with the selector in 'L', the transmission starts in first gear and will remain locked in that gear irrespective of road speed and accelerator position. This gear provides maximum engine braking.

When the transmission is in the 'D' range, the selection of 'L' will immediately give second gear ratio at road speeds over 5 mile/hr, or first gear ratio at road speeds under 5 mile/hr, with engine braking. First gear may also be obtained at speeds up to 19 mile/hr (diesel models 17 mile/hr) by fully depressing the accelerator pedal (kick-down).

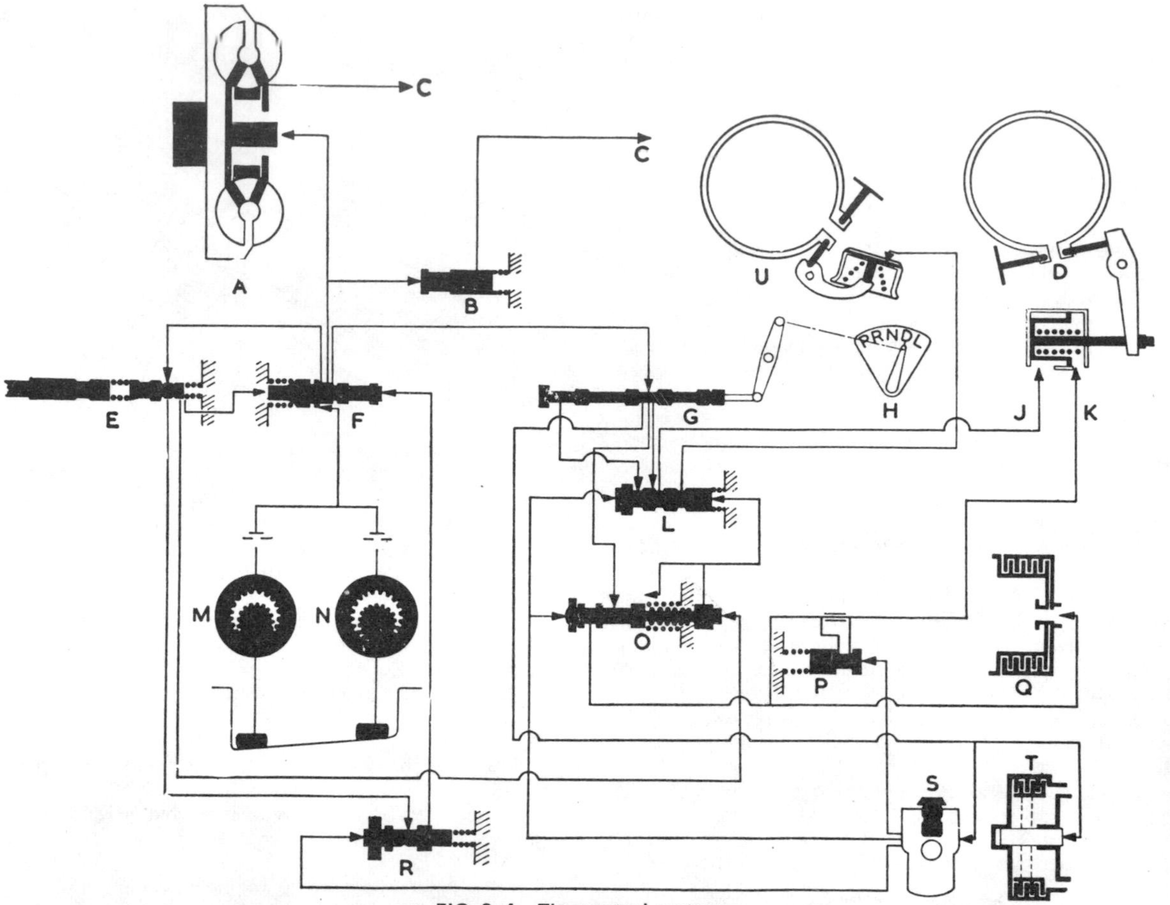

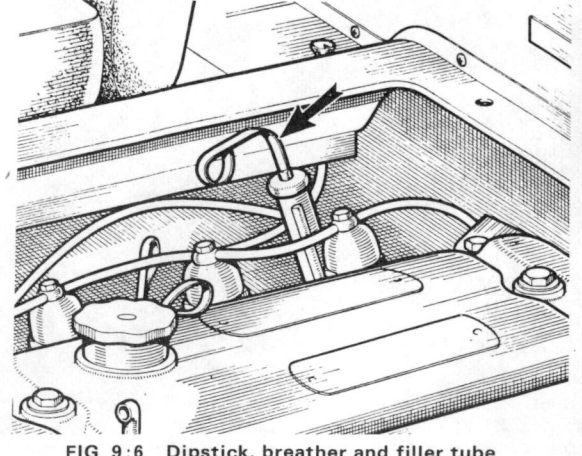

FIG 9:4 The control system

Key to Fig 9:4   **A** Torque converter   **B** Secondary regulator valve   **C** Lubrication   **D** Front band   **E** Downshift and throttle valve   **F** Primary regulator valve   **G** Manual control valve   **H** Selector quadrant   **J** Front servo 'apply'   **K** Front servo 'release'   **L** 1–2 shift valve   **M** Front pump   **N** Rear pump   **O** 2–3 shift valve   **P** Orifice control valve   **Q** Rear clutch   **R** Modulator valve   **S** Governor   **T** Front clutch   **U** Rear band

FIG 9:5 The selector lever and quadrant, early vehicles

FIG 9:6 Dipstick, breather and filler tube

Driving procedure:

A starter inhibitor switch embodied in the gearbox ensures that the starter will only operate when the selector is in the 'P' or 'N' position. With 'N' selected, apply the hand or footbrake before starting the engine.

Always select 'P' and apply the handbrake before attempting to start the engine by means of the solenoid switch under the bonnet or the starting handle, also when tuning or adjusting the engine.

When the engine has been started from cold with the use of mixture control, stalling will be avoided if this control is left out just sufficiently to increase idling speed until the engine has warmed up.

The more apparent transmission engagement under these conditions is not detrimental to the car or the transmission.

Normal driving:

After starting the engine, release the accelerator, apply the footbrake, and move the selector lever to the appropriate forward or reverse position. Release the brake and depress the accelerator.

With the selector in 'D', all forward gears up and down will be automatically and progressively engaged as the speed of the car increases or decreases. Thus all ratio changes are automatically made to suit the speed of the car as well as the torque demanded.

Minimum accelerator pressure will result in low-speed up-changes. If the accelerator is depressed up to the detent the up-changes will occur at higher road speeds. Depressing the accelerator past the detent will .produce up-changes at maximum road speeds.

Irrespective of the accelerator position, starts from rest are always smooth, but the usual delicacy of accelerator control is necessary on slippery surfaces and for maximum fuel economy.

Increased acceleration:

When a lower gear ratio is required for rapid overtaking or hill climbing, kick-down changes are fully under the drivers control except that the maximum downchange speeds for the 3-2, 3-1 and 2-1 gear ratios are preset to give optimum performance without overspeeding the engine. Kick-down does not operate at speeds above:

Changes	Petrol	Diesel
3-2	37 mile/hr	28 mile/hr
2-1	19 mile/hr	17 mile/hr

Engine braking:

When descending steep hills, use the footbrake to reduce the road speed to below 45 miles/hr for petrol models or 40 miles for diesel models when 'L' may be selected. The transmission will instantly change to second gear and thus provide appropriate engine braking.

Driving on soft surfaces:

When the rear wheels fail to grip a surface due to snow, mud or sand, the car may be rocked backwards and forwards by alternately selecting 'R' and 'D' with a small throttle opening.

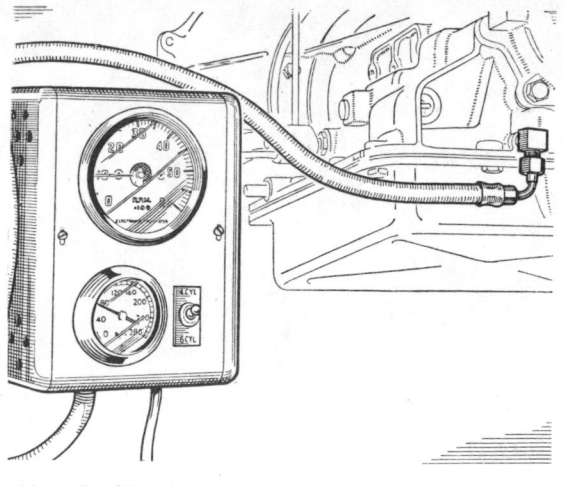

FIG 9:7 Showing use of line pressure gauge and tachometer. Petrol model illustrated

Stopping:

To stop the car, release the accelerator and apply the brakes in the normal way.

Parking:

Stop the car, select 'P' and apply the handbrake as an additional precaution.

Emergency starting:

Cars may be push or tow started. Pushing is recommended as it avoids the danger of the car over-running the towing vehicle.

Select 'N', switch on the ignition, set the mixture control, and release the handbrake. Allow the car to attain a road speed of approximately 25 mile/hr, then select 'D', while fully depressing the accelerator.

Towing for recovery:

Before towing always check the automatic transmission fluid. If there is any reason to suspect that the transmission is faulty or damaged, the propeller shaft must be removed or, alternatively, the rear wheels lifted from the ground before towing commences.

Tow in 'N' and ensure that the handbrake has been released.

9:3 Routine maintenance

In countries where the ambient temperature is unusually high, dust and/or mud must not be allowed to decrease the effective areas of the stoneguards in the converter housing.

On cars which are frequently used on unmade roads, the transmission oil pan must not be allowed to remain caked in mud as this would act as a temperature insulator.

Checking fluid level:

The transmission filler tube with breather and dipstick is located under the engine cowling on the righthand side (see **FIG 9:6**).

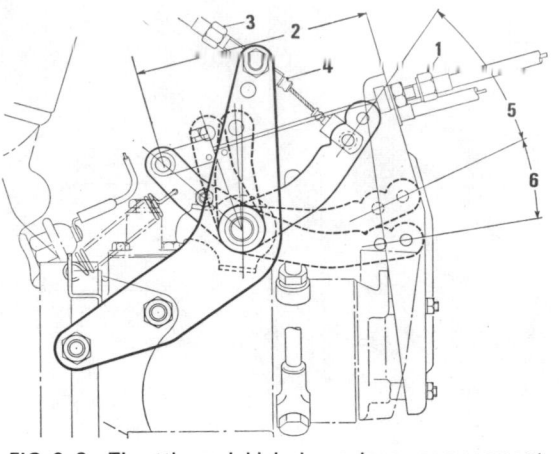

FIG 9:8 Throttle and kick-down lever arrangement. Diesel model illustrated

Key to Fig 9:8   1 Throttle cable adjuster   2 Throttle lever initial setting 4¼ in (11cm)   3 Kick-down cable adjuster   4 Crimped collar   5 Kick-down lever (31 deg. of travel to fully open throttle)   6 Kick-down lever (17 deg. of travel to operate the downshift valve)

The car should be on a level surface and the transmission should be at normal running temperature, i.e. as reached after about five miles of driving.

Select 'P' and allow the engine to idle for two minutes. With the engine still idling in 'P', wipe the dipstick with a non-fluffy rag or clean paper, insert, withdraw immediately. If necessary, add fluid to bring the level to the 'high' mark. The difference between the 'high' and 'low' marks on the dipstick is 1 imperial pint (.6 litre). Do not overfill.

If checked when the fluid is cold, the level must be at least ⅜ inch (10 mm) below the high mark with the engine idling in 'P' as described. The level must be verified at normal running temperature as soon as possible.

Frequent need for topping up is indicative of leakage, which should be rectified immediately to prevent damage to the transmission.

Periodic fluid changes are not recommended.

9:4 Adjustments

Under normal operating conditions no periodic adjustments are required.

Kick-down (down-shift and throttle) cable:

Correct alignment and adjustment is most important. Ensure that the cable trunnion is set to allow the inner cable to follow a natural line throughout the full range of throttle movement.

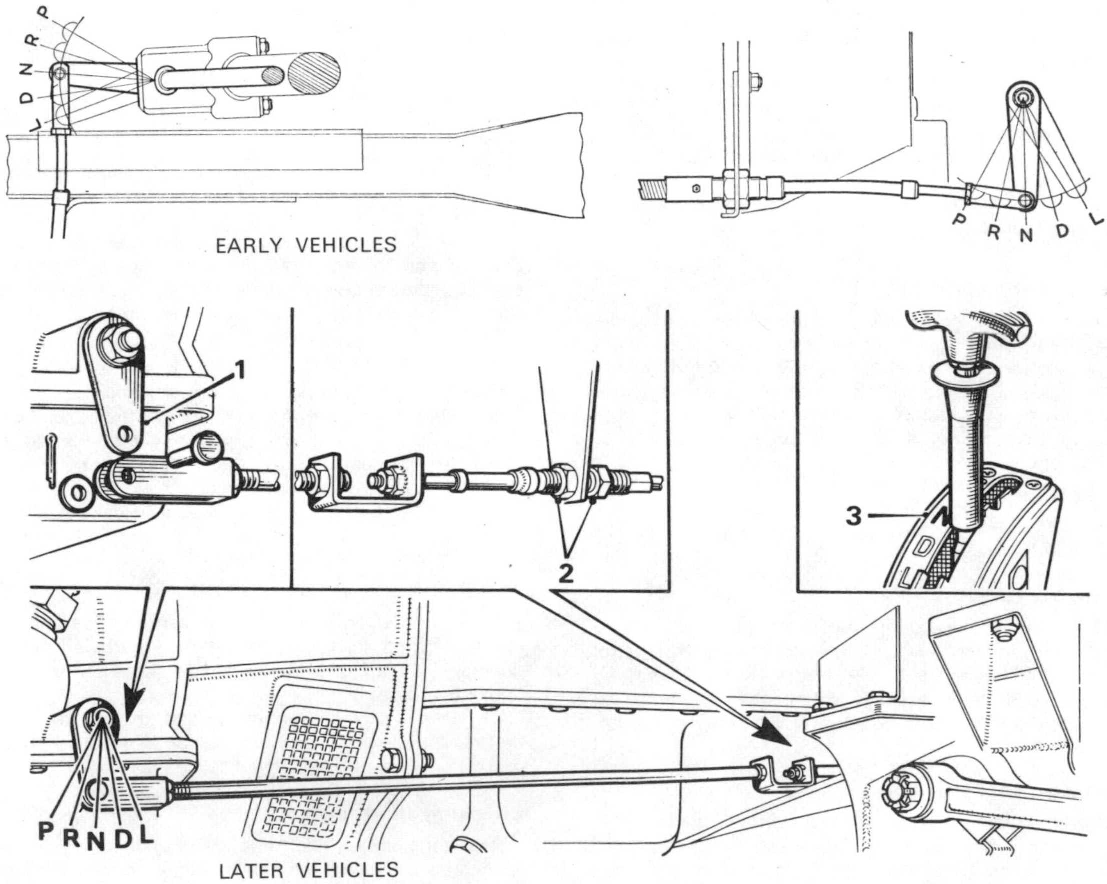

EARLY VEHICLES

LATER VEHICLES

FIG 9:9 Selector levers and linkage adjustment

Cable adjustment is preset by means of a collar crimped on the inner cable between the yoke end and the outer cable adjuster. A check may be made with a line pressure gauge and tachometer (see **FIG 9 : 7**).

With brakes applied and wheels chocked when the engine speed in D is increased from the correct idling by 500 rev/min the line pressure should rise by 15 to 20 lb/sq inch (1.05 to 1.40 kg/sq cm). If the rise is less, the effective length of the outer cable should be increased by means of the adjuster provided. If the rise is more than 20 lb/sq inch the effective length of the cable should be decreased (see **FIG 9 : 8**).

Note that the cable is impregnated with silicon or molybdenum disulphide and must not be oiled.

Selector linkage, early models:

Disconnect both ends of the selector control inner cable from the selector levers.

Select and secure N on the selector lever quadrant and see that the selector lever on the transmission casing is in the central one of the five positions (see **FIG 9 : 9**).

Adjust the control cable at both yoke ends until the holes in the yoke ends and levers line up to allow the clevis pins to be inserted with neither strain nor slackness on the inner cable. If necessary to eliminate any slackness, renew the yoke ends and clevis pins.

Check the linkage in all five positions and feel a definite click in each position.

Selector linkage, later models:

Disconnect linkage at lever 1, slacken locknuts 2 at cable abutment. Select and secure selector lever in 'N', and ensure transmission casing lever is in the central position. Adjust the position of the cable in the abutment until the holes in the yoke and lever line up, and the clevis pin can be inserted without strain or slackness of the inner cable.

Check the operation as before.

Accelerator pedal button:

With the accelerator pedal detent button touching the pedal, the carburetter throttle should be seven-eighths open. On diesel models the throttle lever must be against the maximum fuel stop.

Starter inhibitor switch:

This switch has four terminals, two for the starter inhibitor and two, angled at 45 deg., for the reversing light when fitted.

In the event of a failure, disconnect the four switch leads from the vehicle wiring, which can then be checked by joining together the vehicle leads of each circuit. Both the starting control and the reversing light should then operate in all selector positions. Note that the terminals for each circuit are opposite, i.e. 1-3 starter inhibitor and 2-4 for the reversing light.

Adjusting the switch:

Before starting any adjustments, apply the brakes and chock the wheels, as the vehicle may move off if the engine is started in 'D', 'L' or 'R'. Before adjusting the switch, check the manual linkage adjustment.

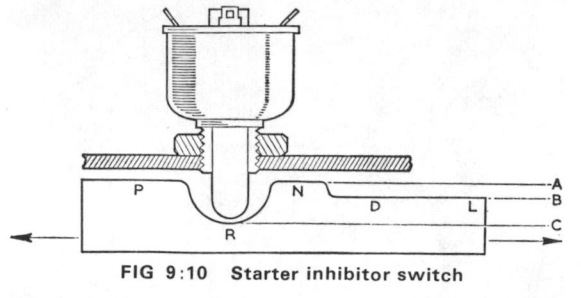

FIG 9:10   Starter inhibitor switch

Key to Fig 9:10   A Starter operative   **B** Starter inoperative
C Starter inoperative, with reversing light on

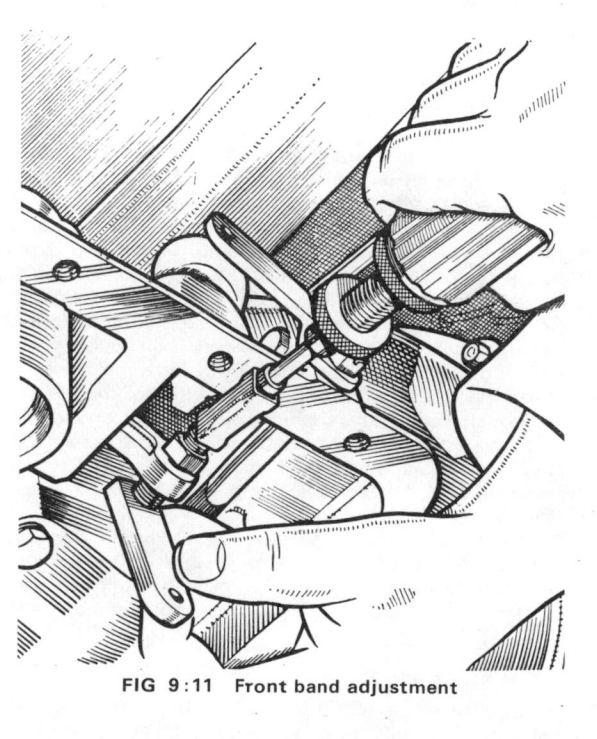

FIG 9:11   Front band adjustment

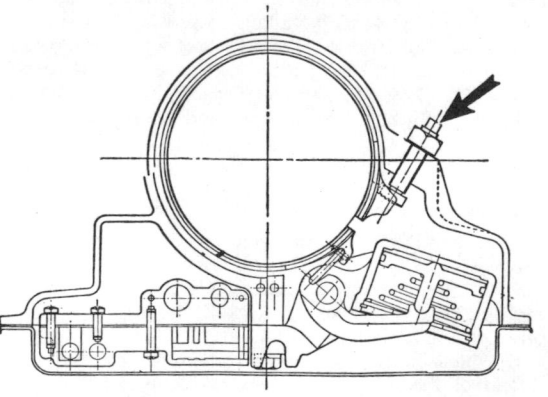

FIG 9:12   Rear band adjustment

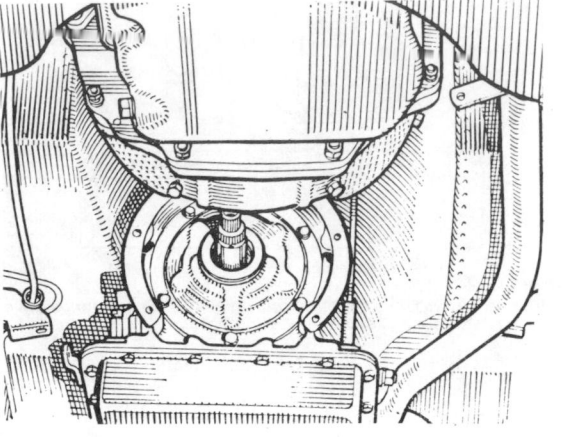

FIG 9:13 Withdrawing gearbox from converter housing

To adjust the switch (see **FIG 9:10**) place the selector lever in 'D' or 'L'. Connect a small bulb and battery across the starter inhibitor terminals and another across the reversing light terminals. Loosen the locknut, fully unscrew the switch from the main case, and then screw it in until the reversing light terminals break. Note and mark the position of the switch in relation to the case. Screw in the switch further, until the starter inhibitor terminals make, again mark the position. Then unscrew the switch until it is in a position midway between the two marks made. In this position, tighten the locknut. Refit the switch leads to the appropriate connectors and verify that the starting control operates only when the selector is in 'P' or 'N' and not in 'D', 'L' or 'R'. Check also that the reversing light if fitted, operates only when the selector is in 'R'.

The boss on some switches may be .030 inch (.76 mm) oversize. Where a switch cannot be adjusted, reduce the thickness of the locknut by .025 inch (.64 mm). If the switch still fails to operate correctly, it must be renewed.

Front brake band:

For this adjustment the gearbox oil pan must be removed. Slacken the locknut (see **FIG 9:11**), move the servo lever outwards, and place the .25 inch (6.35 mm) gauge block between the adjusting screw and the servo piston pin. Tighten the servo adjusting screw to a torque of 10 lb inch (.115 kg m). There is a special torque screwdriver, 18G.681 and spanner 18G.678 to make this job easier. Tighten the locknut and then remove the gauge block.

Rear brake band:

This band has an external adjusting screw in the right-hand wall of the transmission case (see **FIG 9:12**). Slacken the locknut and tighten the adjusting screw to a torque of 7 lb ft (.97 kg m). Back off the adjusting screw one turn and tighten the locknut.

On the second type assembly, identified by the coarse thread of the adjusting screw, back off the adjusting screw threequarters of a turn and tighten the locknut.

9:5 Removing and refitting the transmission

The normal operating temperature of the fluid is between 100 and 115°C (212 and 239°F). To avoid the possibility of scalding, extreme caution must be exercised when draining a transmission which has recently been operating.

Removing gearbox:

1 Before raising the car on a lift, disconnect the downshift cable from the carburetter and outer cable adjuster from the bracket.
2 Drain the fluid from the gearbox oil pan.
3 Remove the propeller shaft.
4 Remove the exhaust system.
5 Disconnect the speedometer cable from the gearbox extension and the leads from the starter inhibitor switch.
6 Disconnect the manual linkage from the selector lever on the gearbox and remove the cable anchor bracket.
7 Disconnect the fluid filler tube and remove the rubber plug from the righthand side of the engine bearer plate.
8 Support the engine beneath the sump and remove the tie-rod from the gearbox mounting bracket and the floor crossmember.
9 Extract the four crossmember bolts and lower the transmission sufficiently to give access to the two top bolts to the converter housing.
10 Place a unit lift under the gearbox or support under the **flange** of the sump.
11 Starting with the two lowest bolts remove the gearbox to converter housing bolts, then place a suitable container in position to catch the fluid as the gearbox is withdrawn to the rear (see **FIG 9:13**).

Removing torque converter:

1 Slacken the starter motor bolts and ease the motor forward.
2 Remove the converter housing bolts and locking washers and withdraw the housing.
3 Remove the four bolts and washers securing the converter to the crankshaft adaptor plate. Access is between the starter ring and the engine mounting plate.
4 Withdraw the converter.

Refitting:

If it is intended to refit the gearbox with the converter still in position great care must be taken in lifting the gearbox and attaching it to the converter without damaging the front pump oil seal (see **FIG 9:14**).

To ensure the correct engagement of the front oil pump drive, rotate the converter so that the driving tangs on the hub are at 9 o'clock and 3 o'clock and the slots of the front oil pump driving gear are rotated to a similar position.

Torque converter and gearbox:

It is recommended that the gearbox and converter be assembled prior to installation in the vehicle.

1 Align the driving tangs of the converter with the slots of the front pump driving gear and fit the converter.

2 Lift up the complete assembly to the engine and tighten up the securing bolts evenly, noting the dowel on each side of the mounting plate for converter alignment.

3 Refit the starter motor and filler tube.

4 Secure the rear crossmember and refit the tie-rod.

5 Fit the starter, the starter inhibitor switch leads and the speedometer cable. Refit the exhaust system.

6 Drain and remove the engine sump and refit the four converter bolts and locking plates.

7 Replace the rubber plug in the bearer plate and refit the engine sump. Lower the vehicle and refill the transmission and the engine sump.

8 Reconnect the selector linkage and the downshift/throttle cable and adjust.

9 : 6 Removing and refitting the selector

Disconnect the flashing indicator and horn leads, then extract the four steering box mounting bolts, release the column support bracket from the parcel shelf and lower the column.

Take out the three grub screws from the steering wheel centre and withdraw the horn push and stator tube from the steering column.

Unscrew the steering wheel nut and withdraw the steering wheel from the tapered shaft.

Slacken the upper support bracket clamp bolt and remove the bracket locating screw.

Remove the clevis pin from the front end of the control cable. Cut the locking wire and remove the square headed screw to release the selector lever lower end of the control rod.

Withdraw the upper support bracket, hand lever and control rod upwards from the steering column (see **FIG 9 : 15**).

Refitting is a reversal of the above procedure, not forgetting to adjust the linkage as described in **Section 9 : 4.**

9 : 7 Stall speed and road test procedure

Stall speed test:

This test provides a rapid check on the correct functioning of the converter as well as the gearbox.

The stall speed is the maximum speed at which the engine can drive the torque converter impeller while the turbine is held stationary. As the stall speed is dependent both on engine and torque converter characteristics, it will vary with the condition of the transmission. It is necessary, therefore, to determine the condition of the engine in order to interpret a low stall speed.

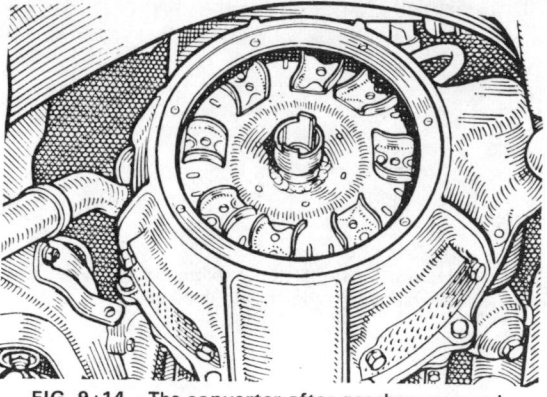

FIG 9 : 14   The converter after gearbox removal

To obtain the stall speed, connect a tachometer to the engine and place it where it can easily be read from the drivers seat. Allow the engine and transmission to attain normal working temperature, set the handbrake, chock the wheels, and apply the footbrake. Select 'L' or 'R' and fully depress the accelerator. Note the reading on the revolution indicator. To prevent overheating, the period of stall test must not exceed 10 seconds.

Check the results with the following table:

	Rev/min	Conditions indicated
Petrol Models	Under 1000	Stator freewheel slip
	1800-1900	Normal
	Over 2000	Slip in the transmission
Diesel Models	Under 1000	Stator freewheel slip
	1450-1550	Normal
	Over 1600	Slip in the transmission

Changespeed chart—petrol engines 1622cc:

Selector	Throttle	Gearshift	Mile/hr
D	Minimum	1-2	3-7
		2-3	11-15
D	Full	1-2	12-15
		2-3	26-30
D	Kick-down	1-2	24-27
		2-3	38-42
		3-2	34-37
		2-1	16-19
L	Minimum	3-2	Above 5
		3-1	Below 5
L	Kick-down	2-1	Below 16-19

On selecting L from D the maximum safe road speed to prevent over-speeding the engine is 45 mile/hr.

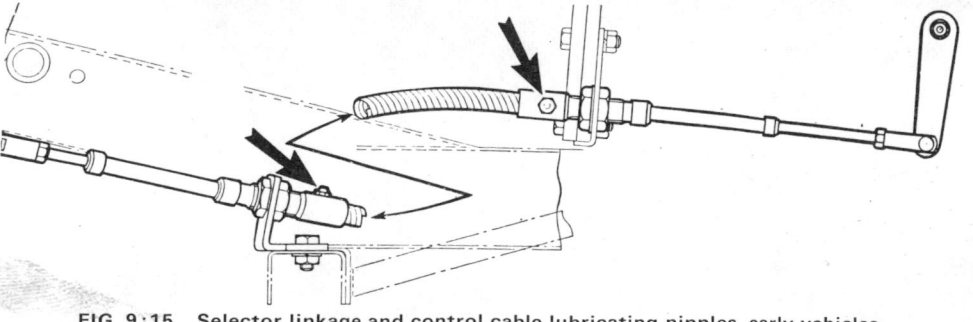

FIG 9 : 15   Selector linkage and control cable lubricating nipples, early vehicles

Changespeed chart—diesel engines:

Selector	Throttle	Gearshift	Mile/hr
D	Minimum	1-2	2-5
		2-3	9-12
D	Full	1-2	11-14
		2-3	20-23
		3-2	25-28
		2-1	14-17
L	Minimum	3-2	Above 5
		3-1	Below 5
L	Kick-down	2-1	Below 14-17

On selecting L from D the maximum safe road speed to avoid overspeeding the engine is 40 mile/hr.

Road test procedure:

1 Check that the starter will operate only with the selector in 'P' and 'N' and that the reverse light operates only in 'R'.

2 Apply the brakes and with the engine at normal idling speed, select 'N-D', 'N-L', 'N-R'. Transmission engagement should be felt in each position selected.

3 Check the converter stall speed.

4 Select 'D' release the brakes and accelerate with minimum throttle opening. Check the shift speeds with the change-speed chart.

5 At just over 30 mile/hr select 'N' switch off the ignition and let the car coast. At 30 mile/hr, switch on the ignition and select 'D'. The engine should start through the rear wheels.

6 (a) Stop and restart, using full throttle acceleration, i.e. detent. Check the 1-2 and 2-3 shifts according to the shift speed table.

(b) At 25 mile/hr petrol models, 20 mile/hr diesel models in 3rd gear, depress the accelerator to full throttle position. The car should accelerate and not change down to second gear.

(c) At 30 mile/hr petrol models, 25 mile/hr diesel models, in 3rd gear depress the accelerator to kick-down position through the detent. The transmission should down-shift to second gear.

(d) At 15 mile/hr petrol models, 12 mile/hr diesel models in 3rd gear, depress the accelerator to kick-down position. The transmission should down-shift to first gear.

7 (a) Stop and restart, using forced throttle acceleration through the detent. Check 1-2 and 2-3 shifts according to the shift speed table.

(b) At 25 mile/hr petrol models, 19 mile/hr diesel models in third gear, release the accelerator and select 'L'. Check for 3-2 downshift and engine braking. Check for roll out 2-1 downshift and engine braking.

8 Stop and with 'L' still engaged, release the brakes and, using full throttle, accelerate to 15 mile/hr petrol models, 12 mile/hr diesel models. Check for no clutch slip and no upshifts.

9 Stop and select 'R'. Release the brakes and reverse using full throttle if possible. Check for clutch slip.

10 Stop on brakes facing downhill on gradient and select 'P'. Release the brakes and check that the parking pawl will hold the car. Repeat with car facing uphill. Check that the selector is trapped by the gate in 'P' position.

CHAPTER 10

PROPELLER SHAFT, REAR AXLE, REAR SUSPENSION

10:1 Description of propeller shaft

The propeller shaft and universal joints are of the Hardy Spicer type with needle roller bearings.

A single shaft connects the rear axle and the gearbox. To accommodate fore and aft movement of the axle a sliding joint of the reverse spline type is fitted between the gearbox and the front universal joint flange. Each joint consists of a centre spider, four needle roller bearing assemblies and two yokes.

On early types, a lubricator is fitted to each front and rear spider, and should be charged fully after overhauling and subsequently given three or four strokes with the lubrication gun at regular intervals.

If a large amount of grease exudes from the oil seal the joint should be dismantled and new oil seals fitted. The sliding joint is automatically lubricated from the gearbox.

10:2 Servicing universal joints

Testing for wear:

Wear on the thrust faces is ascertained by testing the lift in the joint either by hand or with the aid of a length of wood suitably pivoted.

Any circumferential movement of the shaft relative to the flange yokes indicates wear in the needle roller bearings, or in the splined shaft in the case of the forward joint.

Removing the propeller shaft:

1 Mark the two universal joint flanges so that they can be refitted in the same relative position. This is important.
2 Unscrew the flange bolts and remove the shaft downwards and backwards.

Refitting the propeller shaft:

1 Wipe the faces of the flange clean and place the propeller shaft in position. Refit the flange with the marks in line, ensuring that the registers engage correctly and that the flange faces bed down evenly all round.
2 Insert the bolts and tighten the self-locking nuts.

Dismantling, universal joints with lubrication nipple:

1 Remove the enamel and dirt from the snap rings and bearing faces. Remove all the snap rings by pinching

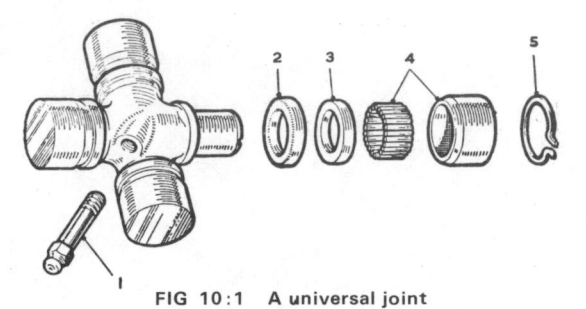

FIG 10:1   A universal joint

Key to Fig 10:1   1 Lubricator   2 Gasket retainer
3 Gasket   4 Needle rollers and bearing   5 Circlip

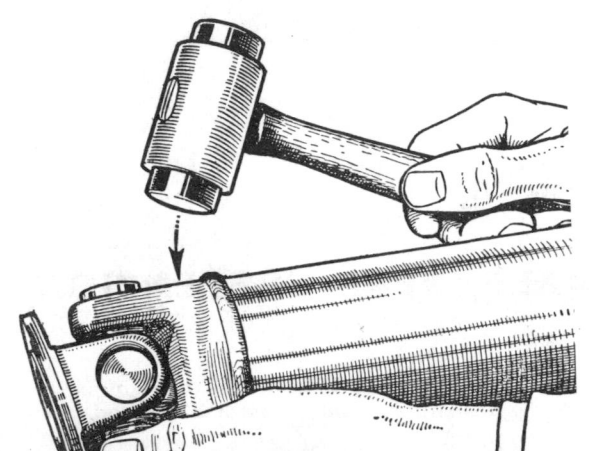

FIG 10:2   Loosening the bearing. Apply light blows to the yoke after removing the retaining clip

their ears together with a pair of thin-nosed pliers and prising them out with a screwdriver. If a ring does not slide readily out of its groove, tap the end of the bearing race slightly to relieve the pressure against the ring. An exploded view of the universal joint is shown in **FIG 10:1.**

2 Remove the lubricator from the journal.

3 Hold the joint in one hand, tap the radius of the yoke lightly with a copper hammer as shown in **FIG 10:2.** The bearing should begin to emerge. Turn the joint over and finally remove the bearing with the fingers. If necessary tap the bearing race from inside with a small diameter bar as shown in **FIG 10:3.** Alternatively, grip the needle bearing race in a vice and tap the flange yoke clear. Care must be taken not to damage the bearing face during removal. Holding the bearing in a vertical position, and when free, remove the race from the bottom to avoid dropping the needle rollers.

4 Repeat this operation for the opposite bearing.

5 Rest the two exposed trunnions on wood or lead blocks to protect their ground surfaces, and tap the top lug of the flange yoke to remove the bearing race.

6 Turn the yoke over and repeat the operation.

Inspection:

The parts most likely to show signs of wear are the bearing races and the spider journals. Should looseness or load markings be observed, the affected parts must be renewed. No oversize journals or races are available.

It is essential that the bearing races are a light drive fit in the yoke trunnions. If the cross holes in a fixed yoke are worn a new propeller shaft assembly must be fitted. New sleeved and flanged yokes must be fitted if their cross holes are worn.

Reassembly:

See that all the drilled holes in the journals are thoroughly cleaned out and free from grease.

1 Smear the walls of the races with grease, assemble the needle rollers in the bearing races, and fill with grease.

2 Insert the spider in the flange yoke, ensuring that the lubricator boss is fitted away from the fixed yoke. Using a soft-nosed drift slightly smaller than the hole in the yoke, tap the bearing into position. Repeat this operation with the other three bearings.

3 Replace the circlips and be sure that these are firmly located in their grooves. If the joint appears to bind, tap lightly with a wooden mallet. This will relieve any pressure of the bearings on the ends of the journals.

4 It is always advisable to replace the cork gasket and the gasket retainers on the spider journals by means of a tubular drift as shown in **FIG 10:4.** The spider shoulders should be covered with shellac prior to fitting the retainers to ensure a good oil seal.

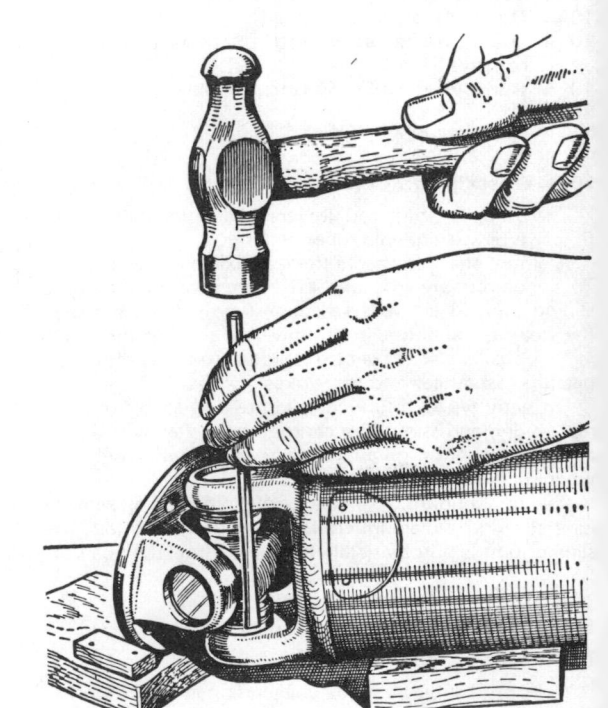

FIG 10:3   Tapping out the bearing with a thin rod

Dismantling universal joints, sealed type:

Dismantling:

Carry out operations 1, 3, 4, 5 and 6 for dismantling universal joints with lubrication nipple. The joint bearing is shown in **FIG 10:5**.

Inspection:

As detailed for joints with lubrication nipple. Wash all parts thoroughly in petrol to remove old grease.

Reassembly:

It is of extreme importance that the assembly of the journals be carried out under absolutely clean, dust free conditions.

1 Fill the reservoir holes in the journal spider with grease, taking care to exclude all air pockets. Fill each bearing assembly with grease to a depth of $\frac{1}{4}$ inch (3 mm).
2 Fit new seals to the spider journals and insert the spider into the flange yoke, tilting it to engage in the yoke bores.
3 Fit a bearing assembly into the yoke bore in the bottom position, and using a soft-nosed drift slightly smaller than the diameter of the hole in the yoke, tap it into the yoke bore until it is possible to fit the circlip. Repeat this operation for the other three bearings, starting opposite the bearing first fitted.
4 After assembly, carefully remove all surplus grease with a soft cloth. If the bearing appears to bind, tap lightly with a wooden mallet. This will relieve any pressure of the bearing on the ends of the journals.

10:3 Description of rear axle

The rear axle is shown in exploded form in **FIG 10:6**. It is of the threequarter floating type, incorporating hypoid final reduction gears. The axle shafts, pinion and differential assemblies can be withdrawn without removing the axle from the vehicle.

The rear wheel bearing outer races are located in the hubs, and the inner races are mounted on the axle tube and secured by nuts and lockwashers. Wheel studs in the hubs pass through the brake drums and axle shaft driving flanges. Brake drums are located on the hub flange by two countersunk screws in each.

The differential and pinion shaft bearings are preloaded, the amount of preload being adjustable by shims. The position of the pinion in relation to the crownwheel is determined by a spacing washer. The backlash between the gears is adjustable by shims.

The semi-elliptic leaf springs provided for rear suspension are secured beneath the rear axle by U-bolts.

The front ends of the springs are anchored in flexing rubber bushes, while the rear ends are mounted in similar bushes in swinging shackles.

10:4 Lubrication, servicing parts without axle removal

Lubrication:

The axle is filled or topped up through the filler level plug at the rear of the axle casing by means of an oil gun with a special adaptor.

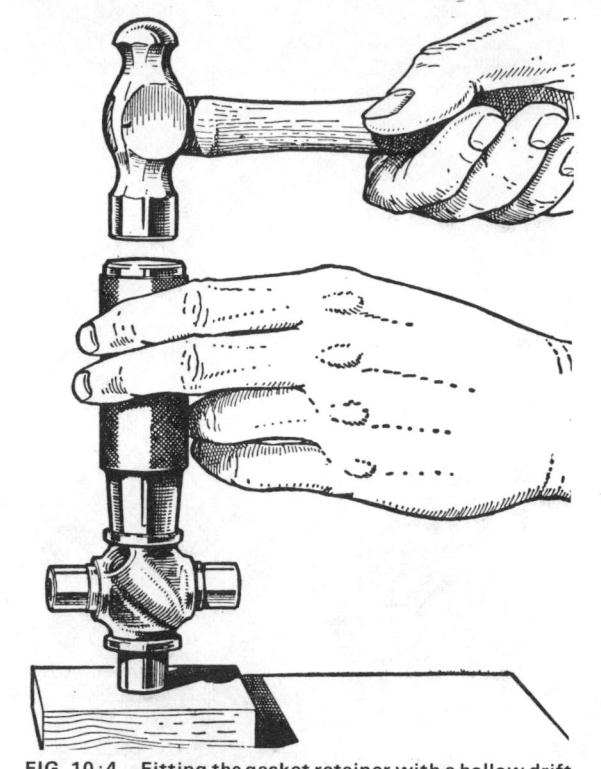

FIG 10:4   Fitting the gasket retainer with a hollow drift

It is of utmost importance that only Hypoid oils of the approved grades and manufacture be used if satisfactory service is to be obtained from the hypoid gears.

Inspect the oil level periodically. Top up as necessary to the level of the filler opening with oil of the approved grade.

Remove the plug from the bottom of the casing to drain the oil. The most suitable time for draining is after a long journey, whilst the oil is still warm. Clean the drain plug, replace and tighten. Refill with fresh oil.

The hub bearings are automatically lubricated from the axle and no provision is made for any other attention. A drain hole is provided in the back of the bearing housing. Oil seepage through this hole does not indicate a defective oil seal unless the amount is excessive.

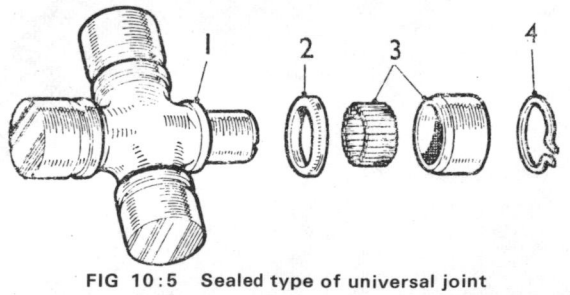

FIG 10:5   Sealed type of universal joint

Key to Fig 10:5   1 Journal spider   2 Rubber seal
3 Needle rollers and bearing   4 Circlip

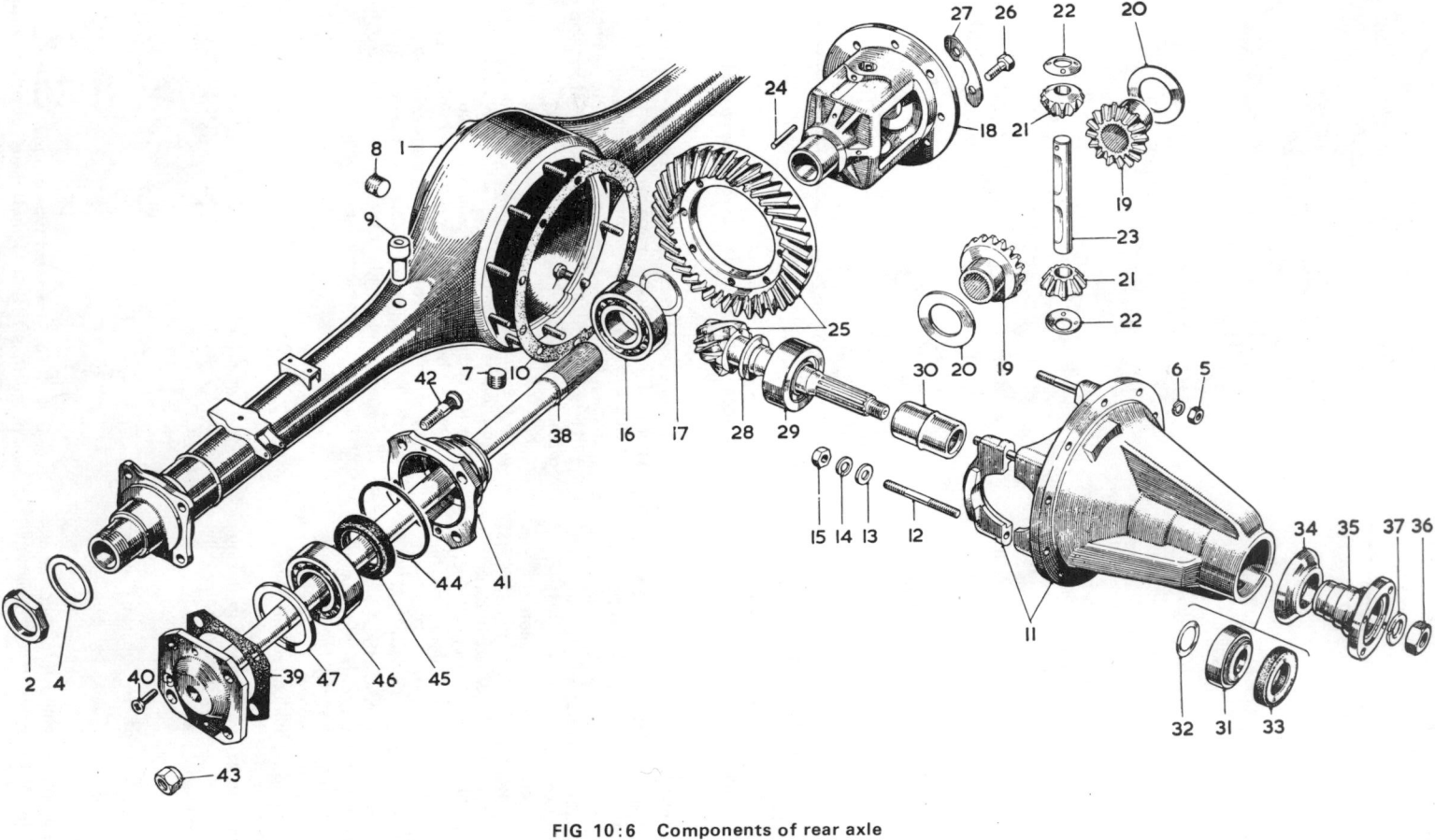

FIG 10:6 Components of rear axle

Key to Fig 10:6   1 Case assembly   2 Nut—bearing retaining   3 Stud for gear carrier   4 Washer for bearing retaining nut   5 Nut—gear carrier to axle case   6 Washer for nut (spring)   7 Plug—drain   8 Plug—filler   9 Breather assembly   10 Joint—gear carrier to axle case   11 Carrier assembly   12 Stud for bearing cap   13 Washer for bearing cap (plain)   14 Washer for bearing cap (spring)   15 Nut for stud   16 Bearing-differential   18 Case—differential   19 Wheel—differential   20 Washer—thrust for differential wheel   21 Pinion-differential   22 Washer—thrust for differential pinion   23 Pin for pinion   24 Peg for pinion pin   25 Crownwheel and pinion   26 Bolt—crownwheel to differential cage   27 Washer for bolt (lock)   28 Washer—pinion thrust   29 Bearing—pinion inner   30 Spacer for bearing   31 Bearing—pinion outer   32 Shim—outer bearing   33 Seal—oil   34 Cover—dust   35 Flange—universal joint   36 Nut to pinion   37 Washer for nut (spring)   38 Shaft—axle   39 Joint—shaft to hub   40 Screw—countersunk—shaft to hub   41 Hub assembly   42 Stud—wheel   43 Nut—wheel stud   44 Ring—oil seal   45 Seal—oil   46 Bearing   47 Spacer—bearing

Removing and refitting brake drum and axle shaft:

1 Jack up the car and place blocks under the spring as close as possible to the axle.
2 Remove the wheel.
3 Release the handbrake.
4 Unscrew and remove the two countersunk brake drum locating screws and tap the drum from the hub. It may be necessary to slacken off the brake adjustment slightly if the shoes hold the drum.
5 Unscrew the countersunk locating screw in the axle shaft driving flange.
6 Withdraw the axle shaft by gripping the flange or carefully prising it with a screwdriver (see **FIG 10 : 7**). If the latter method is used, the paper washer may be damaged and must then be renewed when re-assembling.
7 To replace the shaft and drum, reverse the sequence of operations.

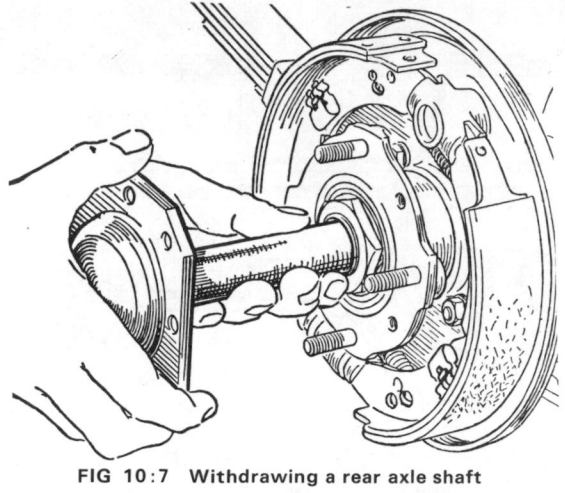

FIG 10:7   Withdrawing a rear axle shaft

Removing and replacing a hub:

1 Remove the brake drum and axle shaft as detailed in the preceding paragraphs.
2 Knock back the tab of the locking washer and unscrew the nut. The lefthand hub bearing nut on the axle has a lefthand thread (turn clockwise to unscrew). The righthand hub nut is righthand threaded. Tilt the locking washer to disengage the peg from its location in the threaded end of the axle casing and remove the washer.
3 Withdraw the hub assembly using a suitable extractor (see **FIG 10 : 8**). The bearing and oil seal will be withdrawn with the hub and can be removed from the hub and replaced. The bearing is not adjustable and is replaced in one straight-forward operation.
4 Repack the bearings with grease.
5 When reassembling, the outer face of the bearing spacer must protrude from .001 to .004 inch (.025 to .102 mm) beyond the outer face of the hub and the paper joint washer when the bearing is pressed into position. This ensures that the bearing is gripped between the abutment shoulder in the hub and the driving flange of the axle shaft.
6 Refit the hub assembly onto the axle casing and drift into position (see **FIG 10 : 9**).
7 Replace the locking washer and nut, tighten the nut, and bend back the locking washer over one of the flats on the nut.
8 Assemble the axle shaft and brake drum.

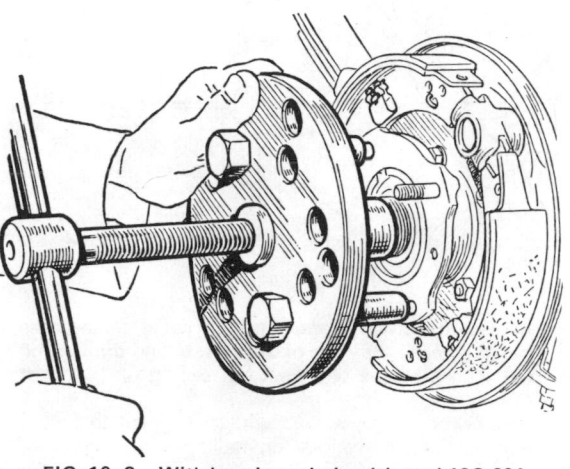

FIG 10:8   Withdrawing a hub with tool 18G.304

Renewing the pinion oil seal:

1 Mark the propeller shaft and pinion shaft driving flanges so that they can be replaced in the same relative positions. Disconnect the propeller shaft, carefully supporting it.
2 Knock back the lockwasher and unscrew the nut in the centre of the driving flange. Remove the nut and washer and withdraw the flange and pressed steel end cover from the pinion shaft.
3 Extract the oil seal from the casing.
4 Press a new seal into the casing with the edge of the sealing ring facing inwards.

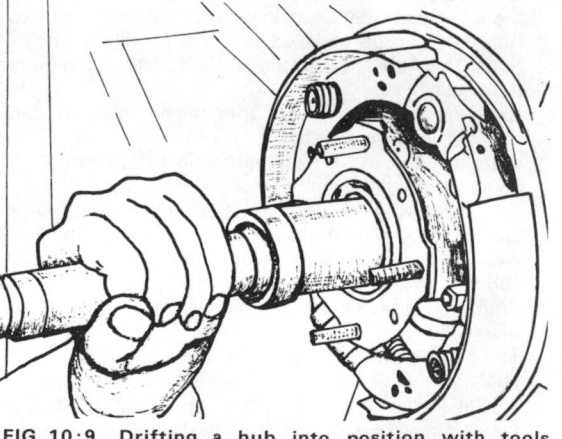

FIG 10:9   Drifting a hub into position with tools 18G.134 and 18G.134P

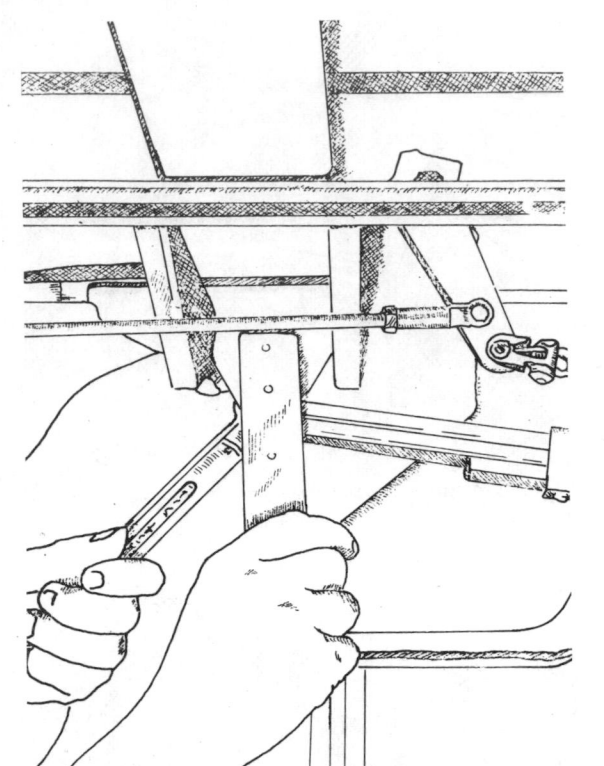

FIG 10:10   Using service tool 18G.312 to remove rear spring

5 Replace the driving flange and end cover, taking care not to damage the edge of the oil seal, and tighten the nut with a torque wrench to a reading of 140 lb ft (19.3 kg m).
6 Reconnect the propeller shaft, taking care to fit the two flanges with the locating marks in alignment.

Removing the differential pinions:

1 Drain the oil from the axle and remove the axle shafts as previously detailed.
2 Mark the propeller shaft and pinion shaft flanges so that they can be replaced in the same relative positions. Unscrew the self-locking nuts and disconnect the joint.
3 Unscrew the eight nuts securing the bevel pinion and gear carrier to the axle banjo.
4 Withdraw the carrier complete with the pinion shaft and differential assembly.
5 Make sure that the differential bearing housing caps are marked so that they can be replaced in their original positions, then remove the four nuts and spring washers.
6 Withdraw the bearing caps and the differential assembly.
7 Tap out the dowel pin locating the differential pinion shaft. It must be tapped out from the crownwheel side as the hole into which it fits has a slightly smaller diameter at the crownwheel end to prevent the pin passing right through.

8 It may be necessary to clean out the metal peened over the entry with a $\frac{3}{16}$ inch drill, to facilitate removal of the dowel pin.
9 Drive out the differential pinion shaft, then the pinions and thrust washers can be removed from the cage.

Replacing the differential pinions:

1 Examine the pinions and thrust washers and renew as necessary.
2 Replace the pinions, thrust washers and pinion shaft in the differential cage and insert the dowel pin. Peen over the entry hole.
3 Reassembly is a reversal of the instructions given for removal. Refill the axle with clean oil.

If it proves necessary to fit any new parts other than those detailed in this Section, the axle assembly must be serviced by a fully equipped service station, as the work involves setting the position of the pinion, preloading the pinion bearing, setting the crownwheel position and adjusting the backlash between the gears.

10:5 Removing and refitting the axle

1 Raise the rear of the car and place suitable stands under the frame forward of the rear springs.
2 Remove the road wheels and release the handbrake.
3 Disconnect the flexible brake hose at the union on the righthand chassis sidemember.
4 Disconnect the brake rod from the relay lever.
5 Support the axle on a stand or trolley jack.
6 Unscrew the U-bolt nuts and locknuts and remove the spring clamp and damper bracket plates.
7 Mark the propeller shaft coupling flanges and disconnect the shaft from the driving flange. Support the rear end of the propeller shaft.
8 Remove the rear shackle nuts and plates and lower the rear ends of the springs to the ground.
9 Withdraw the axle from the car.
10 Reassembly is a reversal of the dismantling procedure, but it will be necessary to bleed the brakes to make sure that no air remains in the system. If the handbrake cable adjustment has been altered it must be re-adjusted (see **Chapter 13**)

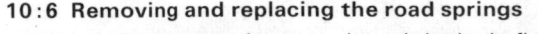

10:6 Removing and replacing the road springs

Using jacks, support the rear axle and the body floor frame to relieve the springs of the weight of the vehicle and axle.

Unscrew the spring fixing bolt nuts and remove the bolts, buffer and plate. Adjust the jacks until the spring is just free of the axle.

Remove the nut from the front anchor pin, while holding it with tool 18G312 (see **FIG 10:10**) and the nuts and spring washers from the bottom rear shackle stud. Drive the pin and the stud out of the spring eyes with a copper drift to avoid damage to the threads.

Withdraw the spring from underneath the vehicle.

Remove the shackle plate stiffener by unscrewing two nuts, then unscrew the top rear shackle nut and remove the pin and bushes.

Refitting the spring is a reversal of the removal procedure with attention to the following points:

Make sure that the spring centre bolt seats properly in the spring seat on the axle.

Fit new bushes in both spring eyes and the rear anchor bracket.

Do not tighten the shackle stud nuts fully until the car is standing on the road normally laden to avoid abnormal flexing of the rubber bushes.

Never permit any lubricant to reach the Harrisflex bushes.

10:7 Dismantling and reassembling the road springs

Remove the bushes from the spring eyes. Grip the spring in a vice between the top and bottom leaves, then remove the countersunk headed screws and rollers from the spring clips, noting that the screws are riveted over the clips.

The front clip and rear clip (third leaf) must be prised open on early vehicles to allow the first three leaves to be dismantled. File down the head of the clip rivet and drill it out.

Unscrew the centre dowel bolt nut and withdraw the bolt to separate the leaves.

Make a note of the positions of the respective leaves and remove them from the vice. Remove all dirt and rust with paraffin and a wire brush.

If any excessive wear or cracks are seen the leaf should be renewed. Indentations caused by leaf ends can be ground smooth.

Examine all other parts for wear and renew as required.

The spring is reassembled in the reverse order, fitting new rollers if necessary and new countersunk headed screws, riveting the ends of the screws over the clip.

Assemble the two new clips on early vehicles on the third leaf and on final assembly bend the ends of the clip 90 deg. inwards, leaving a space of not less than $\frac{1}{8}$ inch (3 mm) between the ends and the leaves to enable the leaves to slide through.

10:8 The dampers

Armstrong lever type hydraulic dampers are fitted, and no adjustment is required and none is provided.

If the dampers do not appear to be functioning correctly, an indication of their resistance can be obtained by carrying out the following check.

Remove the suspected damper from the car and hold it in a vice while moving the lever up and down through a complete stroke.

A moderate resistance should be felt throughout the full stroke. If, however, resistance is erratic or free movement is felt, the presence of air or a lack of fluid is indicated. Free movement at the outer end of the arm should not exceed $\frac{1}{8}$ inch.

If the addition of fluid and a number of full strokes on the arm make no improvement, a new damper should be fitted. Too much resistance making hand operation difficult or impossible suggests a broken internal part or a seizure; again a new damper is indicated.

Removing:

Unscrew and remove the nut securing the damper arm link to the axle bracket.

Remove the two bolts, nuts and spring washers securing the damper to the body brackets and lift it off. When handling dampers that have been removed from a vehicle, they should be kept upright to prevent air entering the operating chamber.

Before finally refitting a damper it is advisable to work the arm a few times to expel any air which may have entered.

Topping up:

This must be done with the damper removed from the vehicle.

Before taking out the filler plug, clean the outside of the unit to prevent any dirt from entering and fill up to the bottom of the filler plug hole with Armstrong Super (thin) Shock Absorber Fluid. Work the damper arm a few times to prime the damper and check the level before fitting.

10:9 Fault diagnosis

(a) Noisy axle

1 Insufficient or incorrect lubricant
2 Worn bearings
3 Worn gears

(b) Excessive backlash

1 Worn gears, bearings or bearing housings
2 Worn axle shaft splines
3 Worn universal joints
4 Loose or broken wheel studs

(c) Oil leakage

1 Defective seals in hub
2 Defective pinion shaft
3 Defective seals on universal joint spiders

(d) Vibration

1 Propeller shaft out of balance
2 Worn universal joint bearings

(e) Rattles

1 Rubber bushes in damper links worn through
2 Dampers loose
3 Spring U-bolts loose
4 Loose spring clips
5 Worn bushes in spring eyes and shackles
6 Broken spring leaves

(f) 'Settling'

1 Weak or broken spring leaves
2 Badly worn shackle pins and bushes
3 Loose spring anchorages

NOTES

CHAPTER 11

FRONT SUSPENSION AND HUBS

11:1 Description

To facilitate repair after accidental damage, and to simplify servicing, the front crossmember complete with the front suspension units, is attached by four main bolts to the underframe and four bolts each side to the engine mounting plate. The four mounting bolts are on rubber packing pieces, which considerably reduces body noises and steering wheel rattles excited by road irregularities.

The two independent suspension units are of wishbone construction. Road shocks are absorbed by low periodicity coil springs mounted between the upper and lower linkages, the springs being controlled by double-acting dampers on the upper linkages.

The front suspension is shown in exploded form in **FIGS 11:1** and **11:2**.

11:2 Routine maintenance

Rubber bushes are used in the suspension. It is therefore of the utmost importance not to use oil or grease on these components.

Normal maintenance is confned to lubrication of the fulcrum pins and swivel pins. Grease nipples are provided for these points.

The maintenance of the hydraulic dampers should include a periodical examination of their anchorages to the chassis and axle and tightening the fixing bolts as required. When examining and replenishing the fluid level, the filler plugs and the surrounding surfaces must be thoroughly cleaned to ensure that no dust or dirt enters the damper interior.

Ensure that only Armstrong recommended fluid is used for topping up. While adding fluid the lever arm must be worked up and down through its full stroke to expel any air that may be trapped in the working chamber. Fluid should be added up to the level of the bottom of the filler plug hole.

The screws securing the coverplate must be kept fully tightened to prevent leakage of the fluid.

11:3 Removing and refitting the front suspension unit

1 Jack-up the front of the car, placing stands under the body crossmember, and remove the road wheels.
2 Support the engine by an overhead sling.
3 Disconnect the negative lead from the battery and remove the horn wires.

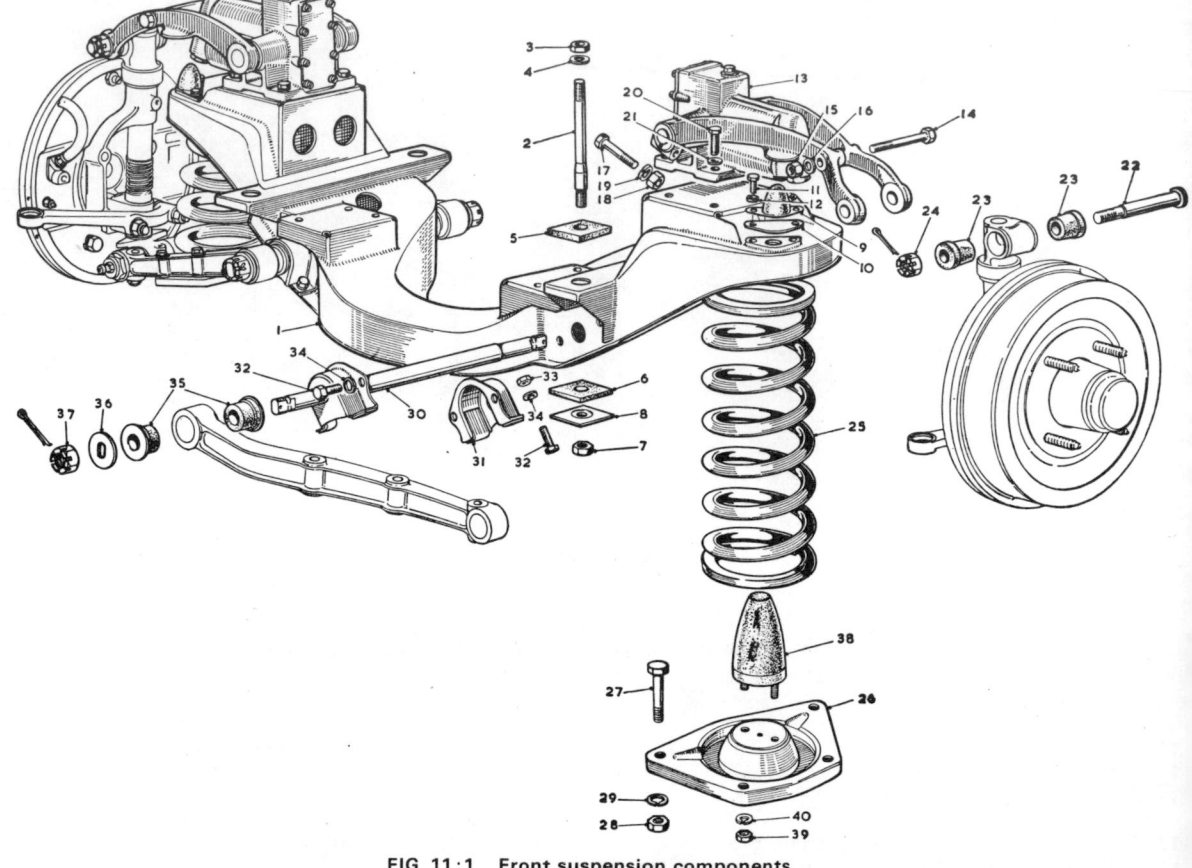

FIG 11:1   Front suspension components

Key to Fig 11:1   1 Crossmember   2 Bolt—crossmember to body   3 Nut for bolt   4 Washer for bolt
5 Washer—crossmember mounting (rubber)   6 Washer—crossmember mounting (rubber)   7 Nut—crossmember to body
8 Washer for nut   9 Buffer—rebound   10 Packing piece for rebound buffer   11 Screw—rebound buffer to crossmember
12 Washer for screw (spring)   13 Damper (with arms)   14 Bolt for damper arm   15 Nut for bolt   16 Washer for nut (spring)
17 Bolt—clamp   18 Nut for bolt   19 Washer for nut (spring)   20 Bolt—damper mounting   21 Washer for bolt (spring)
22 Pin—fulcrum   23 Bearing—top link   24 Nut for fulcrum pin   25 Spring—road (coil)   26 Seating for spring
27 Bolt—spring seat to lower link   28 Nut for bolt   29 Washer for nut (spring)   30 Spindle with fixed bracket—lower link
31 Bracket for spindle (detachable)   32 Screw—bracket to crossmember   33 Nut for screw   34 Washer for screw (spring)
35 Bearing for lower link   36 Washer—locating—lower link spindle   37 Nut for spindle   38 Buffer—suspension
39 Nut for buffer   40 Washer for nut (spring)

4 Drain the hydraulic brake system through one bleed screw into a clean container.

5 Remove the two flexible brake pipes by first removing the upper pipe union nuts. Then, holding the hexagon on the rubber pipes, remove the locknuts retaining the pipes to the engine sidemembers. Unscrew the pipes from the brake backplates.

6 Remove the splitpins and castellated nuts from the draglink ball joints on the steering box and the steering idler drop arm.

7 Release the ball joints, using tool 18G.125.

8 Remove the engine bearer bolts, four from each side.

9 Position a moveable jack under the suspension to just support the unit and remove the four chassis mounting nuts and spring washers with their rubber packing pieces.

10 The unit is now free to be removed from under the car.
    Refitting the suspension unit is an exact reversal of the removal procedure. After completion, the brakes must be bled (see **Chapter 13**).

11:4 Dismantling the suspension unit

1 Remove the hub and the brake backplate (see **Section 11:6**).

2 Remove the coil spring (see **Section 11:7**).

3 The top wishbones are connected at their narrowest point by a clamping bolt. Unscrew the nut and remove the spring washer and bolt.

4 Remove the splitpin and castellated nut from the upper trunnion fulcrum pin on the outer end of the top wishbone arms.

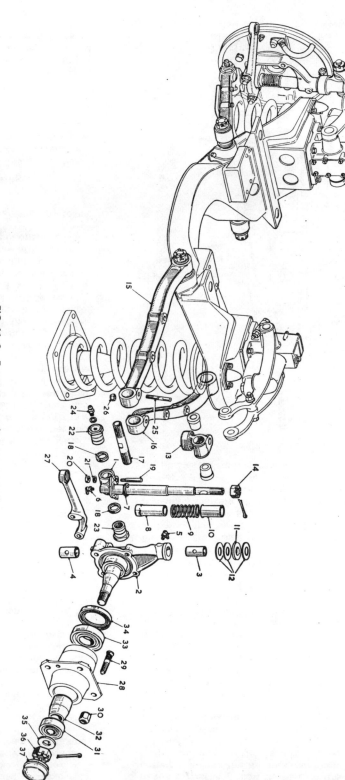

FIG 11:2 Front suspension components

Key to Fig 11:2

1 Pin—swivel
2 Axle assembly—swivel
3 Bush (top)
4 Bush (bottom)
5 Lubricator for swivel axle (upper)
6 Lubricator for swivel axle (lower)
7 Ring (cork)
8 Tube—dust excluder (bottom)
9 Spring for dust excluder
10 Tube—dust excluder (top)
11 Washer (thrust)
12 Washer (floating thrust)
13 Trunnion—suspension link
14 Nut—trunnion to swivel pin
15 Link—lower—LH front and RH rear
16 Link—lower—LH rear and RH front
17 Pin—fulcrum—lower link
18 Ring for fulcrum pin
19 Pin—cotter—fulcrum pin to swivel pin
20 Nut for cotter
21 Washer for nut (spring)
22 Bushes—front for link
23 Bushes—rear for link—swivel pin end
24 Lubricator
25 Pin—cotter—link to bushes
26 Nut for cotter
27 Lever—steering—LH
28 Hub assembly
29 Stud—wheel
30 Nut for wheel stud
31 Bearing for hub (outer)
32 Distance piece for bearing,
early vehicles
33 Bearing for hub (inner)
34 Seal—oil
35 Washer—bearing retaining
36 Nut for swivel axle
37 Cup—grease-retaining

5 The forward arm of the top wishbone is secured to the shock absorber spindle by a clamping bolt. Slacken the clamping bolt and partially withdraw the arm.

6 The trunnion fulcrum pin can now be withdrawn and the damper removed, complete with the top wishbone arms.

7 Withdraw the rubber bearing from each end of the upper trunnion. These bearings fit into a groove in the swivel pin and must be taken out before the swivel pin can be removed.

8 Remove the splitpin and castellated nut from the top of the swivel pin. Remove the upper trunnion and washers and lift off the swivel pin, stub axle, and hub assembly. Detach the cork washer from the lower end of the swivel pin.

9 The outer bearing of the lower wishbone can now be dismantled. Slacken the nut on each of the cotters located in the ends of the lower wishbone arms, screw out the threaded bushes, and detach the arms. Unscrew the nut located in the centre of the lower trunnion and tap out the cotter.

10 Withdraw the fulcrum pin and remove the cork washer from each end of the trunnion.

11 The suspension unit is now dismantled and worn or damaged parts can be renewed.

Inspection:

Swivel pin:

If wear on the swivel pin and bushes is suspected, carefully examine the swivel pin for wear by checking for ovality with a micrometer. Should the pin not show any signs of wear, renewal of the swivel pin bushes may effect a satisfactory cure. When refitting the top bush the oiling holes must line up with the oil hole in the swivel housing and the top of the bush must be flush with the top of the housing. The lower bush must be flush with the housing at the bottom and protrude about $\frac{1}{8}$ inch (3.18 mm) above the upper face of the housing.

Before fitting the swivel pins into their respective housings the bushes must be reamed to their correct size.

If possible the service tool 18G.85 should be used for removing and fitting the bushes (see **FIG 11:3**). This tool enables the swivel axle bushes to be removed and fitted without the distortion which would occur if an improvised drift were used. The shoulder of the driver is recessed to prevent the split bushes from opening when being pressed into position.

The two-piece dust cover is easily removed by telescoping the spring-loaded tubes.

Wishbone arm screwed bush bearing:

If the screwed bushes can be moved forwards or backwards on the fulcrum pin thread they should be renewed. Should new bushes still produce end play, then renew the fulcrum pins also.

11:5 Reassembling the suspension unit

1 Assemble the lower spindle rubber bushes to one of the lower wishbone links and fit the assembly to the lower spindle on the crossmember. Leave the slotted retaining nut sufficiently slack to allow the link to pivot freely.

2 Fit the fulcrum pin to the trunnion on the lower end of the swivel pin, align the flat on the pin with the cotterpin hole in the trunnion, and centralize the pin in the trunnion. Fit the securing cotter and nut and tighten fully.

3 Fit the swivel axle assembly to the swivel pin together with the dust excluder tubes and spring.

4 Fit the thrust washer between the two floating thrust washers, assemble the top trunnion to the swivel pin, fit the trunnion securing nut and tighten down.

5 Check the freelift of the swivel axle on the swivel pin. This should not exceed .002 inch (.05 mm).

6 The floating thrust washers are available in three different thicknesses to enable this clearance to be adjusted. When the correct clearance has been obtained, slacken ·back the retaining nut to ease further assembling.

7 Place a cork ring into the recess on either side of the lower trunnion and pass the appropriate end of the fulcrum pin through the eye in the outer end of the wishbone link.

8 Fit the fulcrum bush retaining cotter to the link and assemble the correct screwed bush to the fulcrum pin and wishbone link.

9 Assemble the other link to its spindle on the crossmember and to the fulcrum pin, fit the bush retaining cotter, and screw in the retaining bush. Do not tighten the bushes fully at this stage.

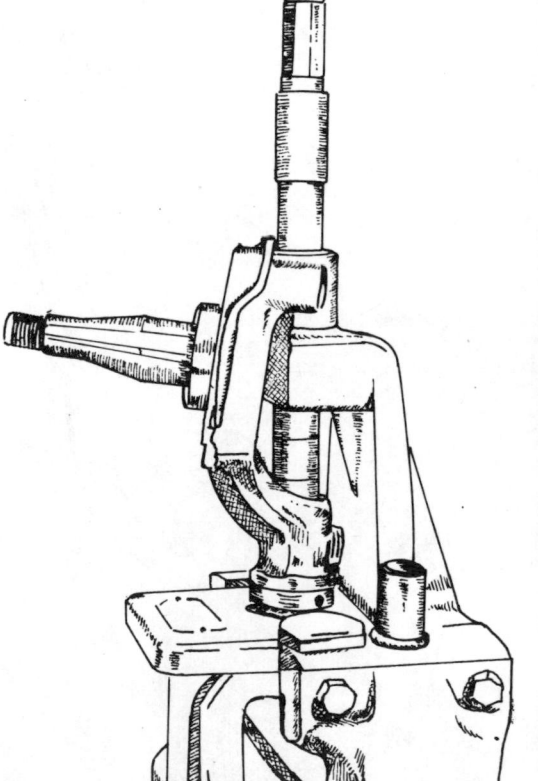

FIG 11:3   Removing or replacing a swivel pin bush

10 Refit the hydraulic damper, reassemble the top
trunnion rubber bushes, and reconnect the damper
arms to the trunnion. Do not tighten the fulcrum pin
retaining nut fully at this stage.

11 Lift the suspension assembly to its approximate
working position and tighten the lower spindle nuts
fully. Refit the spring seat plate to the underside of
the wishbone links.

12 Screw each threaded fulcrum bush fully home, then
slacken off each bush one flat of the hexagon and
tighten the bush retaining cotters. A clearance of
.002 inch (.05 mm) should exist between the inside
face of the hexagonal head of the bush and the outer
face of the wishbone link.

13 Remove the spring seat plate and slacken the spindle
nuts.

14 Refit the suspension spring and the spring plate.

15 The spindle nuts, the top fulcrum pin retaining nut, and
the top trunnion retaining nuts must be finally
tightened and splitpinned after the weight of the
vehicle is taken by the suspension. Lubricate all
appropriate points on the suspension.

11:6 Front hub and brake plate, removal and refitting:

Removing brake drum and hub, early vehicles:

1 Jack-up the car on the side from which the hub is to be
removed

2 Remove the road wheel and prise off the hub cap.

3 Remove the splitpin, castellated nut, and flat washer
from the stub axle.

4 Remove the brake drum by unscrewing the two
countersunk screws. Tap the drum from the hub.
It may be necessary to slacken off the brake adjustment
slightly if the shoes hold the drum.

5 Withdraw the hub, using tool 18G.304 or any suitable
extractor (see **FIG 11:4**). Care must be taken not to
damage the oil seals at the rear of the bearing.

Refitting the hub:

1 Pack each bearing with grease, leaving a small pro-
trusion either side.

2 Insert the inner ballrace into the hub with the thrust
side of the race facing inwards towards the pressed
steel spacer. The thrust side of the bearing has the
part number stamped on it.

3 Lightly smear the spacer with grease and insert it so
that the domed end faces the outer bearing.

4 Replace the outer bearing with the thrust side facing
the spacer. Use a soft metal drift to replace both
bearings, tapping them on diametrically opposite sides
in order to move them evenly into their housings.

5 Replace the oil seal over the inner bearing with its
hollow side facing the bearing.

6 Fill the cavity between the seal and the bearing with
grease.

7 Replace the hub on the stub axle, using a hollow drift
evenly on both inner and outer races of the outer
bearing. Tap the hub into position until the stub axle
nut can be screwed onto the thread.

8 Tighten the nut until the inner race bears against the
stub axle shoulder.

9 Continue tightening the nut and align the slots with
the splitpin hole in the stub axle. Never slacken back
the nut to achieve alignment.

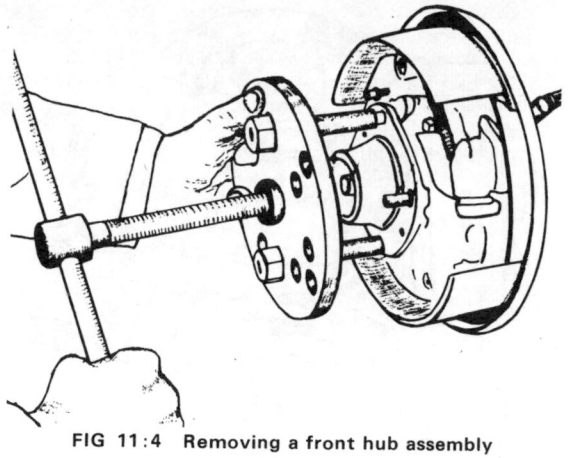

FIG 11:4   Removing a front hub assembly

10 Finally, lock the nut with a splitpin and replace the hub
cap. Do not fill the cap with grease.

On later vehicles a modified front hub with taper roller
bearings and no distance piece is fitted, and adjustment is
as follows:

1 Fit the bearing washers and tighten the nut to 10 lb ft,
back off the nut to the nearest splitpin hole.

2 Check that the bearing end float is between .002 and
.008 inch.

3 Insert a new splitpin and replace the hub cap.

Removing and refitting a brake plate assembly:

Removing:

1 Remove the brake drum and hub as previously
described.

Early type:

2 Disconnect the flexible brake pipe from its union on
the wing valance, remove the locknut and detach the
pipe from the bracket.

3 From inside the brake plate, knock back the tabs of the
locking washers on the two top retaining screws and
remove the screws.

4 Remove the two self-locking nuts and shakeproof
washers, retaining the steering arm and brake plate.
Withdraw the two bolts and lockwashers and detach
the brake plate.

The brake plate can be removed from the hub without
removing the assembly from the vehicle and it can then be
supported or hung in a convenient position without disconnecting the flexible pipe.

Later type:

5 Disconnect the union on the flexible brake hose at the
support bracket on the brake plate. Disconnect the
other end of the bundy pipe from its union at the
wheel cylinder and detach the bundy pipe.

6 Unscrew the locknut retaining the flexible brake pipe
to the support bracket and withdraw the pipe. Seal
the end of the pipe to prevent the loss of brake fluid,
or place the open end in a clean container to catch
the fluid.

7 Remove the self-locking nut and shakeproof washer
retaining the pipe support bracket and detach the
bracket.

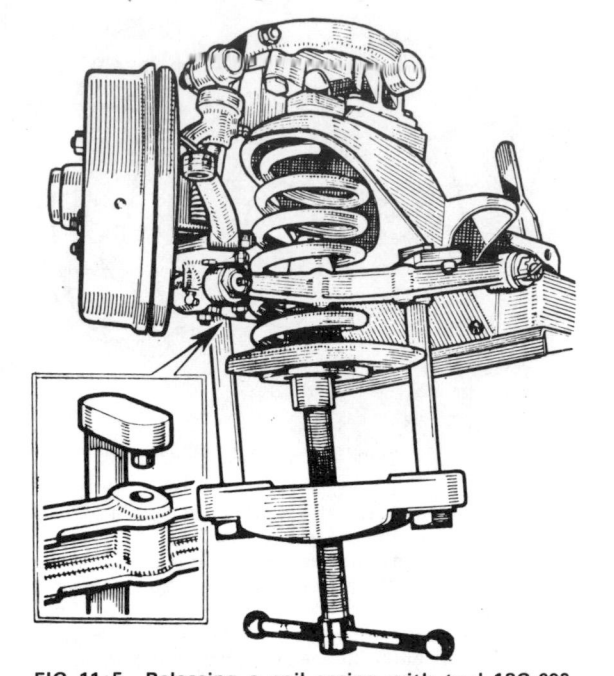

FIG 11:5 Releasing a coil spring with tool 18G.693. Insert shows location of spigot in the rear wishbone outer bolt hole

8 From inside the brake plate, knock back the tabs of the locking washers on the two top retaining screws and remove the screws.

9 Remove the two self-locking nuts and shakeproof washers retaining the steering arm and brake plate. Withdraw the two bolts and lockwashers and detach the brake plate.

Refitting:

Refitting is a reversal of the removing instructions, noting that on the later type, the longer of the two back-plate retaining screws must be fitted to the rear fixing position of the brake plate.

When the flexible brake line has been disconnected, the brake system must be bled after assembly (see **Chapter 13**).

11:7 Removing and refitting a coil spring:

1 Jack-up the side of the car from which the spring is to be removed.

2 Place a stand under the frame sidemember to the rear of the suspension assembly.

3 Use tool 18G.693 or two $\frac{3}{8}$ inch (9.52 mm) slave bolts to release the compression from the spring. These bolts must be at least 4 inches (100 mm) long and threaded their entire length. The method of fixing the service tool for releasing the tension is shown in **FIG 11:5.**

4 There are four nuts and bolts securing the spring plate to the lower wishbone arm. Remove two which are diagonally opposite to each other and replace with the previously prepared slave bolts, screwing the nuts down hard onto the wishbone arms.

5 Remove the other two short bolts and unscrew the nuts from the slave bolts, each a little at a time, until the spring is fully extended.

6 The bolts, together with the spring plate and spring can now be removed.

7 When the spring has been removed it should be checked for free length, see **Technical Data** at the end of this Manual. If there is any excess variation from nominal, the spring should be renewed.

8 Refitting of the coil spring is a reversal of the removal procedure.

11:8 Damper removal, topping up, testing

Removal:

1 Raise the front of the car and remove the road wheel. Place a stand beneath the front body crossmember.

2 Place a further jack beneath the outer end of the lower wishbone arm and raise it until the damper arms are clear of their rebound rubbers on the top of the wishbone arms.

3 Extract the cotterpin and castellated nut from the upper trunnion fulcrum pin and take out the pin.

4 On removing the four setscrews and spring washers, the damper may be removed from its mounting on the front suspension crossmember assembly.

When handling dampers that have been removed from the car it is essential to keep the assemblies upright as far as possible, otherwise air may enter the operating chamber, resulting in free movement.

Refitting is a reversal of the removal instructions, but before fitting the upper trunnion fulcrum pin, work the damper arms a few times through their full travel to expel any air which may have found its way into the operating chamber.

Topping up with fluid:

The front dampers may be replenished in position, providing the tops have been thoroughly cleaned to ensure that when the filler plug is extracted no dirt falls into the filler orifice. This is most important, as it is absolutely vital that no dirt or foreign matter should enter the operating chamber.

The use of Armstrong Super (thin) Shock Absorber Fluid in the Armstrong dampers is recommended. If this fluid is not available, any good quality mineral oil to Specification SAE.20/20W should be used, but this alternative is not suitable for low temperature operation.

Fluid should be added to the level of the bottom of the filler plug hole. When fluid has been added, the damper arm should be worked throughout its full stroke before the filler plug is replaced to expel any air that might be present in the operating chamber.

Testing the dampers:

If there is any doubt that the road springs are adequately damped, the condition of the springs and the tyre pressures must also be considered, as these have an appreciable bearing on the results obtained.

If the hydraulic dampers do not appear to be functioning satisfactorily, an indication of their resistance can be obtained by carrying out the following check:

Remove the dampers from the car.

Hold them in a vice and move the lever arm up and down through its complete stroke. A moderate resistance throughout the full stroke should be felt. If however, the resistance is erratic, or free movement in the lever is noted, lack of fluid is indicated, or there may be air in front of the piston. The free movement should not exceed $\frac{1}{8}$ inch (3 mm) at the outer end of the arm.

If the addition of fluid to the correct level, and working the arm over its full range of travel a number of times gives no improvement, a new damper should be fitted.

Refit the damper to the vehicle, remove the filler plug to ensure correct fluid level and replace.

Too much resistance, i.e. when it is not possible to move the lever arm slowly by hand, indicates a broken internal part or a seized piston. In such cases the damper should be changed for a new or reconditioned one.

11:9 Fault diagnosis

(a) Wheel wobble

1 Worn hub bearings
2 Broken or weak front springs
3 Uneven tyre wear
4 Worn suspension linkage
5 Loose wheel fixings

(b) 'Bottoming' of suspension

1 Check 2 in (a)
2 Rebound rubbers worn or missing
3 Dampers not working

(c) Heavy steering

1 Neglected swivel pin lubrication
2 Wrong suspension geometry

(d) Excessive tyre wear

1 Check 4 in (a); 3 in (b); and 2 in (c)

(e) Rattles

1 Check 2 in (a)
2 Pivot lubrication neglected, rubber bushes worn
3 Damper mountings loose
4 Radius arm mountings loose or worn

(f) Excessive rolling

1 Check 2 in (a); 3 in (b)

NOTES

CHAPTER 12

THE STEERING GEAR

12:1 Description

The steering gear is the cam and lever type, with the cam in the form of a worm, integral with the steering shaft and running in ballbearings. The rocker shaft moves in a phosphor-bronze bush, with the cam peg and roller carried in the lever portion.

The peg is conical in shape and as it does not touch the bottom of its groove it is possible to make adjustment for wear by means of a screw in the side cover. The steering arm is attached to the rocker shaft on tapered splines.

Two idlers are employed, connected together by an adjustable ball jointed track rod, each idler being connected to the wheel swivel arm by a ball jointed side rod of fixed length.

The components of the steering gear assembly are are shown in the two exploded views of **FIGS 12:1** and **12:2**.

12:2 Removing the steering gear assembly

Jack up the vehicle and support it on stands. Detach the drag link from the steering lever (tool 18G.125).

On early vehicles disconnect the flashing indicator and horn cables at the snap connectors and pull the assembly from the steering column.

On later vehicles, lever the centre cover from the steering wheel, and detach the lights and horn control from the outer steering column.

Unscrew the securing nut and tap the steering wheel from its tapered shaft. A sharp blow with the hand is usually adequate.

Remove the four bolts securing the steering box bracket to the frame and suitably support the box while removing the drivers floor and toe plates and releasing the clamp from the steering column support bracket.

Remove the brake pedal return spring, then lower the steering box and column and withdraw underneath the vehicle.

12:3 Dismantling the steering gear

Mark the steering lever and the end of the rocker shaft, then using a suitable extractor pull off the steering lever.

Prepare to catch the oil and remove the side cover and gasket. Pull out the rocker shaft and oil seal and then press out the cam roller peg assembly from the shaft.

Hold the steering box horizontally in a vice and extract the felt bush from the top of the steering shaft.

On early vehicles remove the stator tube nut, olive and adaptor from the bottom cover and lift out the stator tube. On later vehicles mark for assembly and remove the indicator switch striker and locating peg if fitted. Where a steering column lock is fitted ensure the locking pin is disengaged from the inner column. Remove the bottom cover, shims and gasket.

The steering shaft should now be tapped out from the top, using a hard wooden dolly. This will force out the bottom ball cup and cage and the shaft and cam assembly can be withdrawn complete with the ball cage loose on the shaft.

Examination:

Clean all the parts in paraffin and dry and inspect for excessive wear or damage such as pitting of ball races,

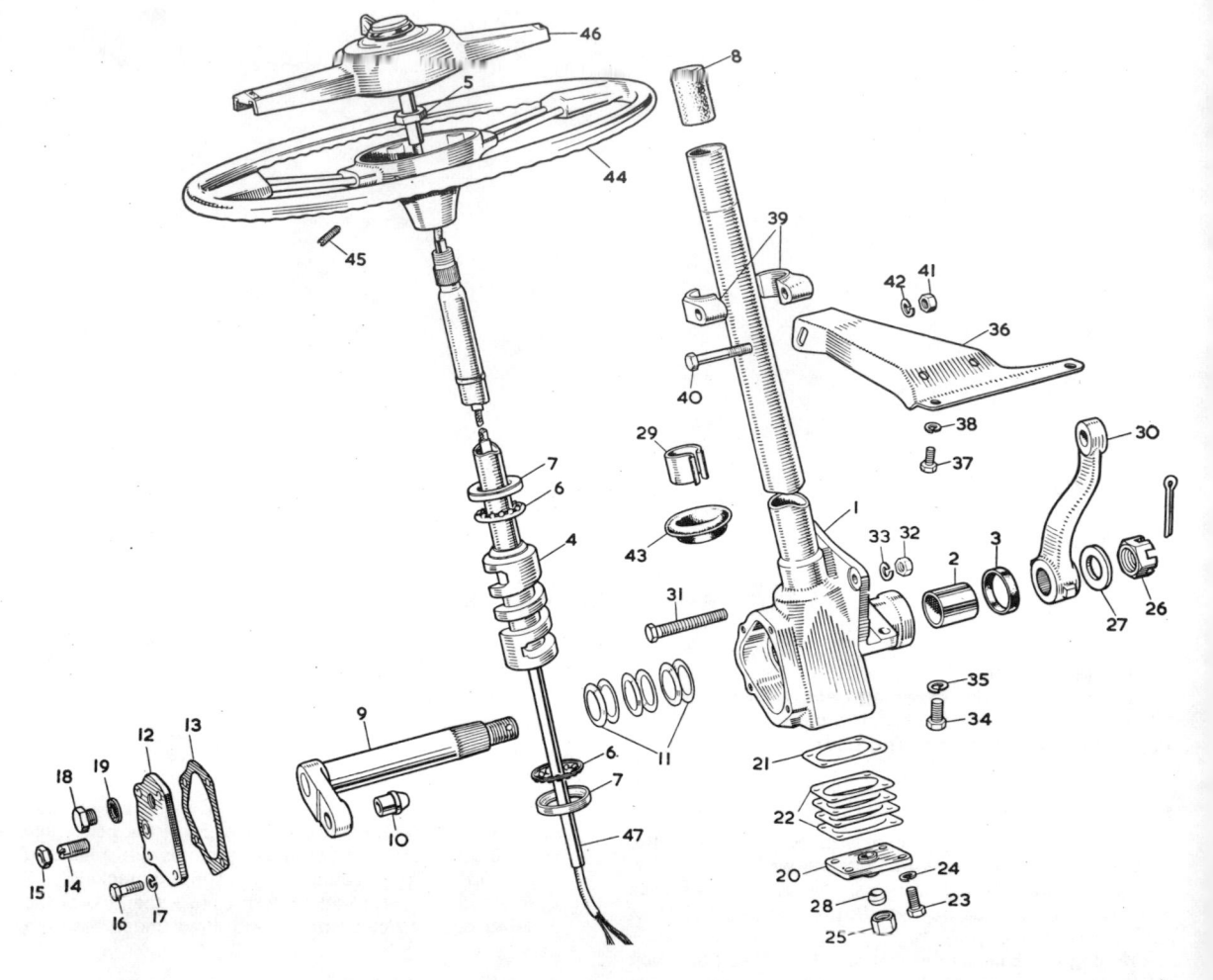

FIG 12:1 Components of the steering gear

Key to Fig 12:1   1 Box and outer column   2 Bush for rocker shaft   3 Oil seal   4 Column with cam   5 Nut for steering wheel   6 Ball cage assembly   7 Cap for ball cage   8 Bush (felt)   9 Rocker shaft assembly   10 Peg   11 Washer (Belleville)   12 Side cover   13 Joint   14 Thrust screw   15 Nut for thrust screw   16 Bolt for side cover   17 Washer   18 Oil plug   19 Washer for plug   20 End cover   21 Joint   22 Shims   23 Bolt   24 Washer   25 Nut for stator tube   26 Nut—lever to steering gear   27 Washer   28 Olive for stator tube   29 Clip for oil filler hole   30 Steering lever   31 Bolt—steering box to frame   32 Nut   33 Washer   34 Screw—steering box to frame   35 Washer   36 Steering column support bracket   37 Bolt   38 Washer   39 Clamps for steering column   40 Bolt   41 Nut   42 Washer   43 Draught excluder for steering column   44 Steering wheel   45 Grubscrew for stator ring   46 Horn control assembly

and track, flattening on the conical peg on the rocker shaft lever or wear in the cam grooves.

If the rocker shaft bush is worn it will be necessary to tap it out and press in a new bush and ream it to size.

Reassembly:

Before commencing work it is advisable to lubricate the cam bearings and rocker shaft bush with oil and soak a new oil seal in engine oil ready for use.

Press the top ball cup into the steering box, then mount the box in a vice while the cam and shaft assembly are inserted. Thread the top ball cage and balls over the shaft,

lip of the cage first, and insert the assembly into the steering box, engaging the ballrace with the ball cup. Then insert the bottom ball cage and balls, lip of the cage foremost, followed by the ball cup.

Fit a new joint washer, the original shims and then secure the bottom and cover in position.

Move the assembly in the vice to bring the column horizontal, temporarily fit the steering wheel, test for end play and adjust as described in **Section 12:6** if necessary.

Fit a new rocker shaft oil seal into the housing and insert the rocker shaft. Fit a new gasket and the side cover.

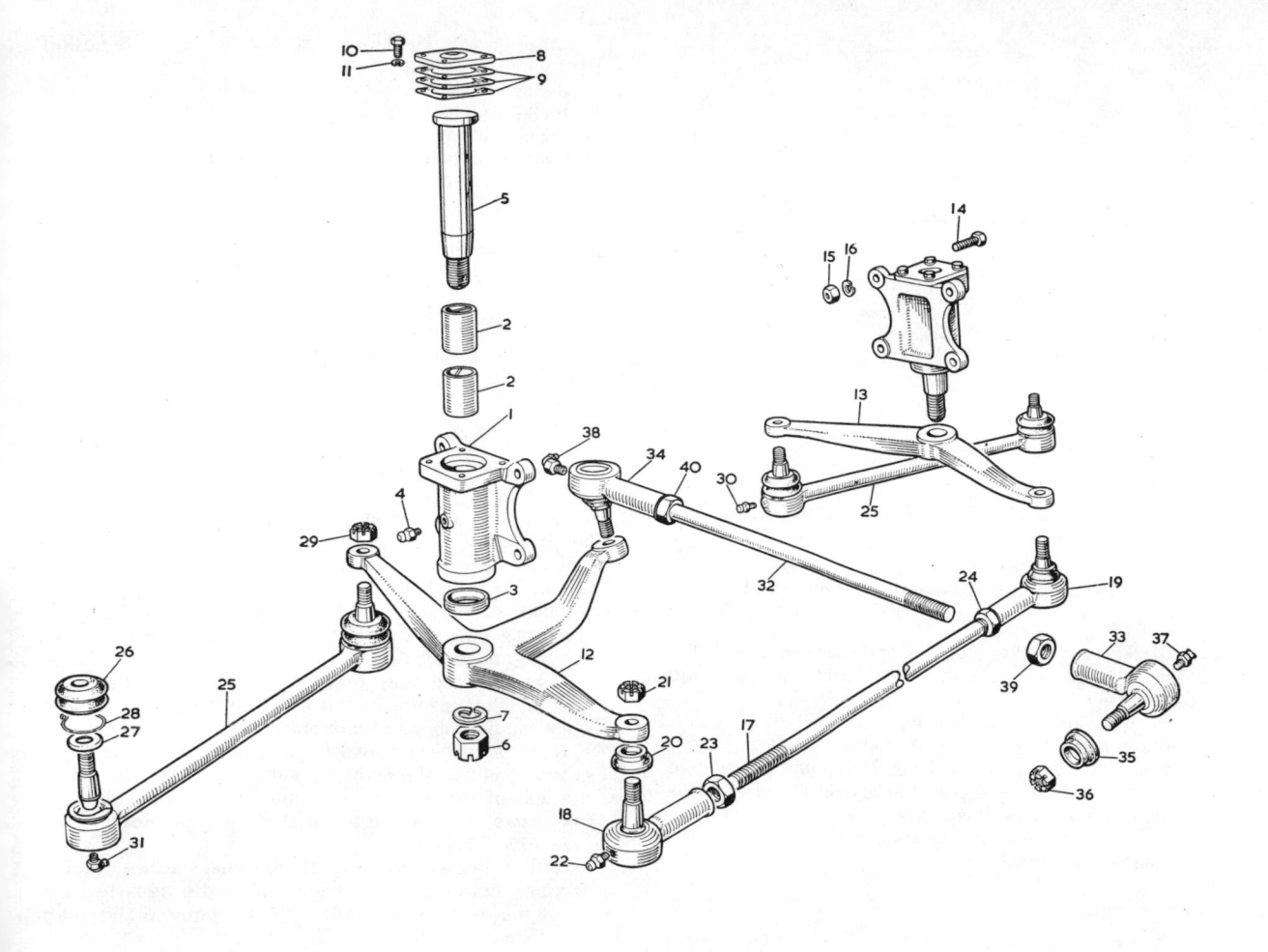

FIG 12:2 Steering gear idlers, rods and drag link assembly

Key to Fig 12:2   1 Idler body   2 Bush   3 Seal   4 Lubricator   5 Shaft   6 Nut for shaft   7 Washer
8 Cover   9 Joint for cover   10 Bolt   11 Washer   12 Lever for idler gear—RH   13 Lever for idler gear—LH
14 Bolt—idler to frame   15 Nut for bolt   16 Washer   17 Track rod assembly   18 End assembly—RH
19 End assembly—LH   20 Dust cover for ball joint   21 Nut for ball pin   22 Lubricator   23 Locknut—RHT
24 Locknut—LHT   25 Side rod assembly   26 Dust cover   27 Washer   28 Clip for dust cover   29 Side rod nut for
ball pin   30 Lubricator (straight)   31 Lubricator (angular)   32 Draglink assembly   33 End assembly—RHT
34 End assembly—LHT   35 Dust cover   36 Nut for ball pin   37 Lubricator (straight)   38 Lubricator (angular)
39 Locknut—RHT   40 Locknut—LHT

Fit the steering lever, mating up the marks made earlier, test for backlash in the central position and adjust if necessary.

Remove the steering wheel and insert a new felt bush in the top of the steering column. Fill the steering box with the recommended grade of oil.

12:4 Refitting the steering gear

This is carried out by reversing the sequence given in **Section 12:2** observing the following precautions:

Line up the steering column carefully before tightening the securing bolts to ensure that no undue bending loads are imposed.

Make sure that the steering wheel is in its middle position and that the front wheels are in the straight-ahead position when installing the draglink.

Pull down the steering wheel nut to a torque of 41 lb ft.

12:5 Draglink assembly

Withdraw the splitpins and remove the nuts from the ball pins at the steering lever end and the idler arm end of the draglink.

Loosen the ball pins from each end by using tool 18G.1063 and remove the draglink.

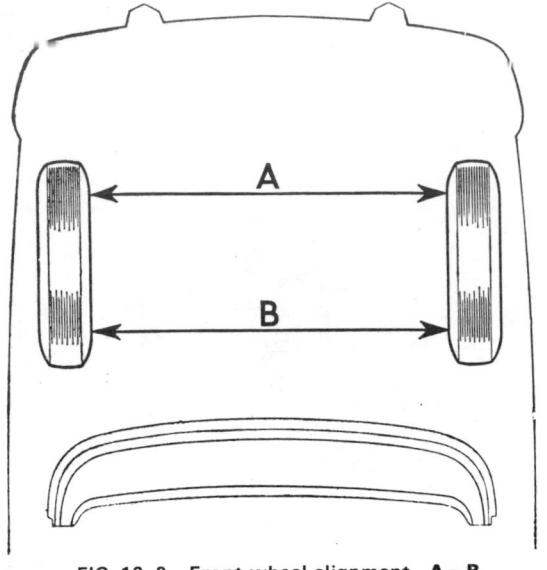

FIG 12:3 Front wheel alignment. **A = B**

Slacken the socket locknuts and unscrew the socket assemblies which are screwed lefthand and righthand respectively.

Remove the dust covers from the ball pin sockets. Further dismantling is not permissible.

Check the ball pins for wear. They must permit free movement without end play and should be renewed as complete assemblies if necessary.

Renew damaged dust covers and check the draglink for damage or distortion.

Reassembly:

Fit the dust covers on the ball pins and sockets, then screw the socket assemblies on to the rod an equal number of turns to give a measurement of $13\frac{1}{8}$ inch (33.33 cm) between ball pin centres and secure them by tightening the locknuts.

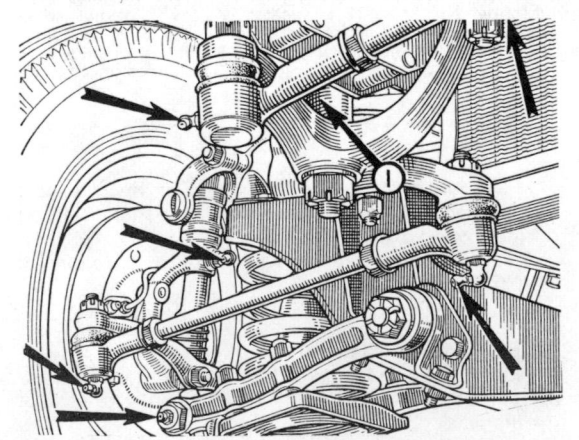

FIG 12:4 Showing the idler **1**, track rod and side rod with lubrication points

Continue with the removal procedure in reverse noting the following points:

Make sure that the steering wheel is in the centre of its travel and that the front wheels are in the straight-ahead position.

Tighten the ball pin nuts and fit new splitpins.

Lubricate all points according to the lubrication chart.

12:6 Adjustments

Front wheel alignment:

Of the four angles which make up the geometry of the steering, three, namely camber, castor and swivel pin inclination, are built into the vehicle and should only need attention in the event of damage being incurred. This would be a matter for professional assistance.

The fore and aft alignment of the front wheels can be adjusted when necessary by the simple means of lengthening or shortening the central track rod seen at 17 in **FIG 12:2**.

In the unladen condition, the two front wheels should be parallel, and although it is advisable to have them checked with specialised equipment, it is possible to obtain satisfactory results as follows.

Make sure that the tyres are correctly inflated and stand the car on a level road with the wheels in the straight-ahead position.

Measure accurately the distance between the inner rims at wheel centre height at the front of the wheels. Mark the two points of reference.

Roll the vehicle forward so that the wheels make exactly one half of a revolution and the marks are now at the rear of the wheels. Measure the distance between the marks, it should be equal to the previous figure (see **FIG 12:3**).

If the measurements are not the same, slacken the nuts securing both ball joint assemblies to the track rod and rotate the rod as appropriate until the required alignment is obtained.

Steering cam bearing adjustment:

This is to eliminate steering column end play.

Disconnect the draglink from the steering lever.

Disconnect the flashing indicator switch and horn cables at the snap connectors below the steering box. From inside the car, gently draw out the indicator switch and horn push until the cables have been drawn into the stator tube and so clear of any oil.

Place a tray under the steering box and remove the nut and olive from the end cover and also the end cover by removing the four retaining bolts.

Add or subtract the necessary shims at 22 in **FIG 12:1** to obtain the correct adjustment. The steering wheel should turn freely when held lightly at the rim with the thumb and forefinger.

Rocker shaft adjustment:

This is to eliminate excessive backlash or play in the steering and is set after adjusting the cam bearings as detailed above.

With the draglink still disconnected, slacken the locknut 15 and screw in the thrust screw 14.

Check for backlash by pressing lightly on the lower end of the steering lever in each direction while an assistant turns the steering wheel slowly from lock to lock.

Play is not constant, there should be less in the centre than in the full lock positions. The correct setting is when the adjuster is screwed in sufficiently to give a barely noticeable tight spot as the steering wheel is moved through its centre position. At this point lock the adjusting screw and fill up with the correct grade of oil.

Reconnect the draglink and any other components in the reverse order of removal.

12:7 Fault diagnosis

(a) Wheel wobble

1 Unbalanced wheels and tyres
2 Slack steering connections
3 Incorrect steering geometry
4 Excessive play in steering gear
5 Broken or weak front springs
6 Worn hub bearings

(b) Wander

1 Check 2, 3 and 4 in (a)
2 Front suspension and rear axle mounting points out of line
3 Uneven tyre pressures
4 Uneven tyre wear
5 Weak dampers or springs

(c) Heavy steering

1 Check 3 in (a)
2 Very low tyre pressures
3 Neglected lubrication
4 Wheels out of track
5 Steering gear maladjusted
6 Steering column bent or misaligned

(d) Lost motion

1 End play in steering column
2 Loose steering wheel, worn splines
3 Worn steering box and idler
4 Worn ball joints
5 Worn suspension system

NOTES

CHAPTER 13

THE BRAKING SYSTEM

13:1 Description

The brakes on all four wheels are hydraulically operated by a foot pedal directly coupled to a master cylinder, in which the hydraulic pressure of the brake operating fluid is originated. A separate supply tank provides a reservoir and also incorporates the fluid reservoir for the clutch system. Steel pipelines, flexible hoses, and unions interconnect the master and wheel cylinders.

The pressure generated in the master cylinder is transmitted with equal and undiminished force to all wheel cylinders simultaneously. This moves each wheel cylinder piston outwards, expanding the brake shoes and thus producing automatic equalization and efficiency in direct proportion to the effort applied at the pedal.

In the rear drums a single wheel cylinder, operated both hydraulically and mechanically, floats on the backplate and operates the brake shoes, giving one leading shoe and one trailing shoe in each direction of rotation, and so provides adequate braking in reverse.

The handbrake is mounted beneath the facia panel, being of the pistol grip pattern. It operates on the rear wheels only by means of cables and rods through a compensator mounted on the rear axle and transverse rods to the wheel cylinder levers.

Refer to **FIG 13:1**. Two leading shoes in each front assembly are expanded by individual, single-acting hydraulic cylinders connected by tubing and bolted to the backplate. Each shoe pivots and slides on one of the cylinders with its opposite end in contact with the piston diametrically opposite. Two pull-off springs are fitted, each connected from one shoe to the backplate.

An adjuster controls the movement of each shoe without interfering with its normal braking function.

Refer to **FIG 13:2**. Two shoes, one leading and one trailing, are expanded in each rear brake assembly by a single-acting hydraulic cylinder and piston assembly floating on the backplate and acting against the adjuster.

Two springs are connected between the shoes which slide on their abutments and centralize in the drum. The shoes are supported by steady pins and springs.

The handbrake lever is pivoted in the cylinder body, and when operated, the lever tip expands the leading shoe independently of the hydraulic piston and the pivot moves the cylinder body to apply the trailing shoe.

13:2 Routine maintenance, brake shoe adjustment

Check the level of the fluid in the master cylinder reservoir and maintain it at the level indicated on the outside of the cylinder, by the addition of Unipart 410 or 550 brake fluid, if unobtainable, a brake fluid to specification SAE.J1703C. **Do not use any other fluid.** The necessity for frequent topping up is an indication of a leak in the system which should be traced and immediately rectified. Access to the reservoir is gained by removing the seat and the inspection plate.

To safeguard against the possible effects of wear, or deterioration, it is recommended that drum brake linings, hoses and pipes, should be examined at intervals laid down in the Drivers Handbook.

Brake fluid should be changed completely every 18 months or 18,0000 miles (30,000 km) whichever is the sooner.

All fluid seals in the hydraulic system and all flexible hoses should be examined and renewed if necessary every 3 years or 36,000 miles (60,000 km), whichever is the sooner. At the same time the working surfaces of the pistons and of the bores of the master cylinder, wheel cylinders, and other slave cylinders should be examined and new parts fitted where necessary.

Care must be taken always to observe the following points:

1 At all times use the recommended brake fluid.
2 Never leave fluid in unsealed containers. It absorbs moisture quickly and this can be dangerous if used in this condition.
3 Fluid drained from the system or used for bleeding is best discarded.
4 The necessity for absolute cleanliness throughout cannot be over-emphasized.

Brake shoe adjustment:

The brake shoes must be adjusted to compensate for wear of the linings. The need for adjustment is shown by excessive movement of the brake pedal before solid resistance is felt.

Adjustment of the rear brake shoes also automatically adjusts the handbrake, and no separate adjustment is required.

Front brake adjustment:

1 Jack-up the wheel or wheels requiring adjustment.
2 Turn one of the squared adjuster screws on the backplate in a clockwise direction until the drum is locked against rotation (see FIG 13:3).
3 Slacken off the adjuster just enough to free the drum, generally two 'clicks' of the adjuster.
4 Repeat the adjustment with the other shoe adjuster.

Rear brake adjustment:

Chock up the front wheels and release the handbrake. Jack-up the rear end of the car.

Rotate the squared end of the adjuster screw in a clock-wise direction until the drum is locked, and then back off enough to enable the drum to rotate freely. Two clicks is usually sufficient.

Apply the footbrake to centralize the shoes and recheck.

Repeat for the other rear wheel.

13:3 Removing and refitting brake shoes

Front:

For identification and positioning of components, refer to FIG 13:1.

1 Jack-up and remove the wheel and brake drum.
2 Remove the steady springs by turning the top retaining washer slot to line up with the locating peg.

3 Lift off the washer, spring and washer, and take out the locating peg from the rear of the backplate. On later models, remove the steady spring and pin.
4 Lift the trailing end of a shoe from the abutment on the wheel cylinder and the leading end from the piston of the opposite cylinder.
5 Detach the spring and shoe.
6 Repeat with the other shoe.
7 Prevent the pistons from falling out of the cylinders by the use of rubber bands or wire.

If the linings are worn down to the rivets, renewal is necessary. It is not recommended that owners should reline brake shoes themselves. It is important that the linings should be perfectly bedded down on the shoes and then ground to perfect concentricity with the brake drums. For this reason it is best to obtain sets of replacement shoes already lined. Do not fit odd shoes and do not mix lining material or unbalanced braking will result.

Do not allow oil or grease to come into contact with the brake shoe linings. If the original linings are contaminated with oil or grease do not attempt to clean them as nothing useful can be achieved.

Refitting:

1 Before refitting the shoes, lightly smear the steady posts and both ends of the shoes with Girling White Brake Grease, but take care to keep all grease from the rubber parts and pistons, and from the linings.
2 Fit the shoes. The shorter hook of each spring must be connected to a brake shoe.
3 Refit the steady posts and springs.
4 Refit the brake drum and adjust the brakes as detailed in Section 13:2.

Rear:

For identification and positioning of components refer to FIG 13:2.

1 Jack-up and remove the wheel and brake drum.
2 The method of removing the rear brake shoes is similar to that detailed for the front. Note that the lining of the leading shoe is fitted towards the trailing end and that of the trailing shoe towards the leading end. Both springs are connected between the shoes the lighter spring at the wheel cylinder ends.
3 Before refitting the shoes, lightly smear the steady posts and both ends of the shoes with Girling White Brake Grease, but take care to keep all grease away from the rubber parts and pistons and from th linings.
4 Fit the shoes and drums and adjust the brakes a detailed in Section 13:2.

13:4 The master cylinder

Removal and refitting:

Prepare to catch the escaping fluid, then disconnect th pipes from the master cylinder.

Disconnect the brake pedal return spring and uncoupl the pedal from the master cylinder pushrod by removin the clevis pin.

Remove the two securing bolts from the flange of th master cylinder flange and lift it off. On later vehicles not the parallel and taper shims, where fitted, between th master cylinder flange and the vehicle body, and ref them in their original position to maintain a clearanc

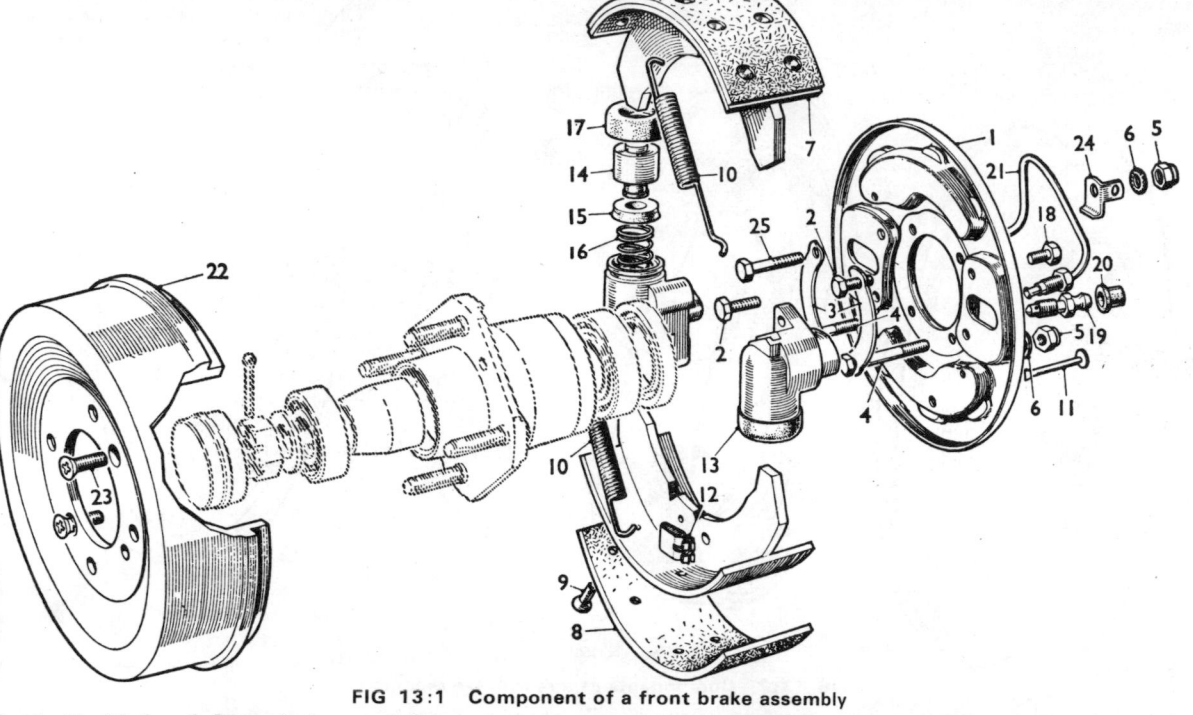

FIG 13:1 Component of a front brake assembly

Key to Fig 13:1   1 Plate—brake   2 Screw—brake plate to swivel axle   3 Washer for screw (lock)   4 Bolt—brake plate and steering lever to swivel axle   5 Nut for bolt   6 Washer for nut (shakeproof)   7 Shoe assembly—brake   8 Liner 9 Rivet   10 Spring—brake shoe return   11 Pin—brake shoe steady   12 Spring for steady pin   13 Cylinder assembly—wheel 14 Piston   15 Seal   16 Spring   17 Cover—dust—for piston   18 Screw—wheel cylinder to brake plate   19 Screw—bleed 20 Cover—dust—for bleed screw   21 Pipe—brake   22 Drum—brake   23 Screw—drum to hub   24 Bracket—brake hose * 25 Bolt—brake backplate and steering lever to swivel axle *   *Later models*

of .025 inch between the master cylinder and the steering idler. On LHD vehicles this will be the clutch master cylinder.

Refitting is the reverse of the above, after which the system must be refilled with the recommended grade of fluid and bled as described in **Section 13:7**.

13:5 Instructions on servicing hydraulic internals

All hydraulic brake parts should be washed in commercial alcohol, methylated spirits, or approved brake fluid.

Do not use mineral oils, or cleaning fluid extracted from mineral oil, e.g. petrol, paraffin, carbon tetrachloride, etc. as they will cause the rubber seals to swell and become ineffective. The slightest trace of mineral oil could soon render the brakes inoperative. Methylated spirits or commercial alcohol must always be used for flushing out the system, washing brake housings, components and any container that comes into contact with brake fluid.

Any foreign matter should be washed from components with methylated spirits or commercial alcohol. If any foreign matter finds its way into the system it may score the pistons or damage the seals, and render the brakes either wholly or partly inoperative.

Pistons and seals should be carefully stored away from grease or oils and handled carefully at all times. The seals should be inspected carefully before fitting, even if they are new.

See that the sealing lips are perfectly formed, concentric with the bore of the seal, free from knife edges, surface blemishes or marks. Any seal that is not perfect, no matter how minute the blemish may be, should be rejected. Seals should not be turned inside out when inspecting them, since this strains the surface skin and may eventually lead to a failure.

All pistons and housings must be carefully inspected before assembly. Any imperfections or scores on a piston or cylinder bore may provide a track for fluid leaks under pressure, and any damaged parts must be discarded. All parts of the components must be handled very carefully to avoid any possibility of accidental scoring.

Prior to assembly, immerse hydraulic components in clean approved brake fluid to facilitate fitting and provide initial lubrication for working surfaces.

Removing a flexible hose:

Do not attempt to release a flexible hose by turning either end with a spanner as this will twist the hose and may damage it. It should be removed as follows:

Unscrew the metal pipeline union nut from its connection to the hose.

Hold the hexagon on the flexible hose and remove the locknut securing the flexible hose union to the bracket. Unscrew the flexible hose from the cylinder.

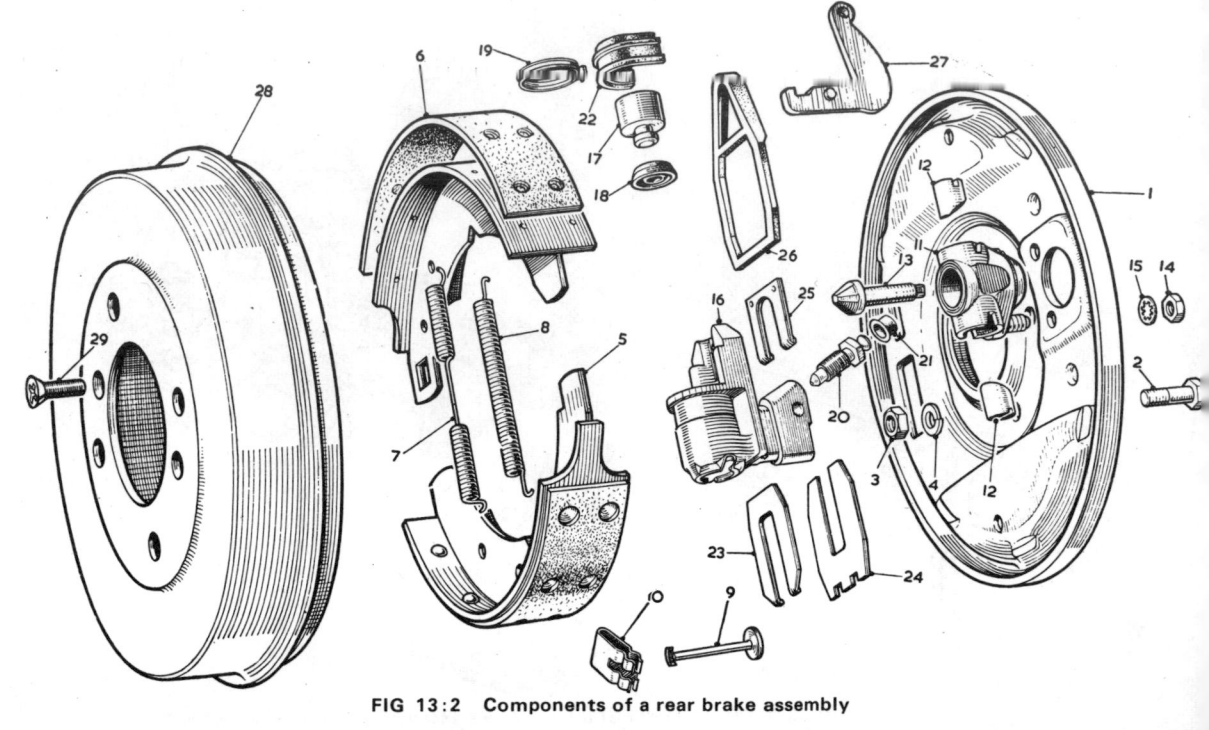

FIG 13:2   Components of a rear brake assembly

Key to Fig 13:2   1 Plate—brake   2 Bolt—backplate to axle case   3 Nut for bolt   4 Washer for bolt (spring)
5 Brake shoe assembly   6 Liner   7 Spring—shoe return—cylinder end   8 Spring—shoe return—adjuster end
9 Pin—brake shoe steady   10 Spring—brake shoe steady   11 Body—adjuster   12 Tappet   13 Wedge   14 Nut—adjuster
to backplate   15 Washer for nut (shakeproof)   16 Body—wheel cylinder   17 Piston   18 Seal for piston   19 Retainer for
dust cover   20 Screw—bleeder   21 Cover—dust—bleed screw   22 Cover—dust—piston   23 Spring—retaining—wheel cylinder
24 Plate—locking   25 Washer (distance)   26 Cover—dust—wheel cylinder to backplate   27 Lever assembly—handbrake
28 Drum—brake   29 Screw—drum to hub

13:6 Servicing the master and wheel cylinders

Master cylinder, dismantling:

1 Remove the master cylinder as detailed in **Section 13:4.**
2 Pull back the dust cover and remove the circlip. The pushrod and dished washer can then be removed (see **FIG 13:4**).
3 Remove the plunger assembly complete.
4 Lift the thimble leaf over the shouldered end of the plunger.
5 Depress the plunger return spring to allow the valve stem to slide through the elongated hole of the thimble and release the spring tension.
6 Remove the thimble, spring and valve complete. Detach the valve spacer, taking care of the spacer spring washer located under the valve head. Remove the seal from the valve head. Later models incorporate a taper seal on the plunger.

Examine all parts for wear and distortion and renew where necessary.

Reassembly:

Assembly is mainly a reversal of the dismantling instructions but note the following:

1 Make sure that the flat side of the valve seal is correctly seated on the valve head.

2 Locate the spring washer with the domed side against the underside of the valve head.
3 The legs of the valve spacer must face towards the valve seal.

Replace the plunger, return spring centrally on the spacer, insert the spring and depress until the valve stem engages through the elongated hole of the thimble. Make sure the stem is correctly located in the centre of the thimble.

Check that the spring is still central on the spacer and fit the plunger seal, with the flat of the seal against the face of the plunger.

Insert the reduced end of the plunger into the thimble until the thimble leaf engages under the shoulder of the plunger, then press home the leaf.

Smear the assembly with recommended brake fluid and insert the assembly into the cylinder bore. Be careful not to damage the seal as it is pushed into position.

Refit the pushrod, circlip and finally the dust cover.

Front wheel cylinder, removal and refitting:

1 Jack-up and remove the wheel, brake drum and brake shoes.
2 Disconnect the bridge pipe unions from the cylinder.
3 Unscrew the two securing nuts and remove the cylinder(s).

Refitting is a reversal of the removal operations. Tighten the wheel cylinder nuts to a torque wrench reading of 5 to 7.5 lb ft (.7 to 1.0 kg m). On completion the brakes must be bled.

Rear wheel cylinder, removal:

1 Jack-up the wheel and remove the wheel, drum and shoes.
2 Disconnect the pipe from the union, the cable at the handbrake lever and remove the rubber boot from the rear of the backplate.
3 With a screwdriver, prise the retainer and spring plates apart and tap the retaining plate from below the neck of the wheel cylinder.
4 Withdraw the handbrake lever from between the backplate and the wheel cylinder.
5 Remove the spring plate and distance pieces, and finally the cylinder from the backplate.

Refitting:

1 Smear the backplate and cylinder with Girling White Brake Grease, and mount the cylinder onto the backplate with the neck through the large slot.
2 Replace the distance piece between the cylinder neck and the backplate with the open end away from the handbrake location. The two cranked lips must also be away from the backplate.
3 Replace the handbrake lever.
4 Locate the retaining plate between the distance piece and the spring plate, with the open end towards the handbrake lever. Tap into position until the two cranked lips of the spring plate locate in the retaining plate.
5 Fit the rubber cover. Connect the pipe to the union and the cable to the handbrake lever.
6 Replace the brake shoes, brake drum and the road wheel.
7 Bleed and adjust the brakes.

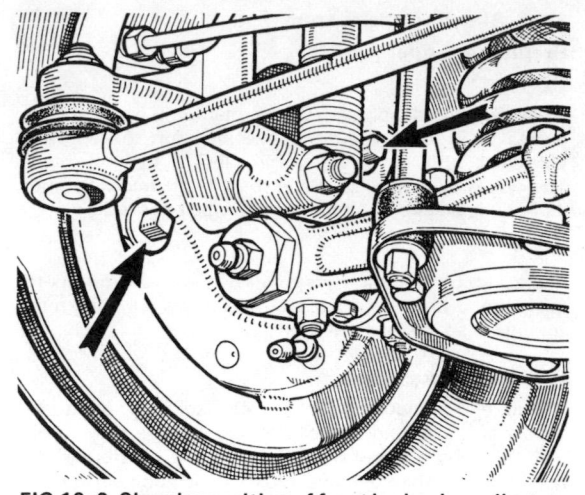

FIG 13:3 Showing position of front brake shoe adjusters

Dismantling and reassembling wheel cylinders:

Front:

1 Remove the wheel cylinder.
2 Remove the dust cover.
3 Withdraw the piston seal, spreader and spring. Use air pressure to extract the remaining components from the cylinder.
Reassembly is a reversal of the dismantling procedure.

Rear:

1 Remove the cylinder.
2 Remove the spring clip and rubber dust cover.
3 Blow out the piston and seal.
Reassembly is a reversal of the dismantling procedure.

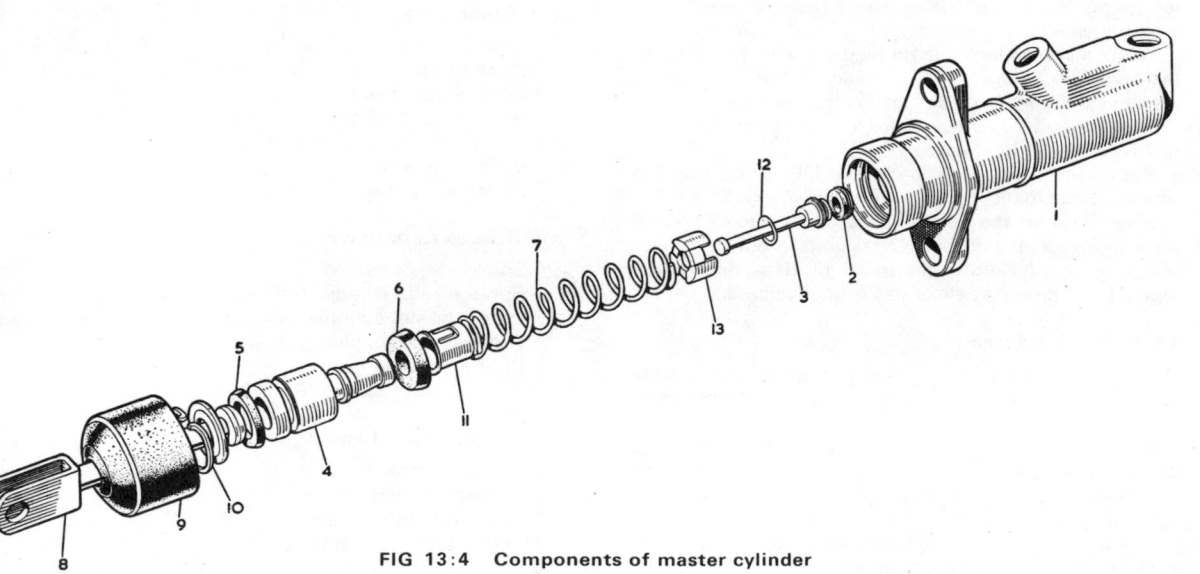

FIG 13:4 Components of master cylinder

Key to Fig 13:4   1 Body   2 Valve seal   3 Valve stem   4 Plunger   5 Seal   6 Taper end seal   7 Spring   8 Pushrod assembly   9 Dust cover   10 Circlip   11 Spring retainer (thimble)   12 Washer for spring   13 Valve spacer

13:7 Bleeding the system

Preliminary operations:

Rear:

Release the handbrake. Check that the wheel cylinder is free to slide on the backplate and turn the adjuster clockwise until the drum is fully locked by the shoes. The wheel cylinder piston will then be pushed right into its bore, leaving a minimum of air to be expelled.

Front:

Slacken off the adjusters to allow the shoe springs to push the pistons into their bores, leaving a minimum amount of space for air or fluid.

Bleeding procedure:

Before commencing, make sure that an adequate supply of brake fluid is available and that the reservoir is well filled, as a quantity of fluid is used up during the operation and the fluid level must not be allowed to drop to a point where air may be drawn into the system.

Attach the bleeder tube to the wheel cylinder furthest from the master cylinder and allow the free end of the tube to be submerged in a small quantity of fluid in a clean glass jar.

Open the bleeder screw half-a-turn.

Begin bleeding with a fairly fast full stroke followed by two or three rapid, short strokes of the pedal, allowing it to fly back freely. Lift the floor covering if this prevents free movement of the pedal.

Watch the flow of fluid into the glass jar, and when air bubbles cease to appear, close the bleeder screw during the last, slow pedal application.

If the bleeding of any cylinder continues for any length of time, without success, it is possible that air is being drawn in past the bleeder screw threads. In such cases, tighten the bleeder screw at the end of each down stroke of the pedal and allow the pedal to return fully before reopening the screw. Close the bleeder screw finally during the last pedal application.

A check should be made for fluid seepage from around the stoplamp switch. If this occurs, a further packing washer (total 2) should be fitted in the switch seating.

Tighten the bleeder screws to a torque wrench setting of 4 to 6 lb ft (.5 to .8 kg m).

Repeat the operation on each wheel, finishing with the wheel nearest to the master cylinder.

After bleeding, top up the master cylinder to its correct level and adjust the brakes in the normal manner. If there is any spongy feeling to the pedal, bleed again at each nipple to confirm that all air has been eliminated.

13:8 The handbrake

The handbrake operates the rear brake shoes only through a system of rods and cables, with a compensator mounted on the rear axle.

Handbrake adjustment is dealt with by the adjustment of the rear brake shoes described in **Section 13:2** and no attempt should be made to adjust them by interfering with the cables or rods.

If, after ensuring that the brake shoes are correctly set, there is still too much slackness in the handbrake mechanism, the adjuster in the cable may be used to take up any stretch.

Slacken the locknut and turn the adjuster in a clockwise direction until the handbrake is hard on when pulled up four or five notches.

Check that the drums are free to rotate when the handbrake is off. Tighten the locknut when the correct setting has been obtained.

13:9 Fault diagnosis

(a) Pedal travel excessive

1 Brake shoes require adjusting
2 Leak at one or more joints
3 Master cylinder cup worn

(b) Pedal feels spongy

1 System requires bleeding
2 Linings not bedded in
3 Master cylinder fixings loose
4 Master cylinder cup worn

(c) Brakes inefficient

1 Shoes not correctly adjusted
2 Linings not bedded in
3 Linings greasy
4 Linings wrong quality
5 Drum badly scored
6 Linings badly worn

(d) Brakes grab

1 Shoes require adjusting
2 Drums distorted
3 Greasy linings
4 Broken or loose road spring
5 Scored drums
6 Worn suspension linkage

(e) Brakes drag

1 Shoes incorrectly adjusted
2 Shoe springs weak or broken
3 Pedal spring weak or broken
4 Handbrake mechanism seized
5 Wheel cylinder piston seized
6 Blocked pipeline
7 Filler cap vent hole blocked

(f) Brakes remain on

1 Shoes over-adjusted
2 Handbrake over-adjusted
3 Port in master cylinder covered by swollen rubber cap
4 Swollen wheel cylinder cups
5 Choked flexible hose
6 Broken return spring

(g) Unbalanced braking

1 Greasy linings
2 Distorted drums
3 Tyres unevenly inflated
4 Brake plate loose on the axle
5 Worn steering connections
6 Worn suspension linkage
7 Different types of grades of linings fitted

CHAPTER 14

THE ELECTRICAL SYSTEM

14:1 Description

A 12-volt electrical system is employed with positive earthing.

Most components are common to both petrol and diesel engined vehicles, the notable exception being the starter motor which is of the pre-engaged type for use with diesel engines and of which there are two versions.

The electrical supply is provided by either a DC generator or an alternator, mounted on the righthand side of the cylinder block and driven by a belt from the crankshaft pulley, which also drives the cooling fan. The tension of the drive belt is adjustable by means of a rotatable mounting for the generator.

Double filament bulbs are fitted in the headlamps, with vertical dipping or to left or right according to local regulations in the country concerned.

14:2 Battery maintenance and testing

Routine maintenance:

Keep the battery, particularly the top, clean and dry and brush away dirt or dust present.

The terminals should be kept clean and coated with petroleum jelly (not grease).

If distilled water or electrolyte has been spilled on top of the battery, it should be cleaned off immediately, as even weak electrolyte will quickly attack and corrode the cable connections. Use a rag soaked in a weak solution of hot water and ammonia, to counteract the action of spilled electrolyte.

Distilled water should be added if the level in any cell is below the top of the separator guard. It is good practice to top up the battery just prior to running the car, especially in cold weather, to ensure thoroughly mixing of the electrolyte and water and so prevent freezing.

If the battery is found to need frequent topping up, steps should be taken to determine the reason. For example the battery may be receiving an excessive charge, in which case the regulator settings should be checked. If one cell in particular needs topping up more frequently than another, check the condition of the battery case. If there are signs of an electrolyte leak, trace the fault and take corrective action.

Testing the battery:

Examine the condition of the battery by taking hydrometer readings. The hydrometer contains a graduated float on which is indicated the specific gravity of the acid in the cell from which the sample is taken. The specific gravity readings should be as follows:

Climates normally below 27°C (80°F):

1.270 to 1.290	..	Cell fully charged
1.190 to 1.210	..	Cell half-discharged
1.110 to 1.130	..	Cell completely discharged

Climates frequently above 27°C (80°F):

1.210 to 1.230	..	Cell fully charged
1.130 to 1.150	..	Cell half-discharged
1.050 to 1.070	..	Cell completely discharged

These figures are given assuming an electrolyte temperature of 16°C (60°F). If the temperature of the electrolyte exceeds this, .002 must be added to hydrometer readings for each 2.7°C (5°F) rise to give the true specific gravity. Similarly, .002 must be subtracted from hydrometer readings for every 2.7°C (5°F) below 16°C (60°F).

The readings of all the cells should be approximately the same. If one cell gives a reading very different from the rest, it may be that the electrolyte has been spilled or has leaked from the cell, or there may be an internal fault. In this case it is advisable to have the battery inspected by a battery specialist. Should a battery be in a low state of charge, it should be recharged by taking the car for a long daytime run, or by charging from an external source of DC supply at a current rate of 4 amps (5 amps for nine plate batteries) until the cells are gassing freely.

After examining the battery, check the vent plugs, making sure that the air passages are clear, and screw the plugs into position. Wipe the top of the battery to remove all dirt and moisture.

If a battery is to be out of use for any length of time, it should first be fully charged and then given a freshening charge every fortnight. A battery must never be allowed to remain in a discharged condition as this will cause the plates to become sulphated.

Filling and charging:

Preparing electrolyte:

Electrolyte is prepared by mixing distilled water and concentrated sulphuric acid, usually of 1.840.SG. The mixing must be carried out either in a lead-lined tank or in suitable glass or earthenware vessels. Slowly add the acid to the water, stirring with a glass rod. Never add the water to the acid, as the resulting chemical reaction causes violent and dangerous spurting of the concentrated acid. Heat is produced by mixing acid and water, and the electrolyte should be allowed to cool before taking hydrometer readings.

Charging:

The initial charge rate is 2.5 (7 plate) or 3.5 (9 plate) amps. Charge at this rate until the voltage and specific gravity readings show no increase over five successive hourly readings. On a discharged battery, this will take from 48 to 80 hours.

Keep the current constant by varying the series resistance of the circuit output. This charge should not be broken by long rest periods. If, however, the temperature of any cell rises above 38°C (100°F) the charge must be interrupted until the temperature has fallen at least 5.5°C (10°F) below this figure. Throughout the charge the electrolyte must be kept level with the top of the separator guard by the addition of electrolyte of the same

specific gravity as the original, until the specific gravity and charge readings have remained constant for five successive hourly readings. If the charge is continued beyond that point, top up with distilled water.

At the end of the charge, carefully check the specific gravity in each cell to ensure that when corrected to 16°C (60°F), it lies between the specified limits. If any cell requires adjustment, some of the electrolyte must be siphoned off and replaced either by distilled water or by electrolyte as originally used for filling, depending on whether the specific gravity is too high or too low. Continue the charge for an hour or so to ensure adequate mixing of the electrolyte and again check the specific gravity readings. If necessary, repeat the adjustment process until the desired reading is obtained in each cell. Finally, allow the battery to cool, and siphon off any electrolyte over the tops of the separator guards.

Whenever booster-charging of the battery or electric welding of the body is carried out, the battery earth lead (positive) must be disconnected to prevent damage to the electrical system.

14:3 Generator routine maintenance, tests in situ

The only routine maintenance required is to oil the generator end bearing. Also check the fan belt for wear and tension. It should be possible to deflect the belt approximately $\frac{1}{2}$ inch (13 mm) at the centre of its longest run between two pulleys with moderate hand pressure. If the belt is too slack, tightening is effected by slackening the two generator suspension bolts and the bolt of the slotted adjustment link. A gentle pull on the generator outwards will enable the correct tension to be applied to the belt and all three bolts should then be tightened firmly.

Tests when generator is not charging:

1 Make sure that belt slip is not the cause of the trouble.
2 Check that the generator and control box are connected correctly. The generator terminal 'D' should be connected to the control box terminal 'D' and the generator terminal 'F' connected to the control box terminal 'F'.
3 After switching off all lights and accessories, disconnect the cables from the generator terminals marked 'D' and 'F' respectively.
4 Connect the two terminals with a short length of wire.
5 Start the engine and set it to run at normal idling speed.
6 Clip the negative lead of a moving coil type voltmeter, calibrated 0 to 20 volts, to one generator terminal and the other lead to a good earthing point on the generator yoke.
7 Gradually increase the engine speed, when the voltmeter reading should rise rapidly and without fluctuation. Do not allow the voltmeter reading to reach 20 volts. Do not race the engine in an attempt to increase the voltage. It is sufficient to run the generator up to a speed of 1000 rev/min.

If there is no reading, check the brush gear.

If the reading is low (approximately 1-volt) the field winding may be faulty.

If the reading is approximately 5 volts the armature winding may be faulty.

If the generator is in good order, leave the temporary link in position between the terminals and restore the original connections, taking care to connect the generator

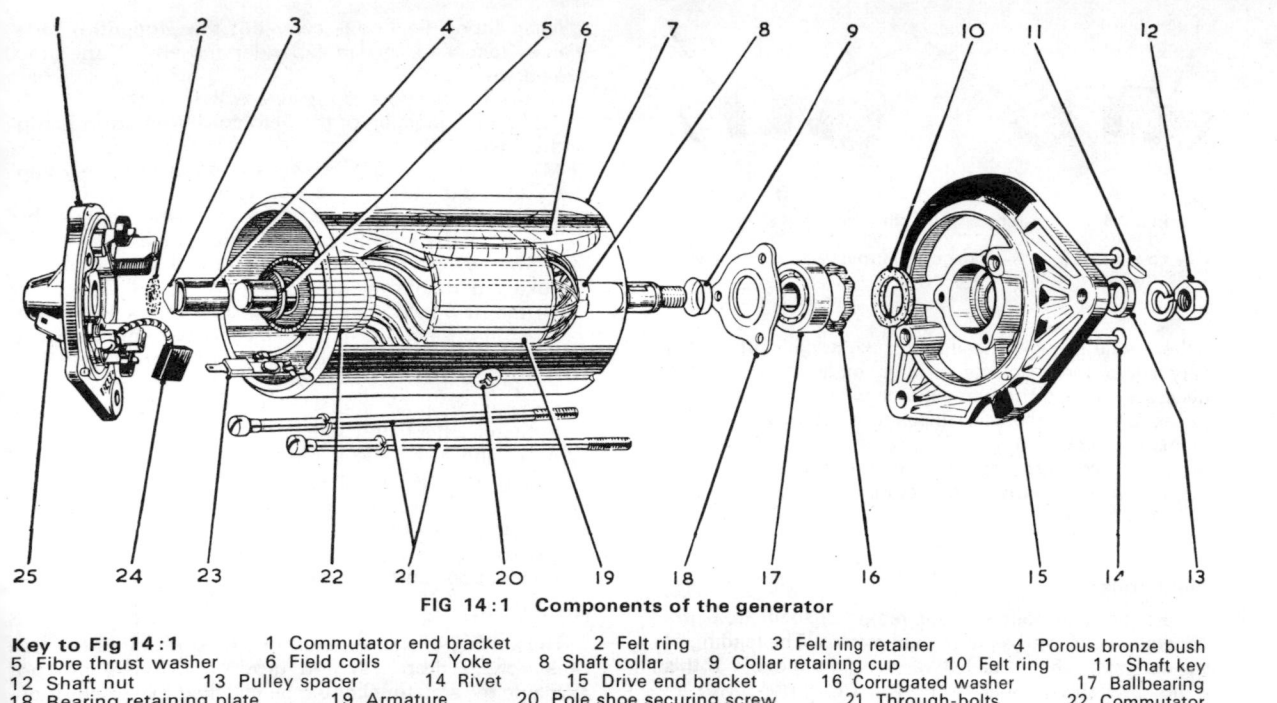

FIG 14:1   Components of the generator

Key to Fig 14:1   1 Commutator end bracket   2 Felt ring   3 Felt ring retainer   4 Porous bronze bush
5 Fibre thrust washer   6 Field coils   7 Yoke   8 Shaft collar   9 Collar retaining cup   10 Felt ring   11 Shaft key
12 Shaft nut   13 Pulley spacer   14 Rivet   15 Drive end bracket   16 Corrugated washer   17 Ballbearing
18 Bearing retaining plate   19 Armature   20 Pole shoe securing screw   21 Through-bolts   22 Commutator
23 Field terminal 'F'   24 Brushes   25 Output terminal 'D'

terminal 'D' to the control box terminal 'D', and the generator terminal 'F' to the control box terminal 'F'. Remove the lead from the 'D' terminal on the control box and connect the voltmeter between this cable and a good earthing point on the vehicle.

Run the engine as before. The reading should be the same as that measured directly on the generator. No reading on the voltmeter indicates a break in the cable to the generator. Carry out the same procedure from the 'F' terminal, connecting the voltmeter between cable and earth. Finally, remove the link from the generator. If the reading is correct, test the control box.

14:4 Removing and dismantling generator

Removal:

1 Disconnect the generator leads from the generator terminals.
2 Slacken all four attachment bolts and pivot the generator towards the cylinder block to enable the fan belt to be removed from the generator pulley.
3 The generator can now be removed by completely removing the two upper and one lower attachment bolts.

Dismantling:

Refer to **FIG 14:1** for identification of components.
1 Remove the securing nut and take off the drive pulley.
2 Remove the Woodruff key from the commutator shaft.
3 Unscrew and remove the two through-bolts and take off the commutator end bracket.

4 The driving end bracket, together with the armature and its ballbearing, can now be lifted out of the yoke. Unless the ballbearing is damaged or requires attention, it need not be removed from the armature.
5 Should it be necessary to remove the bearing, the armature must be separated from the end bracket by means of a hand press.

14:5 Brushes and commutator servicing, field coil testing

Brushes:

Test if the brushes are sticking. Clean them with petrol and if necessary, ease the sides by lightly polishing with a smooth file. Replace the brushes in their original positions.

Test the brush spring tension with a spring scale if available. The correct tension is 20 to 25 oz (567 to 709 gm). Fit a new spring if the tension is low.

If the brushes are worn so that the flexible lead is exposed on the running face, new brushes must be fitted. Brushes are preformed so that bedding to the commutator is not necessary.

Commutator:

A commutator in good condition will be smooth and free from pits or burned spots. Clean the commutator with a petrol-moistened cloth. If this is ineffective, carefully polish with a strip of fine glasspaper while rotating the armature.

To remedy a badly worn commutator, mount the armature (with or without the drive end bracket) in a

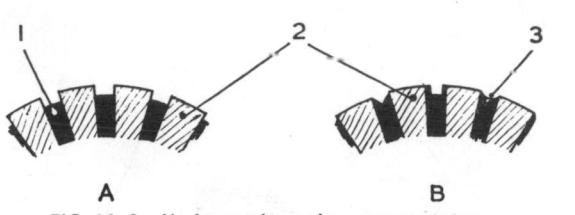

FIG 14:2 Undercutting the commutator

Key to Fig 14:2   **A** Correct   **B** Incorrect   1 Insulator
2 Segments   3 Insulator

lathe, rotate at high speed, and take a light cut with a very sharp tool. Do not remove more metal than is necessary. Polish the commutator with very fine glass-paper. Undercut the mica insulation between the segments to a depth of $\frac{1}{32}$ (.8 mm) with a hacksaw blade ground down to the thickness of the mica. The correct method of undercutting the commutator is shown in **FIG 14:2**.

Field coils:

Test the field coils without removing them from the generator yoke, by means of an ohmmeter. The reading of the ohmmeter should be between 6 and 6.3 ohms. If this is not available connect a 12-volt DC supply with an ammeter in series between the field terminal and the generator yoke. The ammeter reading should be approximately 2 amps. If no reading is indicated the field coils are open-circuited and must be renewed. To test for earthed field coils, unsolder the end of the field winding from the earth terminal on the generator yoke and, with a test lamp connected to a mains supply, test across the field terminal and earth. If the lamp lights, the field coils are earthed and must be renewed.

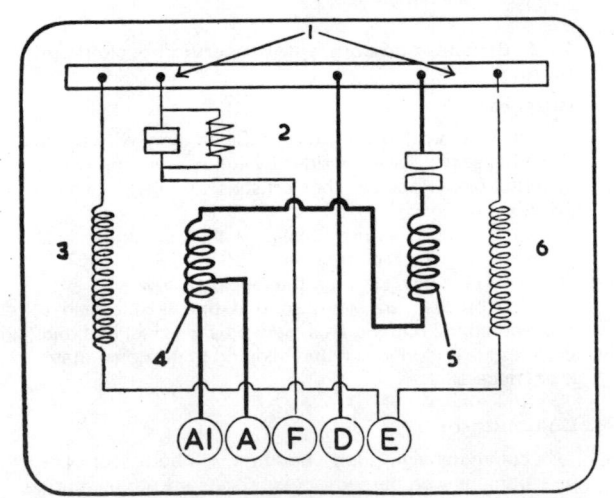

FIG 14:3 Internal wiring and connection of the regulator and cut-out, type RB.106

Key to Fig 14:3   1 Regulator and cut-out frame   2 Field resistance   3 Shunt coil   4 Tapped series coil
5 Series coil   6 Shunt coil

When fitting field coils carry out the procedure outlined as follows, using an expander and wheel operated screwdriver.

1 Remove the insulation piece which is provided to prevent the junction of the field coils from connecting the yoke.
2 Mark the yoke and pole shoes in order that they can be refitted in their original positions.
3 Unscrew the two pole shoe retaining screws by means of the wheel operated screwdriver.
4 Draw the pole shoes and coils out of the generator yoke and lift off the coils.
5 Fit the new field coils over the pole shoes and place them in position inside the yoke. Take care to ensure that the taping of the field coils is not trapped between the pole shoes and the yoke.
6 Locate the pole shoes and field coils by lightly tightening the fixing screw.
7 Insert the pole shoe expander, open it to the fullest extent, and tighten the screws.
8 Finally tighten the screws by means of the wheel operated screwdriver and lock them by caulking.
9 Replace the insulation piece between the field coil connections and the yoke.

Armature:

The testing of the armature winding requires the use of a voltage drop test and growler. If these are not available the armature should be checked by substitution. No attempt should be made to machine the armature core or to true a distorted shaft.

Bearings:

Bearings which are worn to such an extent that they allow side movement of the armature shaft must be replaced by new ones. To fit a new bearing at the commutator end of the generator proceed as follows:

1 Press the bearing bush out of the commutator bracket.
2 Press the new bearing bush into the end bracket using a shouldered mandrel of the same diameter as the shaft which is to fit in the bearing. Before fitting the new bearing bush, allow it to stand completely immersed in thin engine oil for 24 hours to fill the pores of the bush with lubricant. **Do not ream after fitting.**

The ballbearing at the driving end is renewed as follows:

1 Knock out the rivets which secure the bearing retaining plate to the end bracket and remove the plate.
2 Press the bearing out of the end bracket and remove the corrugated washer, felt washer and oil retaining washer.
3 Before fitting the replacement bearing, see that it is clean and pack it with a high melting point grease.
4 Place the oil retaining washer, felt washer, and corrugated washer in the bearing housing in the end bracket.
5 Locate the bearing in the housing and press it home by means of a hand press.
6 Fit the bearing retaining plate. Insert the new rivets from the inside of the end bracket and open the rivets by means of a punch to secure the plate rigidly in position.

14:6 Generator reassembly and refitting

Reassembly of the generator is a reversal of the dismantling procedure, but note the following points:

1 If the end bracket has been removed from the armature, press the bearing end bracket onto the armature shaft, taking care to avoid damaging the end plate and armature winding.

2 Add a few drops of oil through the hole in the armature end cover.

3 When assembling the commutator end bracket, the brushes must first be held clear of the commutator by partially withdrawing them from their boxes, until each brush is trapped in position by the side pressure of the spring. The brushes can be released onto the commutator by a small screwdriver or similar tool when the end bracket is assembled to within about ½ inch (13 mm) of the yoke. Before closing the gap between the end bracket and the yoke, see that the springs are in correct contact with the brushes.

Refitting the generator:

Refitting is an exact reversal of the removal operations detailed in **Section 14:4**. The upper bolts may have flat washers under their heads which must be refitted.

Before tightening the attachment bolts, set the fan belt tension. A gentle pull on the generator outwards will enable the correct tension to be applied to the belt and all three bolts should then be tightened firmly. It should be possible to deflect the belt approximately ½ inch (13 mm) at the centre of its longest run between two pulleys with moderate hand pressure.

14:7 Control box description, regulator adjustments

Description—Type RB.106:

The control box contains two units, a voltage regulator and a cut-out. Although combined structurally, the regulator and cut-out are electrically separate (see **FIG 14:3**). Both are accurately adjusted during manufacture, and the cover protecting them should not be removed unnecessarily. Cable connections are secured by Lucar connections.

Regulator adjustment:

The regulator is carefully set before leaving the works to suit the normal requirements of the standard equipment, and in general it should not be necessary to alter it. If, however, the battery does not keep in a charged state, or if the generator output does not fall when the battery is fully charged, it may be advisable to check the setting, and if necessary, adjust it.

It is important, before altering the regulator setting, when the battery is in a low state of charge, to check that its condition is not due to a battery defect or to the generator belt slipping.

Electrical setting (with unit cold):

The electrical setting of the control unit can be checked without removing the cover. Use a good quality moving coil voltmeter (0 to 20 volts).

Refer to **FIG 14:4**, withdraw the cables from the control box terminals 'A' and 'A1' and connect these cables together.

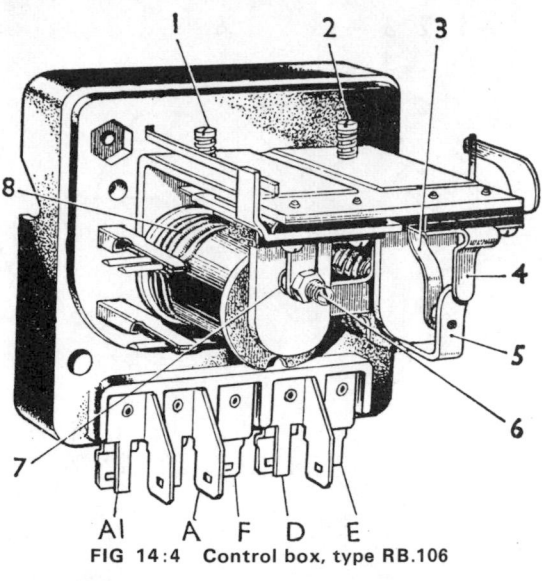

FIG 14:4 Control box, type RB.106

Key to Fig 14:4 1 Regulator adjusting screw 2 Cut-out adjusting screw 3 Fixed contact blade 4 Stop arm 5 Armature tongue and moving contact 6 Regulator fixed contact screw 7 Regulator moving contact 8 Regulator series winding

Connect the negative lead of the voltmeter to the control box terminal 'D' and connect the other lead to terminal 'E'.

Start the engine and increase the speed until the generator speed is about 3000 rev/min (4500 for generator type C42). The voltmeter should then read between the following limits.

Ambient temperature	Open circuit voltage
10°C (50°F)	16.1 to 16.7
20°C (68°F)	16.0 to 16.6
30°C (86°F)	15.9 to 16.5
40°C (104°F)	15.8 to 16.4

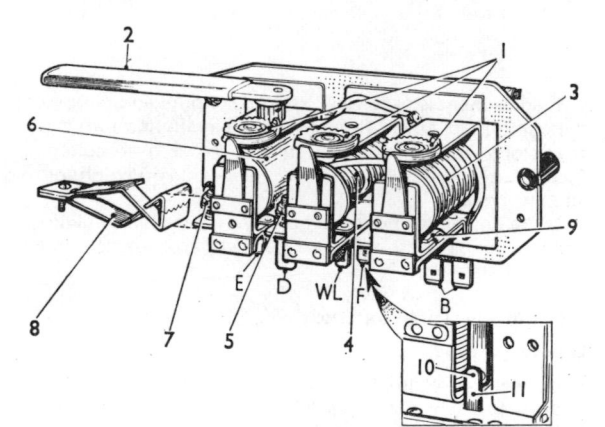

FIG 14:5 Control box, type RB.340

Key to Fig 14:5 1 Adjustment cams 2 Setting tool 3 Cut-out relay 4 Current regulator 5 Current relay contacts 6 Voltage regulator 7 Voltage regulator contacts 8 Clip-contacts 9 Armature back-stop 10 Cut-out contacts 11 Fixed contact bracket

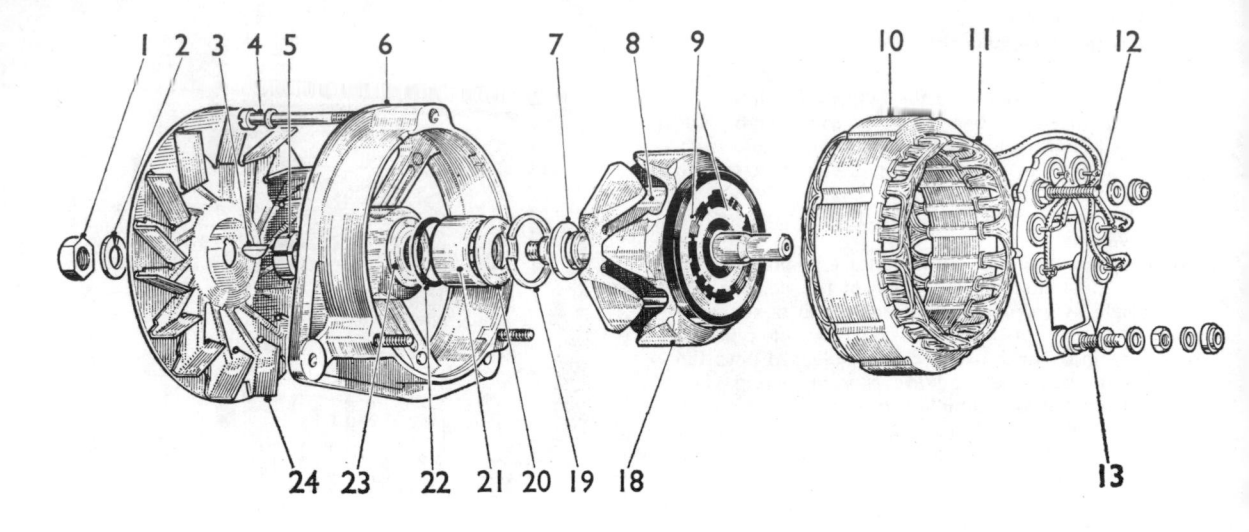

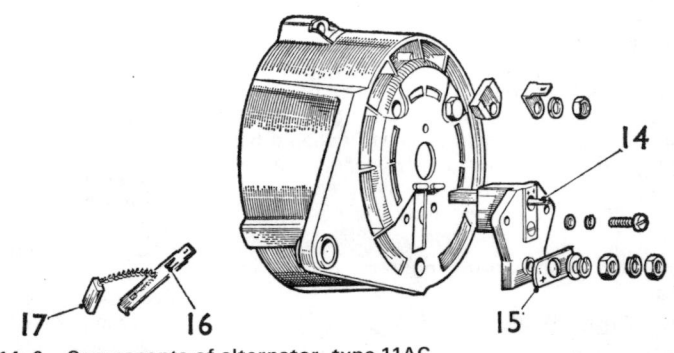

FIG 14:6   Components of alternator, type 11AC

Key to Fig 14:6   1 Shaft nut   2 Spring washer   3 Key   4 Through-bolt   5 Distance collar   6 Drive end bracket   7 Jump ring shroud   8 Rotor (field) winding   9 Slip rings   10 Stator laminations   11 Stator windings   12 Warning light terminal   13 Output terminal   14 Field terminal blade   15 Output terminal plastic strip   16 Terminal blade retaining tongue   17 Brush   18 Rotor   19 Bearing circlip   20 Bearing retaining plate   21 Ballbearing   22 O-ring seal   23 O-ring retaining washer   24 Fan

If adjustment is necessary, stop the engine and remove the control box cover. Run the engine again and turn the regulator adjusting screw 1 in **FIG 14:4** as required. Clockwise rotation of the screw will increase the voltage and vice versa.

Make any adjustments as quickly as possible to avoid overheating. Stop the engine, recheck and replace the connections.

Cut-out electrical setting:

Cut-in voltage:

Connect a voltmeter between terminals D and E, remove the cover and switch on a load such as the headlamps.

Start the engine and slowly increase the speed. At between 12.7 and 13.3 volts the contacts should close, indicated by a slight drop or flick back of the meter needle. Turn the adjusting screw 2 clockwise to increase the voltage and vice versa.

Drop-off voltage:

Disconnect the cables from terminals A and A1 and join them together. Connect a voltmeter between either of these terminals and a good earth.

Run the engine to give a generator speed of approximately 3000 rev/min and then slowly reduce the speed. Note the voltmeter reading at the moment it falls to zero indicating the opening of the contacts. This should occur between 8.5 and 11.0 volts.

Adjust by carefully bending the fixed contact blade, towards the bobbin to reduce and away from the bobbin to increase the drop-off voltage.

Control box type RB.340 (see FIG 14:5):
Voltage regulator adjustment:

Detach the cables from terminals B and bridge the cables.

Detach the cable from WL and connect a voltmeter between the terminal and a good earth.

Run the engine and with the generator speed at 3000 rev/min the voltmeter should be steady between the following limits:

Ambient temperature	Voltage setting limits
Zero to 25°C (32°F to 77°F)	14.5 to 15.5
26°C to 40°C (78°F to 104°F)	14.25 to 15.25

To adjust the reading, if necessary, turn the voltage regulator 6 cam clockwise to raise the voltage or vice versa.

Cut-out relay:

Cut-in voltage:

Remove the cable from WL and connect the voltmeter between the terminal and earth. Switch on a load such as the headlamps.

Start the engine and slowly increase the speed. The voltage indicated should rise steadily and drop slightly at the moment the contacts close. At this point the reading should be between 12.7 and 13.3 volts.

To adjust the cut-out relay 3, if necessary, turn the cam clockwise to raise or anticlockwise to lower the setting.

Drop-off voltage:

Detach the cables from terminal B and bridge the cables. Connect a voltmeter between the terminal and earth. Start up and run the generator at 3000 rev/min.

Slowly reduce speed and note the voltage immediately before the needle drops to zero. This should be between 9.5 and 11 volts.

If adjustment is necessary, carefully bend the fixed contact bracket 11. Reducing the gap will raise the drop-off voltage and vice versa.

Test and readjust again if necessary until the correct setting is obtained.

14:8 The alternator

Two types of alternators have been used on the later vehicles. The Lucas type 11AC being the first type. This alternator has a separate control unit. The Lucas 16ACR which has replaced the 11AC has its control unit incorporated in the alternator. Both types are belt driven from the crankshaft pulley. The mechanical construction of the alternator differs from the generator in that the field rotates (the rotor), and the generator windings are stationary (the stator). An exploded view of the type 11AC alternator can be seen in **FIG 14:6**.

The brush gear from the field system is mounted on the slip ring end bracket. The carbon brushes bear against a pair of concentric brass slip rings carried on a moulded disc attached to the end of the rotor.

The diodes and stator windings are cooled by airflow through the alternator induced by the fan at the drive end

The alternator output is controlled by a control unit. In addition, a warning light is fitted.

Precautions:

The following precautions must be observed when dealing with vehicles fitted with an alternator:

1 When fitting a replacement alternator, ensure that it is of the same polarity as the original. Terminal polarity is clearly marked.
2 Do not reverse the battery connections. Connect up the earth terminal of the battery first.

3 If a high rate battery charger is used to charge the battery in position in the vehicle, damage will occur to the regulator if the ignition/starter switch is turned on. Detach the connectors from the regulator as a safety measure before boost charging. Reconnect after charging.
4 When starting the engine with the aid of a high rate charger, detach the connectors from the regulator prior to using the charger. Do not reconnect the regulator until the charger is disconnected, and the engine is running at idling speed.
5 The battery must never be disconnected while the engine is running, nor must the alternator be run with the main output cable disconnected either at the alternator end or the battery end.
6 The cable connecting the battery and alternator is 'live' even when the engine is not running. Take care not to earth the alternator terminal or the cable end if removed from the terminal.
7 Disconnect the alternator and regulator as a safety precaution when arc welding on the vehicle.

14:9 Alternator tests in situ
Testing the charging circuit, type 11AC:
Alternator:

1 Check that battery voltage is reaching the brush gear by disconnecting the two cables from the alternator field terminals, connecting a voltmeter between the two cables and running the engine. The voltmeter should read battery voltage. If no reading is obtained, check the field circuit wiring.
2 To check the alternator output, stop the engine and disconnect the positive battery terminal. Connect an ammeter between alternator terminal 'B' and its two cables. Connect the alternator field terminals to the battery terminals. Reconnect the battery positive terminal, start the engine and gradually increase its speed to give an alternator speed of approximately 4000 rev/min. The ammeter should register approximately 40 amps.

If a zero reading is obtained, check the brush gear and repeat the test. If a zero reading is still obtained, remove and dismantle the alternator. If a low reading is obtained, check the wiring connections and repeat the test. If a low reading is still obtained, proceed with the next test.
3 Stop the engine and connect a low range voltmeter between the alternator terminal 'B' and the battery negative terminal. Start the engine and note the voltmeter reading. Transfer the voltmeter connections to the alternator frame and the battery positive terminal and again note the voltmeter reading. If either of these two readings exceeds .5 volt there is a high resistance in the charging circuit. If there is no undue resistance, and the output is low, remove and dismantle the alternator.

Control unit:

1 Check the resistance of the wiring circuits of the alternator, control unit, and battery to control unit, including the relay unit. The resistance should not exceed .1 ohm.

Do not use an ohmmeter of the type which incorporates a hand driven generator when testing the rectifiers or transistors.

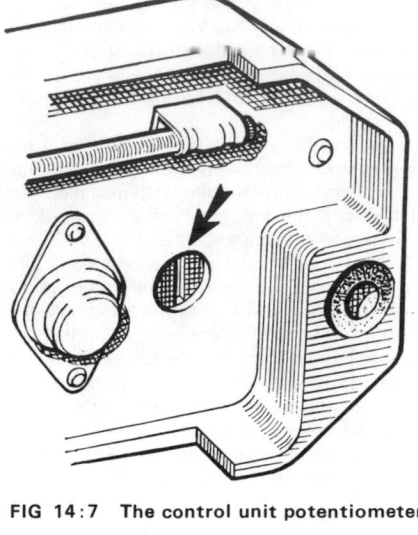

FIG 14:7   The control unit potentiometer

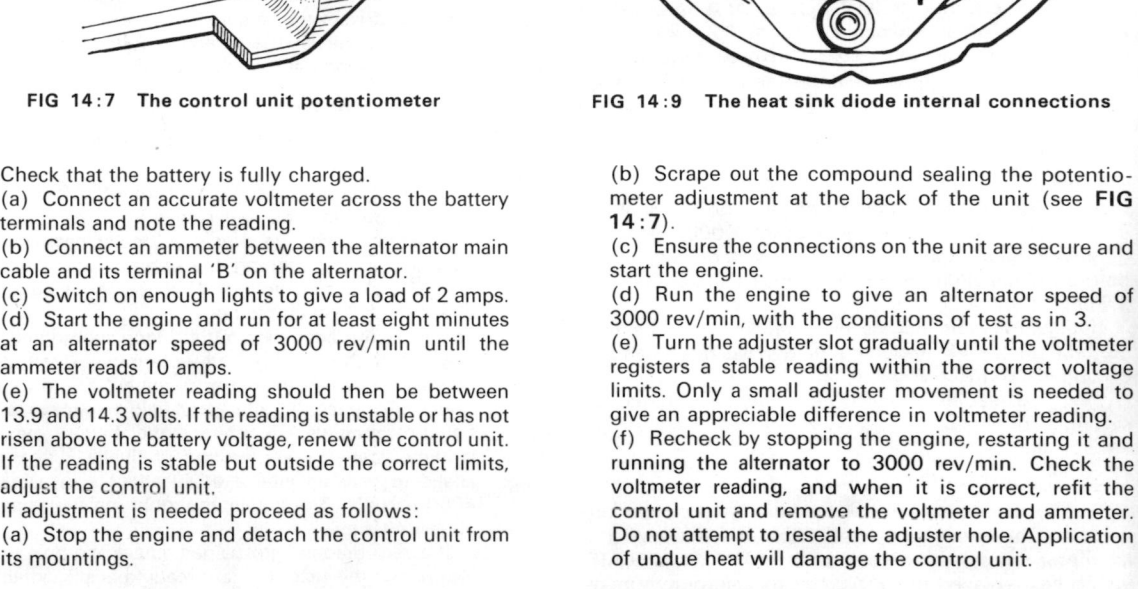

FIG 14:9   The heat sink diode internal connections

2 Check that the battery is fully charged.
(a) Connect an accurate voltmeter across the battery terminals and note the reading.
(b) Connect an ammeter between the alternator main cable and its terminal 'B' on the alternator.
(c) Switch on enough lights to give a load of 2 amps.
(d) Start the engine and run for at least eight minutes at an alternator speed of 3000 rev/min until the ammeter reads 10 amps.
(e) The voltmeter reading should then be between 13.9 and 14.3 volts. If the reading is unstable or has not risen above the battery voltage, renew the control unit. If the reading is stable but outside the correct limits, adjust the control unit.
3 If adjustment is needed proceed as follows:
(a) Stop the engine and detach the control unit from its mountings.

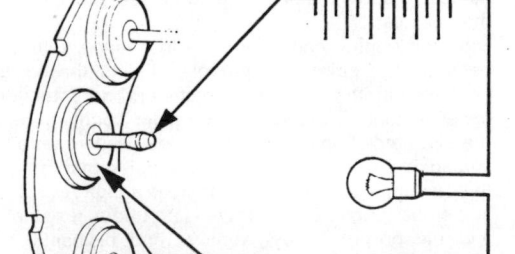

FIG 14:8   Testing the diodes

(b) Scrape out the compound sealing the potentiometer adjustment at the back of the unit (see **FIG 14:7**).
(c) Ensure the connections on the unit are secure and start the engine.
(d) Run the engine to give an alternator speed of 3000 rev/min, with the conditions of test as in 3.
(e) Turn the adjuster slot gradually until the voltmeter registers a stable reading within the correct voltage limits. Only a small adjuster movement is needed to give an appreciable difference in voltmeter reading.
(f) Recheck by stopping the engine, restarting it and running the alternator to 3000 rev/min. Check the voltmeter reading, and when it is correct, refit the control unit and remove the voltmeter and ammeter. Do not attempt to reseal the adjuster hole. Application of undue heat will damage the control unit.

Relay unit:

1 To test the relay unit, remove the lead from relay unit terminal 'C2' and connect to terminal 'C1'.
2 Connect an ammeter between alternator terminal 'B' and its two cables.
3 Start the engine and check the alternator output. If the output is satisfactory, renew the relay unit.

Testing the charging circuit, type 16ACR:

Check the following points before proceeding:
1 Correct drive belt tension.
2 Clean and tighten battery connections.
3 Consistent readings of battery electrolyte specific gravity.
4 That all cables and connections in the charging circuit are in good condition.
If the checks are satisfactory proceed as follows:
1 Check that battery voltage is reaching the alternator by removing the cable connectors from the alternator, connecting the negative of a voltmeter to earth, and switching on the master/starter switch. Connect the positive of the voltmeter to the 'IND' cable connector.

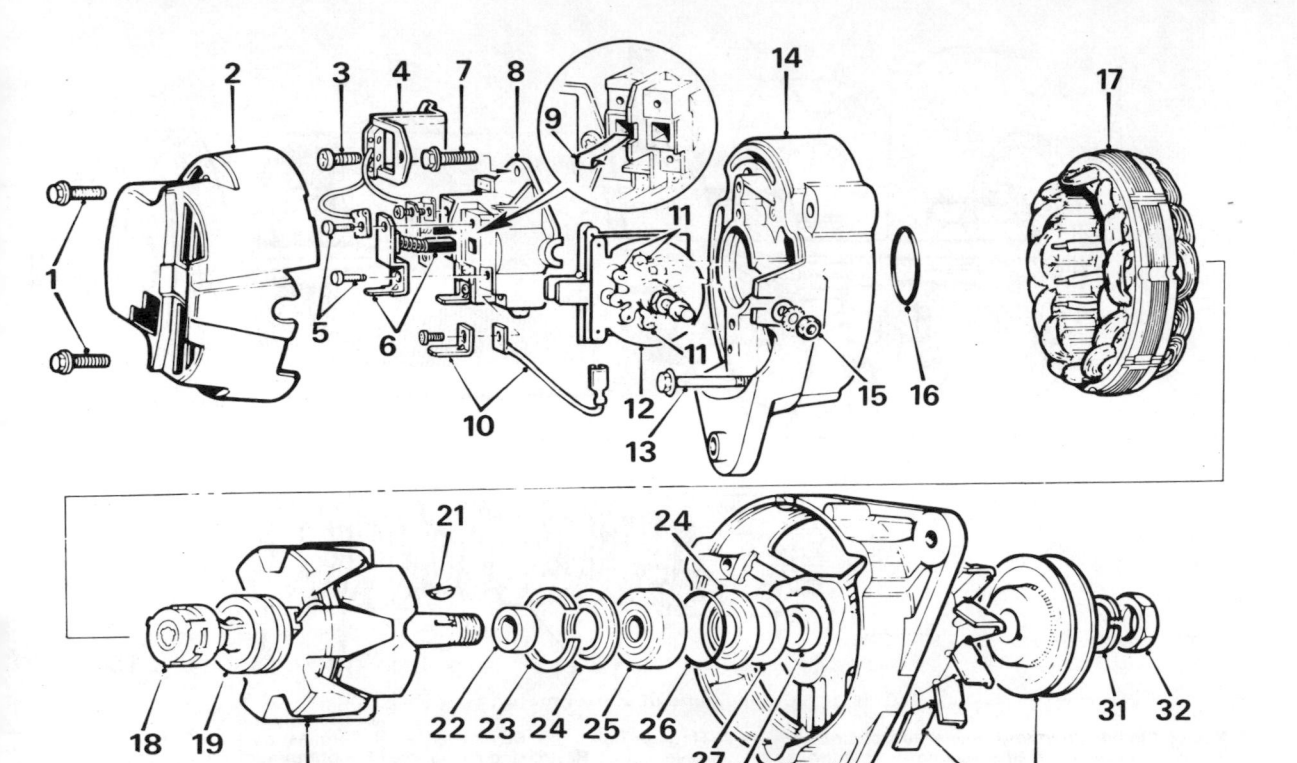

FIG 14:10 Alternator components, type 16ACR

Key to Fig 14:10 1 Screws for end cover   2 End cover   3 Screw retaining regulator   4 Regulator   5 Screws for brush assemblies   6 Brush and spring assembly   7 Screws for brush holder and regulator assembly   8 Brush holder   9 Leaf spring for brush   10 Lead and terminal   11 Diodes   12 Rectifier pack   13 Through-bolt   14 Slip ring end bracket   15 Nut retaining rectifier   16 'O' ring   17 Lamination pack   18 Slip ring   19 Bearing   20 Rotor   21 Key for pulley   22 Distance piece   23 Circlip   24 Bearing cover plates   25 Bearing   26 'O' ring   27 Felt ring   28 Drive-end bracket   29 Fan   30 Pulley   31 Spring washer   32 Nut for pulley

If no voltage is shown check the no-charge warning light and warning light circuit for continuity. Connect the positive of the voltmeter to the main charging cable connector. If no voltage is shown check the circuit between the battery and the alternator for continuity.

2 Reconnect the alternator cables. Disconnect the brown cable from the starter solenoid. Connect an ammeter between the cable and the solenoid terminal. Connect a voltmeter across the battery terminals. Run the engine at 6000 alternator rev/min until the ammeter reading is stable. If the ammeter reading is zero, remove the alternator for overhaul. If the ammeter reading is low, the battery is at fault. The reading should be 34 amp at 14-volt at 600 alternator rev/min. If the ammeter reads below 10 amp with the voltmeter reading below 13.6-volt, or the ammeter reads above 14.4-volt, the alternator regulator is at fault.

Removing and replacing, type 16ACR:

The procedure is similar to the 11AC type except for the following:

1 The cooling system must be drained below the radiator header tank and the top radiator hose removed.

2 Detach the cable from the thermal transmitter, if fitted.

3 Slacken the bolt of the adjusting link.

Refit in the reverse order, tensioning the driving belt to give a deflection of $\frac{3}{8}$ to $\frac{1}{2}$ inch at the centre of the longest run.

14:10 Alternator removal, dismantling and reassembly, type 11AC
Removal:

Disconnect the battery and detach the electrical leads from the alternator. Slacken the alternator securing bolts, push the alternator towards the engine and detach the driving belt from the alternator pulley. Remove the securing bolts and detach the alternator from the engine.

Refitting is a reversal of this procedure. The driving belt must be tensioned so that a deflection of $\frac{1}{8}$ inch (3.18 mm) can be obtained under finger pressure at the mid-point of the longest run on the belt. Do not apply leverage to any point of the alternator other than the front mounting bracket, or run the engine with the battery or alternator disconnected.

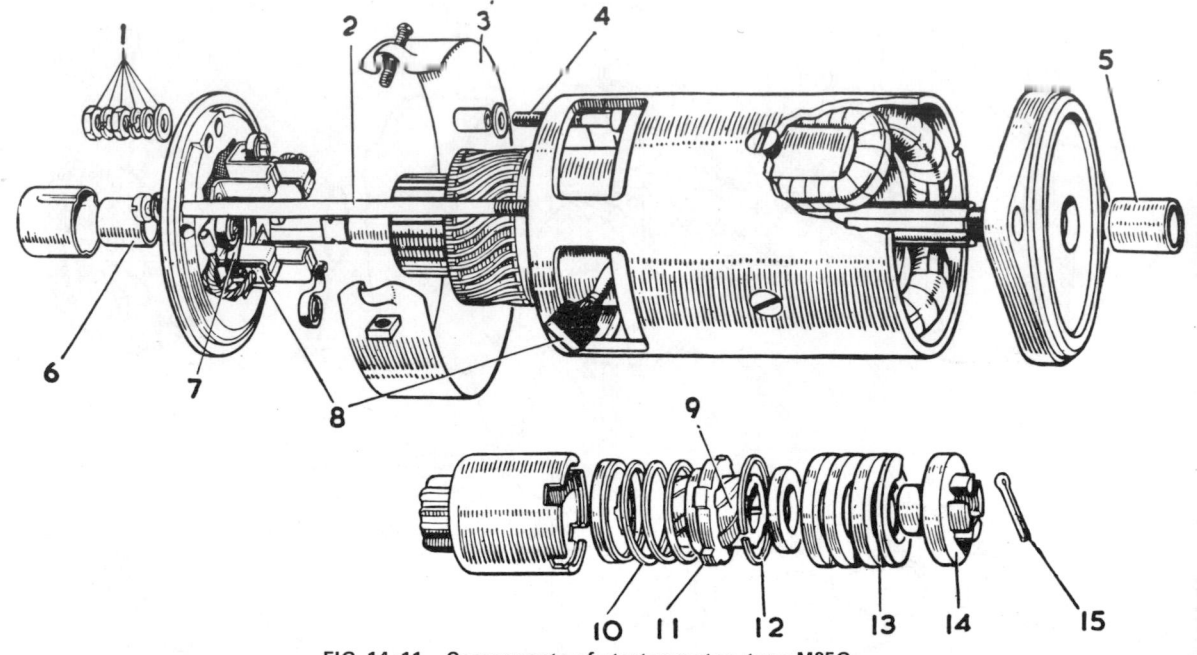

FIG 14:11 Components of starter motor, type M35G

Key to Fig 14:11 1 Terminal nuts and washers   2 Through-bolt   3 Cover band   4 Terminal post   5 Bearing brush
6 Bearing brush   7 Brush spring   8 Brushes   9 Sleeve   10 Restraining spring   11 Control nut   12 Retaining ring
13 Main spring   14 Shaft nut   15 Cotterpin

Dismantling:

1 Refer to **FIG 14:6** to identify component parts. Remove the securing nut and detach the drive pulley, fan and key from the armature shaft.

2 Mark the relative position of the drive end bracket, the stator lamination pack, and the slip ring end bracket for replacement purposes.

3 Remove the through-bolts and detach the drive end bracket and rotor.

4 Press the rotor out of the drive end bracket.

5 Remove the terminal nuts, brush box retaining screws, and the heat sink bolt. Withdraw the stator and heat sink from the slip ring end bracket.

6 Close the retaining tongues on the brush terminal blades and withdraw the terminals from the brush box.

7 Check the brush lengths and if they are worn below the permissible limit of $\frac{5}{32}$ inch (3.97 mm) they must be renewed. Check the spring tensions and renew them if they are below the stated limits as in **Technical Data.**

8 Clean the slip rings with petrol, or if they are burned, with fine glasspaper. The slip rings must not be machined.

9 Test the resistance or current flow of the field winding using an ohmmeter or a 12-volt DC supply and an ammeter. The resistance should be 3.77 plus or minus .18 ohms, and the current flow 3.2 amps.

10 Test the insulation of the windings by connecting a 110-volt AC supply and a 15-watt test lamp between one of the rotor poles and each of the slip rings in turn.

11 Disconnect the three cables from the heat sink, taking care not to overheat the diodes or bend the diode pin.

Test the continuity of the windings by using a 12-volt DC supply and a 1.5-volt test lamp, connected in series with any two of the cables, then repeating the test using the third cable in place of either one of the first two. Test the insulation by connecting a 110-volt AC supply and a 15-watt test lamp between one of the three cables and the lamination pack.

12 Test each diode by connecting a 12-volt DC supply and a 1.5 watt test lamp in series with each diode in turn as shown in **FIG 14:8** and then reversing the connections. Current should flow in one direction only.

13 Remake the cable connections to the heat sink using 'M' grade 45-55 tin lead. Take care not to overheat diodes or bend the pins. Secure the interconnections in the position shown in **FIG 14:9** using a high temperature resistant adhesive.

14 Check that the bearings do not allow excessive side float of the armature shaft. If the needle bearing is faulty, the slip ring end bracket and bearing must be renewed as a complete assembly. If the ballbearing is faulty, renew the bearing, packing the new bearing with high melting point grease.

Reassembly:

Reverse the procedure in 1 to 6 inclusive, bending the retaining tongues of the field terminal blades out at an angle of 30 deg. before fitting. Tighten the through-bolts, brush box fixing screws and diode heat sink fixings to the correct torque figures (45 to 50, 10 and 25 lb inch respectively).

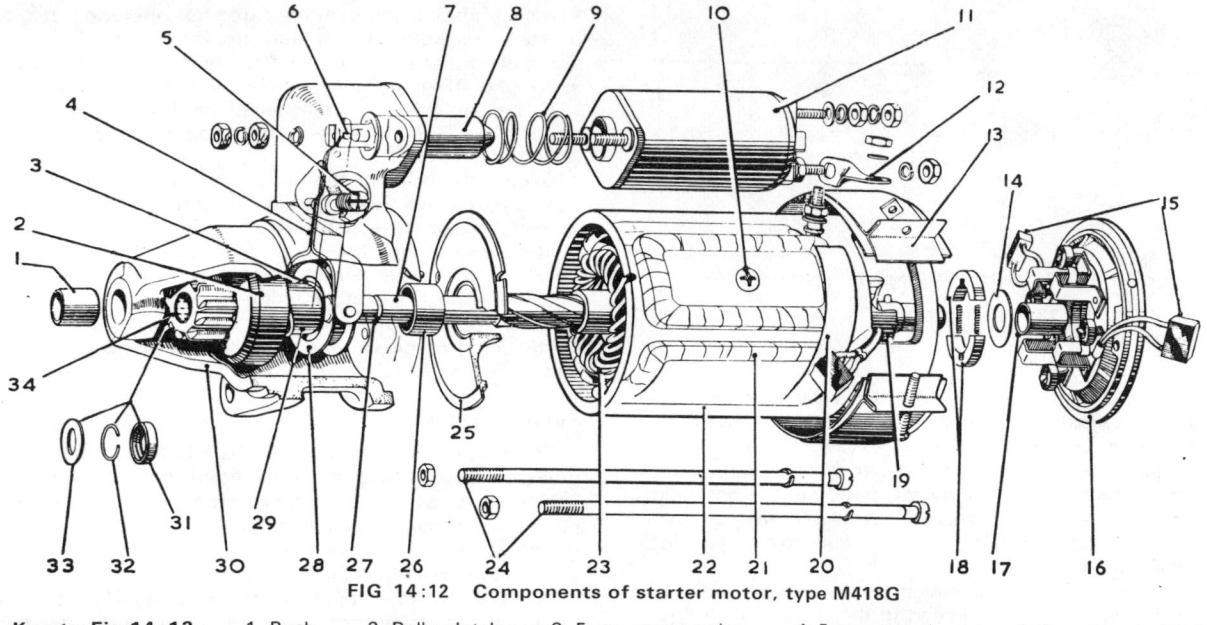

FIG 14:12 Components of starter motor, type M418G

Key to Fig 14:12
1 Bush 2 Roller clutch 3 Engagement spring 4 Engagement lever 5 Eccentric pivot bolt
6 Clevis pin 7 Armature shaft extension 8 Plunger 9 Push-off spring 10 Pole shoe securing screw
11 Actuating solenoid 12 Copper link 13 Band cover 14 Thrust washer 15 Brushes 16 Commutator end bracket
17 Bush 18 Brake shoes 19 Commutator 20 Insulation piece 21 Field coils 22 Yoke 23 Armature
24 Through-bolts 25 Intermediate bracket 26 Bush 27 Groove for retaining ring 28 Operating bush 29 Driving sleeve
30 Driving end bracket 31 Thrust collar 32 Retaining ring 33 Thrust washer 34 Pinion leading face

Dismantling, type 16ACR (see FIG 14:10):

1 Detach the end cover 2, two screws.

2 Detach the cable 10 from the rectifier 12 terminal.

3 Remove the three screws 7, and detach the brush holder and regulator assembly.

4 Check the brush length and spring tension, see **Technical Data**.

5 Disconnect the regulator cables from the brush holder.

6 Detach the regulator 4 from the brush holder 8.

7 Clean the slip rings 18 with a petrol moistened rag, or if necessary, very fine glasspaper.

8 Slacken the nut 15 on the rectifier assembly bolt.

9 Using a pair of long-nosed pliers as a thermal shunt to avoid overheating the diodes, unsolder the three starter cables from the rectifier pack, and withdraw the rectifier assembly.

10 Carry out the tests as for the type 11AC except the resistance of the rotor winding should be 4.33 ohms ± 5% and current flow at 12-volt should be 3 amp.

11 Mark the drive end bracket, the stator, and slip ring end bracket for reassembly and remove the three through-bolts.

12 Drive the bearing 19 out of the slip ring end bracket 14 by using a suitable tube.

13 Unsolder the connections from the slip ring assembly 18 and withdraw the assembly from the rotor shaft.

14 Withdraw the bearing from the rotor shaft.

15 Remove the drive pulley nut 32 and withdraw the spring washer 31, the pulley 30, the fan 29 and the Woodruff key 21.

16 Press the rotor 20 out of the drive end bracket 28 and remove the distance piece 22.

17 Remove the circlip 23 and the bearing cover plate 24.

18 Extract the bearing 25, the 'O' ring 26, the cover plate 24 and the felt ring 27, when fitted.

19 Examine all parts and renew as necessary.

Reassemble in the reverse order noting the following points:

The bearing 19 is fitted with its shielded side towards the slip ring assembly 18.

Use Fry's HT3 solder for the field to slip ring connections.

When refitting the rotor to the drive-end bracket, support the inner race of the bearing.

Use 'M' grade 45-55 tin-lead solder for the starter to rectifier connections. Use a long-nosed pair of pliers as a heat sink to prevent overheating the diodes.

14:11 Starter motor tests in situ

Switch on the lights and operate the starter control. If the lights go dim, but the starter is not heard to operate, an indication is given that current is flowing through the starter windings, but that the starter pinion may be meshed permanently with the geared ring on the flywheel. This was probably caused by the starter being operated while the engine was running. One method to try and free the starter pinion is to engage a gear with the ignition switched off. If the car is now rocked backwards and forwards the jammed pinion should free itself. If it proves impossible to free the jammed starter, it must be removed from the vehicle.

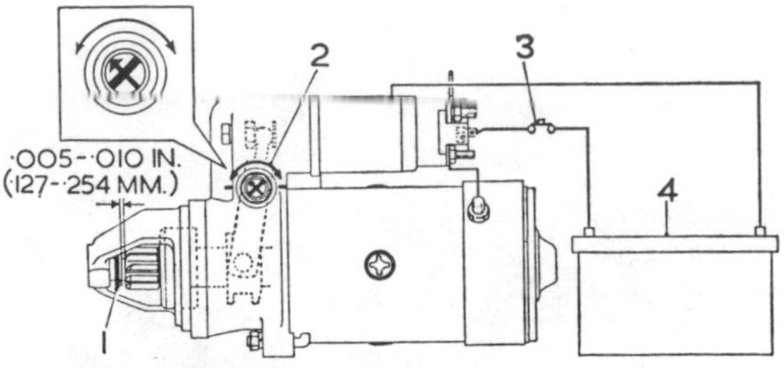

FIG 14:13 Setting the starter pinion travel

Key to Fig 14:13 1 Thrust collar 2 Eccentric pivot bolt
3 Switch 4 6-volt battery

Should the lights retain their full brilliance when the starter switch is operated, check that the switch is functioning. If the switch is in order, examine the connections at the battery, starter switch, and starter, and check the wiring between these units. Continued failure of the starter to operate indicates an internal fault, and the starter must be removed from the engine for examination.

Sluggish or slow operation of the starter is usually caused by a poor connection in the wiring which produces a high resistance in the starter circuit. Check all the connections for cleanliness, tightness, etc.

Damage to the starter drive is indicated if the starter is heard to operate but does not crank the engine.

14:12 Servicing the starter

Four types of starter motors have been used on these vehicles. The type M35G is shown in component form in **FIG 14:11**. The type M35J is similar in construction, but has a face-type commutator, with a brush block rivetted to the end bracket, the brushes being held against the commutator by small coil springs. Servicing can be carried out in a similar manner to the M35G. **FIGS 14:12** and **14:14** show the pre-engaged starter types fitted to diesel engines. These illustrations should enable a reasonably competent home operator to inspect his starter and carry out simple maintenance tasks on it, but in the event of trouble it is usually desirable to take the motor to a qualified service station for repair or replacement.

Removing and testing Type M35G:

This is a conventional type of motor with a spiral sleeve (Bendix) type of engagement and is shown in **FIG 14:11** and is fitted as standard to petrol engines.

Disconnect the battery positive terminal, then release the cable to the starter and remove the two securing bolts. Manoeuvre the starter forwards below the oil filter, then downwards and outwards.

Refitting is the reverse of the above.

Testing:

Refer to **FIG 14:11** and remove the coverband 3, and examine the brushes 8 and the commutator. Hold back each of the brush springs 7 and move the brush by gently pulling on its flexible connector. If the movement is sluggish, remove the brush from its holder and ease the sides by lightly polishing with a smooth file.

Always replace brushes in their original positions. If the brushes are worn so that they no longer bear on the commutator, or if the brush flexible lead has become exposed on the running face, they must be renewed.

If the commutator is blackened or dirty, clean it by holding a petrol-moistened cloth against it while the armature is rotated.

Secure the body of the starter in a vice and test by connecting it with heavy gauge cables to a battery of the correct voltage. One cable must be connected to the starter terminal and the other held against the starter body or end bracket. Under these light load conditions, the starter should run at very high speed.

If the operation of the starter is still unsatisfactory, the starter must be dismantled for detailed inspection and testing.

Type M418G:

This motor which is shown in **FIG 14:12** is one of two types of the pre-engaged starters fitted to diesel engined vehicles. It differs essentially from the previously mentioned model in that the operation of the solenoid engages the starter drive pinion with the flywheel ring gear before the main starting current is applied.

It also incorporates a roller clutch which ensures that in the event of the drive pinion remaining in mesh after the engine has started, the armature is not driven at high speed and damaged as a result.

Testing:

If the motor does not operate, or is sluggish, check the following points before removing it. If it is heard to operate, but does not turn the engine, the motor should be removed for inspection.

Connect a voltmeter (0 to 20) across the battery terminals and operate the starter switch.

1 If the reading drops to about 6 volts but the motor does not operate, this indicates that the current is flowing but the armature is not turning. Remove for inspection.

2 If the voltmeter reading is steady about 12 volts, examine all connections and check the wiring for continuity.

(a) Connect the voltmeter between the small terminal on the solenoid and earth and operate the starter switch. No reading indicates a faulty switch or connection.

(b) Connect the voltmeter between the battery supply terminal on the solenoid and earth. No reading indicates a discharged battery, a faulty cable or a loose connection.

(c) Connect the voltmeter between the large output terminal on the solenoid and earth and operate the starter switch. If the starter is operating normally a reading of 6 to 7 volts should be obtained. A zero reading indicates a faulty solenoid, while a reading of 12 volts indicates a breakdown in the motor windings. Remove the starter for repair or replacement.

Removal and refitting:

Disconnect the battery and the heavy and light cables from the terminals on the base of the solenoid.

Unscrew the two securing bolts and withdraw the motor forwards away from the engine.

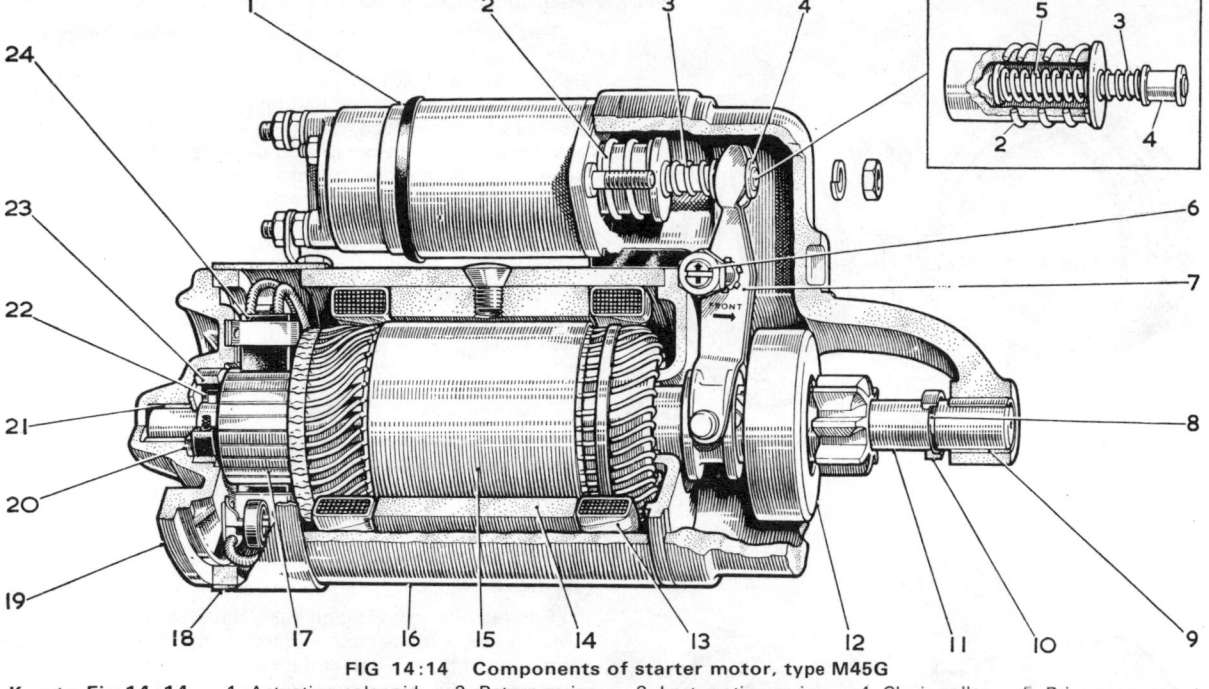

FIG 14:14   Components of starter motor, type M45G

Key to Fig 14:14   1 Actuating solenoid   2 Return spring   3 Lost-motion spring   4 Clevis collar   5 Drive engagement
spring   6 Eccentric pivot bolt   7 Engagement lever   8 Retaining ring   9 Bush   10 Thrust collar   11 Armature shaft
extension   12 Roller clutch   13 Field coils   14 Pole shoe   15 Armature   16 Yoke   17 Commutator   18 Band cover
19 Commutator end bracket   20 Thrust washer   21 Bush   22 Brake shoes   23 Brake ring   24 Brush

Before refitting the starter the travel of the starter
pinion may be checked (see **FIG 14:13**).

Connect the small centre terminal on the solenoid, by
way of a switch, to a 6-volt supply and connect the other
side of the supply to the solenoid body. Close the switch
and the drive will move into the engaged position.
Press the pinion lightly towards the armature to take up
any play and then rotate the eccentric pivot bolt 2 until
the gap between the pinion leading face and the thrust
collar on the armature shaft is .005 to .010 inch (.127 to
.254 mm). Tighten the locknut and check. Note that the
arc of adjustment is 180 deg. and the arrow on the pivot
pin must point towards the arrowed arc on the drive end
bracket.

Refitting of the starter is a reversal of the removal
procedure, noting that the clearance between the leading
edge of the starter pinion and the starter ring on the flywheel should be $\frac{1}{8}$ inch (3.2 mm).

Type M45G:

This second type of pre-engaged starter, fitted to later
diesel models is in most respects similar to the type
M418G.

Reference to **FIG 14:14** will show the construction
of this motor and it should be tested and serviced in a
similar manner to the earlier type.

14:13 Fuses

The fuse holder is adjacent to the control unit and
houses two fuses in use and two spares.

The fuse between 3-4 protects those accessories
which operate only when the ignition/master switch is

on while the fuse between 1-2 protects all those circuits
which operate irrespective of the ignition/master switch.

The units protected by the fuses can be readily
identified from the wiring diagram and a blown fuse is
indicated by the failure of all units in its circuit. Before
renewing a blown fuse inspect the wiring for evidence
of a shortcircuit or other fault and remedy the cause of the
trouble.

14:14 The headlamps and beam setting

The construction of the standard type of headlamp is
shown in **FIG 14:15** and to gain access to the interior
for bulb removal it is necessary first to remove the rim
after extracting the retaining screw from the under side.
Then push the reflector and glass assembly inwards and
turn in an anticlockwise direction until the locating screws
register with the enlarged ends of the slots, then pull
outwards. Press in the back shell to release the bulb
noting the slot in the bulb flange which engages the
keyway in the holder.

Refit the lamp unit by reversing the removal procedure.

Later cars and some export models may be fitted with
the sealed beam light unit shown in **FIG 14:16**. To
remove this type from the car unscrew the rim retaining
screws and lift the rim off the locating lugs at the top of
the headlamp shell. Slacken the three screws securing
the lamp unit retaining plates, turn the plate and remove
it from the lamp unit which may then be withdrawn and
the plug disengaged.

On some units it is necessary to remove the three
retaining screws.

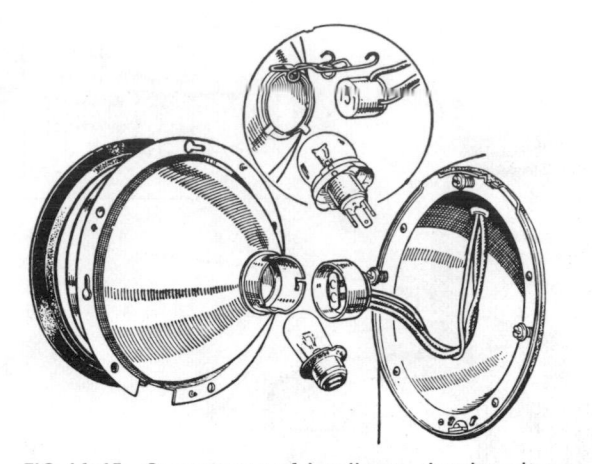

FIG 14:15 Components of headlamp, showing alternative fittings

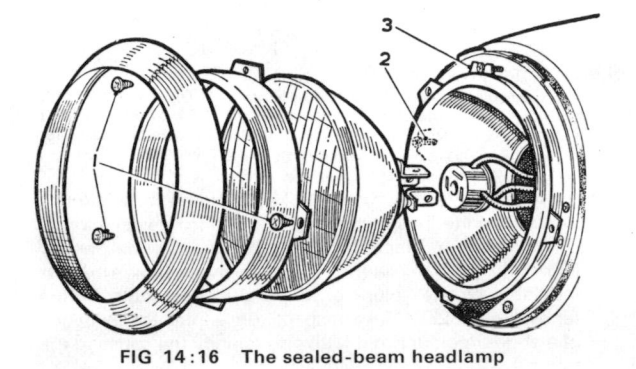

FIG 14:16 The sealed-beam headlamp

Key to Fig 14:16 1 Retaining plate screws 2 Horizontal adjustment screws 3 Vertical adjustment screws

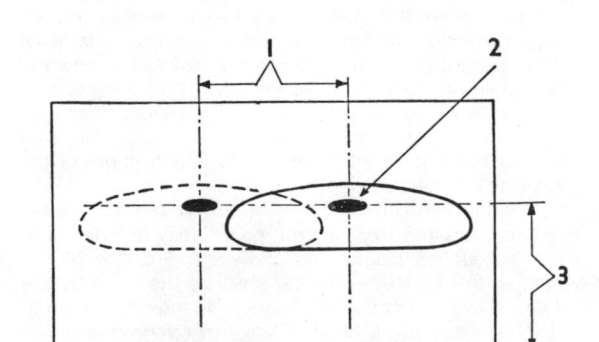

FIG 14:17 Headlamp beam setting

Key to Fig 14:17 1 Distance between lamp centres 2 Concentrated area of light 3 Height of lamp centres from ground

Headlamp beam setting

This operation is best carried out by a service station with an optical beam setter, but an acceptable result can be achieved as follows:

Stand the car on a level surface facing a wall at about 25 feet which has been marked as indicated in **FIG 14:17**. Switch on the main beam and using the three adjusting screws on the rim of the lamp, revealed when the outer decorative rim is removed, adjust the beams until they are parallel to each other and to the road surface.

Vertical adjustment is made by turning the screw at the top of the lamp, while horizontal adjustment is by the two screws on either side of the lamp. It may be found advantageous to cover one lamp while adjusting the other.

14:15 Windscreen wipers

In normal use the windscreen wiper should not require any maintenance apart from the occasional renewal of the rubber blades. In the event of a motor failure the best course is to fit a replacement unit. On later models of the J4 two-speed motors are fitted.

Removal:

Release the springs and take the wiper arms off the splined wheel box spindles. Remove the securing screws and take off the windscreen inner top panel.

Remove the end plates from the wheel boxes and so release the driving rack.

Remove the fuse from the 3-4 terminals of the fuse holder and disconnect the cables from the wiper motor terminals.

Unscrew the three retaining nuts and lift the wiper motor complete with gearbox and flexible drive away from the panel. The two wheel boxes will remain in place.

Reverse the above to refit the wiper, not forgetting to grease the cable rack with a bearing grease.

After long use the mechanism may require some lubrication, or the armature shaft may develop excessive end play and give noisy operation. **FIG 14:18** shows the components of the gearbox assembly and also the thrust screw 14 by which the armature shaft end float may be adjusted. The correct end float is .008 to .012 inch (.21 to .30 mm).

The felt pads in the end brackets may receive a little light oil and the worm gear, cross-head and crank pin a little grease such as Ragosene Listate.

14:16 Heater plugs

To assist in cold starting a 12-volt heater is installed in the combustion chamber of each cylinder. The plugs are connected in parallel and controlled by a switch in the driver's compartment. The loading of each plug is 60-watts and a temperature of 950°C to 1050°C is attained.

When starting from cold the plugs should be switched on for a period of 15 to 30 seconds before operating the starter switch. Even under normal conditions when the engine fails to start it may help to switch the heater plugs on for a few seconds.

At the intervals recommended in the Owners Handbook the heater plugs should be removed and the carbon deposit cleaned from each plug orifice in the cylinder head. This may best be done by inserting an $\frac{11}{64}$ inch twist drill and turning it by hand.

A faulty plug may be located by connecting each plug in turn to the heater plug feed wire with a test lamp or ammeter in circuit. If the plug is in order the lamp will light, or the ammeter show approximately 5 amps when switched on.

When a warning light is fitted it will only indicate the switch position and not the operation or failure of the heater plugs.

14:17 The horn

If the horn fails or becomes erratic in its action, first ascertain that the trouble is not due to a faulty connection or a blown fuse. If the fuse has blown examine the wiring for the fault and renew the fuse after the fault has been rectified.

The performance of the horn can also be affected by a loose mounting.

If after checking these points the horn is still not satisfactory, it should be renewed as it is not practical to overhaul this type of instrument.

14:18 Fault diagnosis

(a) Battery discharged

1 Terminals loose or dirty
2 Lighting circuit shorted
3 Generator not charging
4 Regulator or cut-out units not working properly
5 Battery internally defective

(b) Insufficient charging current

1 Loose or corroded battery terminals
2 Generator driving belt slipping

(c) Battery will not hold charge

1 Low electrolyte level
2 Battery plate sulphated
3 Electrolyte leakage from cracked casing or top sealing compound
4 Plate separators ineffective

(d) Battery overcharged

1 Voltage regulator needs adjusting

(e) Generator output low or nil

1 Belt broken or slipping
2 Regulator unit out of adjustment
3 Worn bearings, loose polepieces
4 Commutator worn, burned or shorted
5 Armature shaft bent or worn
6 Insulation proud between commutator segments
7 Brushes sticking, springs weak or broken
8 Field coil wires shorted, broken or burned
9 Alternator diodes defective
10 Slip rings dirty

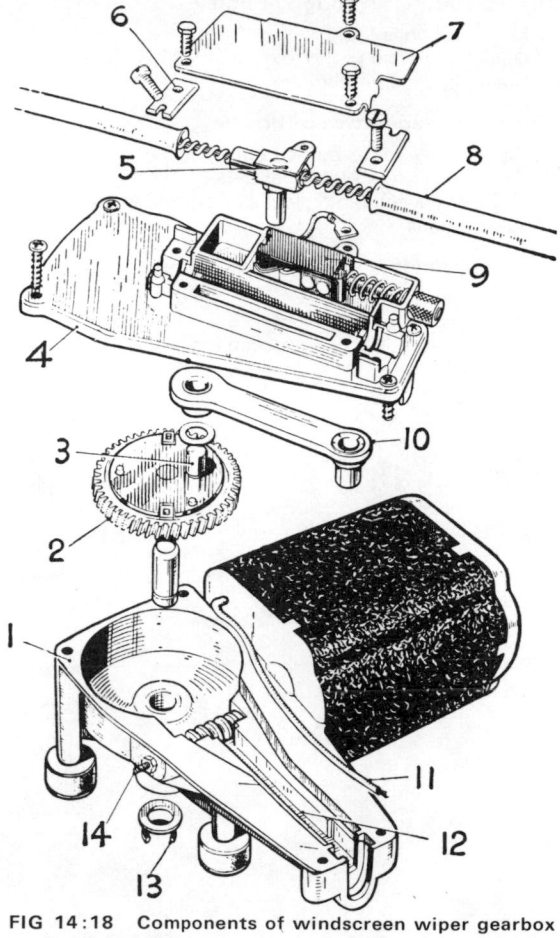

FIG 14:18   Components of windscreen wiper gearbox
Key to Fig 14:18   1 Gearbox   2 Final gear   3 Crankpin
4 Gearbox cover   5 Cross-head   6 Securing strip
7 Limit switch cover   8 Connecting tube   9 Limit switch
10 Connecting rod   11 To limit switch   12 Guide channel
13 Spring ring   14 Thrust screw

(f) Starter motor lacks power or will not operate

1 Battery discharged, loose cable connections
2 Starter pinion jammed in mesh with flywheel gear
3 Starter switch faulty
4 Brushes worn or sticking, leads detached or shorting
5 Commutator worn or dirty
6 Starter shaft bent
7 Engine abnormally stiff

(g) Starter motor runs but does not turn engine

1 Pinion sticking on screwed sleeve
2 Broken teeth on pinion of flywheel gear.

(h) Noisy starter pinion when engine is turning

1 Restraining spring weak or broken

(j) Starter motor inoperative

1 Check 1 and 4 in (f)
2 Armature or field coils faulty

(k) Starter motor rough or noisy

1 Mounting bolts loose
2 Damaged pinion or flywheel gear teeth
3 Main pinion spring broken

(l) Lamps inoperative or erratic

1 Battery low, bulbs burned out
2 Faulty earthing of lamps or battery
3 Lighting switch faulty, loose or broken wiring
  connections

(m) Wiper motor sluggish, taking high current

1 Faulty armature
2 Bearings out of alignment
3 Commutator dirty or shortcircuited

(n) Wiper motor operates but does not drive arm

1 Wheelbox gear and spindle worn
2 Cable rack faulty
3 Gearbox components worn

(o) Fuel gauge does not register

1 No battery supply to gauge
2 Gauge casing not earthed
3 Cable between gauge and tank unit earthed

(p) Fuel gauge reads 'full'

1 Cable between gauge and tank unit broken or
  disconnected

CHAPTER 15

THE BODYWORK

15:1 Maintenance of the bodywork

Regular attention to the body finish is necessary if the vehicle's exterior appearance is to be maintained against the effects of air pollution, rain and mud.

Frequent washing using a soft sponge with plenty of water containing a mild detergent is recommended, remembering that large deposits of mud should be well softened with water before using the sponge. When clean, dry with a damp chamois leather.

Any damaged parts should be covered with paint and a permanent repair effected as soon as possible. When touching-in light scratches and abrasions with paint ensure that all traces of wax polish are first removed from affected area.

Methylated spirits should be used to remove spots of grease or tar from the bodywork, windscreen or bright parts of the vehicle.

The use of a good quality polish is recommended to give lustre and preserve the paintwork, but do not allow it to come in contact with the windscreen as it may have a detrimental effect on the wiper blades.

The interior of the vehicle should be cleaned, preferably before washing the outside by using a stiff brush and a vacuum cleaner. The leather cushions and upholstery trim may be cleaned with a damp cloth and a little neutral soap. Detergents or spirits should not be used.

An oilcan filled with engine oil should be applied occasionally to door hinges, locks and other moving or sliding surfaces.

15:2 Replacing the windscreen or backlight

First extract the rubber locking filler strip from the channel surrounding the window glass, then remove any broken pieces of glass from the groove in the sealing strip.

Take off the sealing strip, clean it thoroughly and inspect it carefully. If it is damaged in any way it should be renewed.

Prepare the edge of the window frame with a soapy solution as a lubricant before fitting the seal.

Fit the seal round the frame and cut it to the correct length.

Place the window glass into the rubber channel, commencing at a lower corner and using the installation tools 18G.468 and 18G.468A. Lift the channel lip over the window and gradually work the window into position.

Inject sealer, Sealastick ST51 is suitable, at the outside face, between the rubber and glass, and between the rubber and aperture flange. Clean off any surplus after fitting the filler strip.

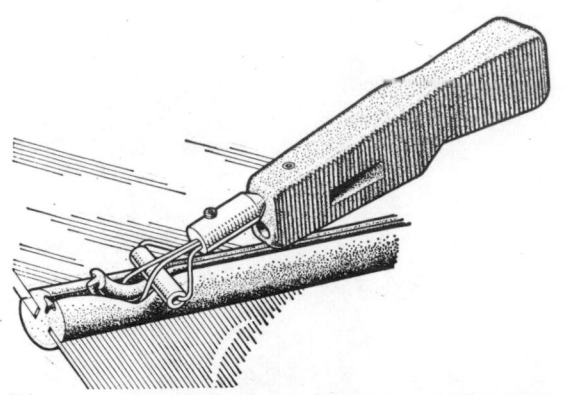

FIG 15:1 Method of using tools 18G.468 and 18G.468A for inserting the filler strip into the rubber channel in order to lock the glass in position

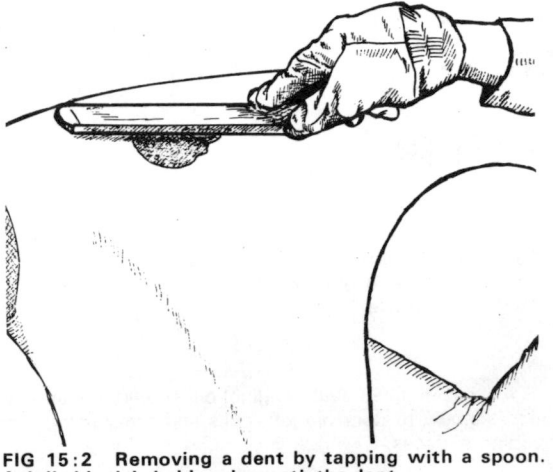

FIG 15:2 Removing a dent by tapping with a spoon. A dolly block is held underneath the dent

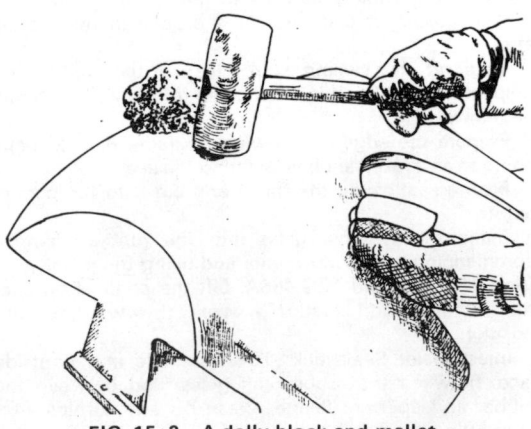

FIG 15:3 A dolly block and mallet

Apply the soapy water solution to the locking filler strip channel and, using the installation tool and eye as shown in **FIG 15:1,** thread the locking filler strip through the tool. Insert the tool into the filler strip channel, hold the end of the filler in position with a thumb and start to pull the tool along the channel, feeding the filler through the tool and into the channel. Progress, particularly round corners, will be assisted by a slight side to side 'wriggling' movement.

After completing the circuit the tool is removed and the filler strip cut off, allowing a small overlap so that, on forcing both ends into place, this results in the joint being under pressure.

15:3 Sliding door locks

To remove a door lock, first unscrew the centre screw from the inside handle then take off the two door handles and escutcheons.

Lever open the retaining spring clips and remove the door trim panel. Take off the coverplate from the aperture in the door panel.

Undo the screws securing the lock and remove the lock through the door panel aperture.

It is not considered practical or economical to effect repairs to these door locks so that if an examination shows that minor attention will not make a suspect lock fit for service, a new lock should be obtained.

Always grease a lock freely before installation which is a reverse of the removal procedure.

15:4 Front door sliding windows

Removal:

Detach both locking plates at the front and rear of the window and then remove the six self-tapping screws holding the surrounding rubber seal and channelling.

Prise out the sealing and withdraw the complete window unit.

Refitting:

First assemble the two glasses in the channel and sealing and fit a drawing cord round the whole sealing flange.

Insert this assembly in the door aperture and then pull on the cord to force the sealing over the flange. Press the assembly firmly inwards and insert the six self-tapping screws, two on each side and two on the top.

Replace the locking plates at the front and the rear of the window.

15:5 Repairs to bodywork

The body on these vehicles is of all-steel construction and for anything other than small jobs it is best to take the work to a service agent with the necessary equipment and experience.

To remove small dents a spoon which is made from a coarse cut file, specially shaped and having the teeth intact, may be used in conjunction with a suitably shaped dolly block. See **FIG 15:2.**

The use of a hammer to remove small dents is not recommended as hammer blows tend to stretch the surrounding metal, giving rise to further complications. For this reason the spoon is advised as by its use a depression can be raised to its original level without stretching.

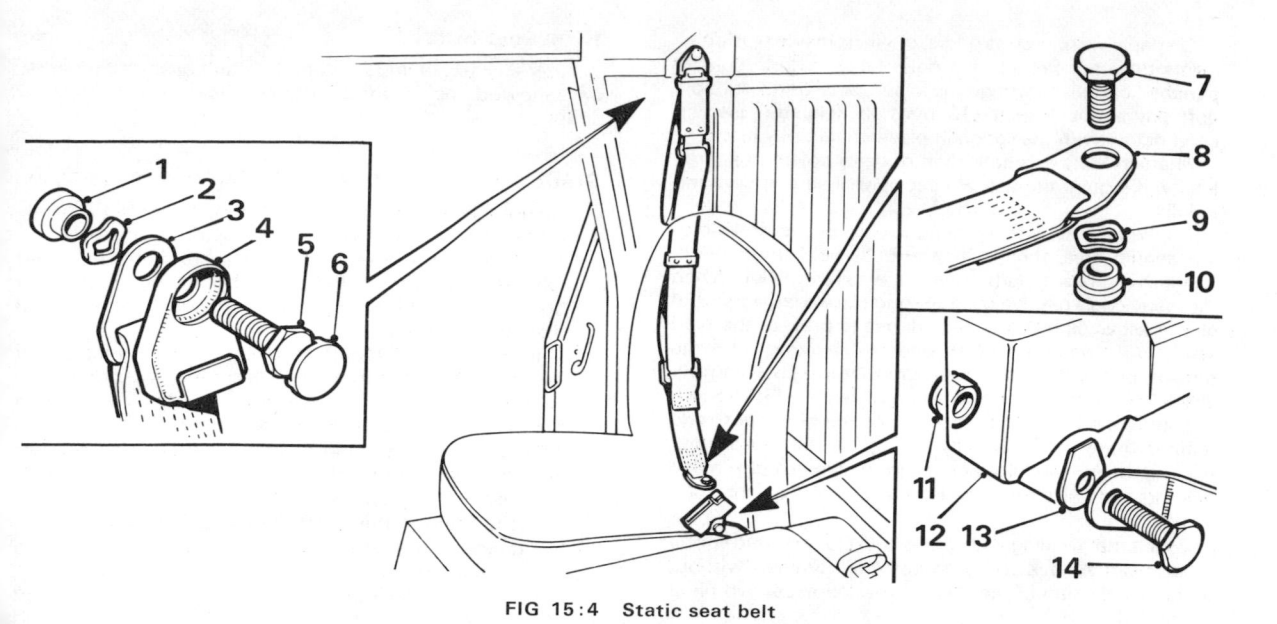

FIG 15:4   Static seat belt

Key to Fig 15:4   1 Shouldered distance piece   2 Anti-rattle washer   3 Upper belt bracket   4 Parking device   5 Bolt
6 Cap   7 Bolt   8 Lower belt bracket   9 Anti-rattle washer   10 Shouldered distance piece   11 Locknut   12 Centre
buckle   13 Fibre washer   14 Bolt

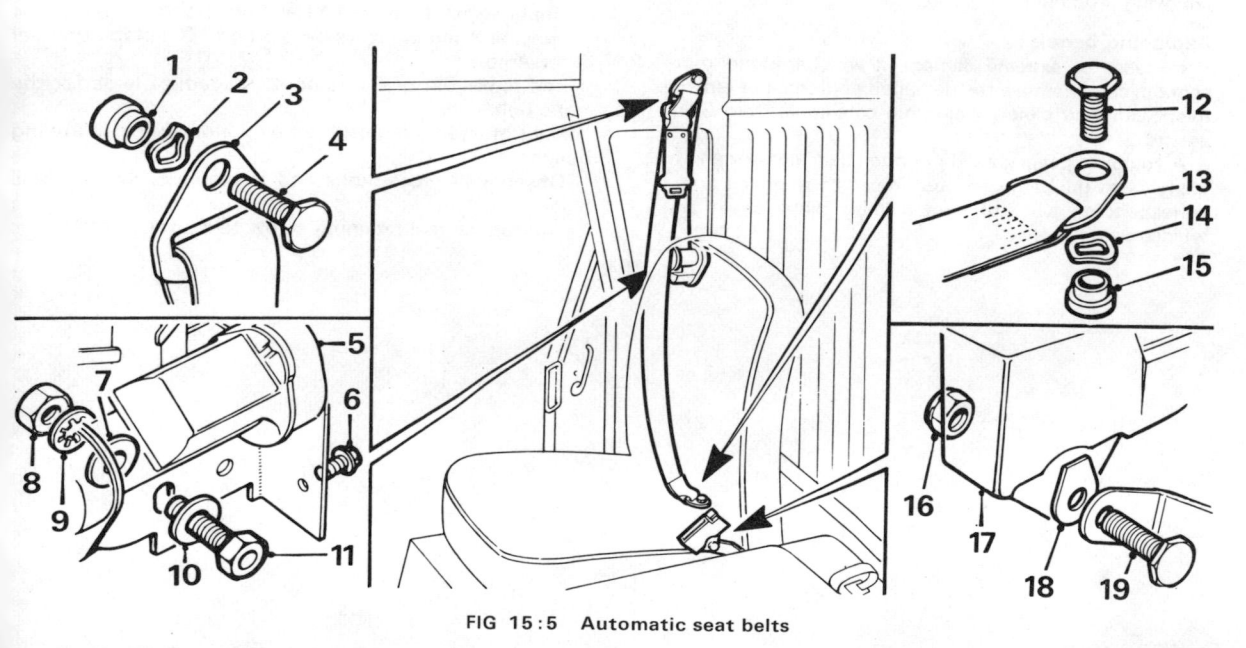

FIG 15:5   Automatic seat belts

Key to Fig 15:5   1 Shouldered distance piece   2 Anti-rattle washer   3 Upper belt bracket   4 Bolt   5 Reel   6 Reel
retaining screw   7 Plain washer   8 Nut   9 Shake-proof washer   10 Plain washer   11 Bolt   12 Bolt   13 Lower belt
bracket   14 Anti-rattle washer   15 Shouldered distance piece   16 Locknut   17 Centre buckle   18 Fibre washer   19 Bolt

On panel work such as doors, or where inside reinforcements prevent the use of a dolly block, a hole can be punched or drilled through the inside panel and a suitable drift pin about $\frac{1}{2}$ inch (13 mm) in diameter used in conjunction with the spoon in place of the dolly block.

Sharper dents or a collection of dents covering a large area will require the use of heat as well as a spoon and a dolly.

Apply heat, as with a welding torch, at the outside of the dented area, then, with the dolly held underneath, hammer the raised portion with a wooden mallet. When the metal cools remove the dolly and place a large handful of wet asbestos over the heated area to prevent the heat spreading. Continue to heat and tap, working from the outside of the damaged area, until the original contour and level is attained as near as possible (see **FIG 15:3**).

Lightly file the surface to show up the high spots and remove these with the dolly and spoon without further heating, being careful when using the file not to remove any more metal than is necessary to show up the high spots.

By alternately filing and raising with the dolly and spoon a flat clean surface will eventually be obtained without undue weakening of the metal, provided excessive filing is avoided.

On completion the surface may be tinned and any small blemishes filled with plumbers solder.

Beadings and mouldings

If difficulty is experienced in straightening or renewing a beading, moulding or corner the original contour may be obtained by careful tinning and filling with plumbers solder.

The finished result should be equal in strength and appearance and at the same time save the necessity for removing inside trimmings, etc.

Replacing panels:

In cases of extreme damage it will be found more economical to remove the damaged portions and replace them with new panels which are obtainable from BMC agents.

A complete panel should not often be necessary and in many cases the damaged portion can be removed and a corresponding part cut from suitable metal sheet and welded in position.

15:6 Seat belts

After any severe impact complete belt assemblies must be renewed including centre buckles and mounting straps.

Static belts, removal and refitting (see FIG 15:4):

1 Remove bolt 7 and detach lower belt bracket 8, anti-rattle washer 9, and shouldered distance piece 10.
2 Remove cap 6 from the upper belt bracket bolt 5 and remove the bolt, collect the hook 4, upper belt bracket 3, anti-rattle washer 2, and shouldered distance piece 1.
3 Unscrew the nut 11, and remove the centre buckle bolt 14, remove the centre buckle and fibre washer 13.
4 Remove the bolt and shake-proof washer and detach the mounting strap and distance piece.

Refit in the reverse order noting the following points:

Distance pieces must make full metal-to-metal contact with the body fixing points.

Refit the fixing in the order shown in **FIG 15:4**.

The deeper shouldered distance piece is fitted at the upper mounting point.

Tighten the centre buckle till it can just be moved by hand.

Tighten belt bracket bolts to 17 lb ft.

Automatic belts, removing and refitting (see FIG 15:5):

1 To prevent the belt retracting during removal, attach a clip to the belt at the entrance to the reel and leave in position until the reel is refitted.
2 Pull out most of the belt from the reel, remove the screw 6 and swivel the reel upwards.
3 Remove nut 8 and bolt 11 and collect the shake-proof washer 9 and plain washers 7 and 10, detach the reel assembly.

The remainder of the removal procedure is as for the static belt.

Refit in reverse order of removal, noting the following points:

Observe all precautions and procedures as for static belts.

Tighten the reel retaining screw to 5 lb ft.

APPENDIX

TECHNICAL DATA

Petrol engine   Diesel engine   Fuel system   Cooling system
Ignition system   Clutch   Gearbox   Rear axle   Steering
Suspension   Brakes   Wheels and Tyres   Electrical   Capacities
Torque wrench settings

WIRING DIAGRAMS

METRIC CONVERSION TABLE

HINTS ON MAINTENANCE AND OVERHAUL

GLOSSARY OF TERMS

INDEX

NOTES

TECHNICAL DATA

Dimensions are in inches unless otherwise stated

PETROL ENGINE

Type—1489 cc	15JE
1622 cc	16JE
Number of cylinders	4
Bore—1489 cc	2.875 (73.02 mm)
1622 cc	3.0 (76.2 mm)
Stroke	3.5 (88.9 mm)
Compression ratio—1489 cc	7.15:1
1622 cc	7.1:1
Firing order	1–3–4–2
Maximum torque—1489 cc...	73 lb ft at 1750 rev/min
1622 cc...	81 lb ft at 2000 rev/min
Oversize bores	.01, .02, .03, .04

Crankshaft:

Main journal diameter	2.0005 to 2.001
Main journal undersizes	.01, .02, .03, .04
Crankpin diameter	1.8759 to 1.8764
Crankpin undersizes	.01, .02, .03, .04
End float (thrust washers at centre main bearing) ...	.002 to .003

Main bearings:

Number and type, 1489 cc	3 steel-backed whitemetal
1622 cc	3 steel-backed copper-lead
Length—1489 cc	1.375
1622 cc	1.25
Clearance—1489 cc	.0005 to .002
1622 cc	.001 to .0027

Connecting rods:

Length between centres	6.5
Big-end, bearing material	Steel-backed whitemetal or copper/lead
side clearance	.008 to .012
running clearance—1489 cc	.0001 to .0016
1622 cc	.001 to .0027

Pistons:

Type—1489 cc	Aluminium alloy, split skirt
1622 cc	Aluminium alloy, solid skirt
Clearance, bottom of skirt—1489 cc	.0007 to .0013
1622 cc	.0015 to .0021

Piston rings:

Type—top	Plain, chrome faced
second and third	Taper
oil control...	Slotted scraper
Width—compression	.078
oil control	.1557
Clearance in ring groove	.002 to .004
Gap—1489 cc	.008 to .013
1622 cc	.012 to .017

Gudgeon pins:

Type	Clamped
Fit in piston	.0003 to .0001
Diameter—1489 cc	.6869 to .6871
1622 cc	.75

Valves:

Head diameter—1489 cc:
- Inlet 1.375
- Exhaust 1.187

Head diameter—1622 cc:
- Inlet 1.5
- Exhaust 1.28

Stem diameter, 1489 cc ... ... .34175 to .34225

Stem diameter, 1622 cc:
- Inlet ... ... .3422 to .3427
- Exhaust ... ... .34175 to .34225

Clearance in guide:
- Inlet ... ... .0015 to .0025
- Exhaust ... ... .002 to .003

Valve timing:

1489 cc:
- Inlet opens ... ... 5 deg. BTDC
-       closes ... ... 45 deg. ABDC
- Exhaust opens ... ... 40 deg. BBDC
-           closes ... ... 10 deg. ATDC

1622 cc:
- Inlet opens ... ... TDC
-       closes ... ... 50 deg. ABDC
- Exhaust opens ... ... 35 deg. BBDC
-           closes ... ... 15 deg. ATDC

Valve to rocker clearance ... ... .015 cold

Seat angle ... ... 45 deg.

Valve guides:

Length—inlet ... ... $1\frac{7}{8}$

        exhaust ... ... $2\frac{13}{64}$

Fitted height ... ... $\frac{5}{8}$ above head

Valve springs:

Free length ... ... $2\frac{1}{64}$

Camshaft:

End float (thrust plate at front) ... ... .003 to .007

Bearing clearance ... ... .001 to .002

Oil pump ... ... Eccentric rotor

Relief valve operates ... ... 50 lb/sq in

Relief valve spring length ... ... 2.859 free   2.156 fitted

Pressure, idling ... ... 15 lb/sq in

DIESEL ENGINE

Types 15Z, 15ZA, 15ZB, 15ZC, 15ZD, 15Z

Capacity ... ... 1489 cc

Bore ... ... 2.8745 to 2.8760

Max. oversize—Linered cylinder ... ... .020

              Unlinered cylinder ... ... .040

Stroke 3.5

Compression ratio ... ... 23 : 1

Firing order 1–3–4–2

Idling speed ... ... 500 to 600 rev/min

Crankshaft:

Journal diameter ... ... 2.0005 to 2.001

Crankpin diameter ... ... 2.0005 to 2.001

Undersizes ... ... —.010, —.020

End float ... ... .002 to .003

Main bearings:

Number and type...	3 steel-backed copper/lead
Length	1.213 to 1.223
Inner diameter	2.0025 to 2.0032
Clearance...	.0010 to .0027

Big-end bearing:

Material	Steel-backed copper/lead
Length	.963 to .973
Diameter	2.0025 to 2.0032
Clearance...	.0010 to .0027
End float	.008 to .012

Camshaft:

Journal diameter—Front	1.78875 to 1.78925
Centre	1.72875 to 1.72925
Rear	1.62275 to 1.62325
End float	.003 to .007
Running clearance	.001 to .002

Valves:

Head diameter—Inlet	1.370 to 1.375
Exhaust	1.151 to 1.156
Stem diameter—Inlet	.3422 to .3427
Exhaust	.34175 to .34225
Clearance to guide—Inlet	.0015 to .0025
Exhaust	.002 to .003
Rocker clearance	.015 cold
Seat face angle	$44\frac{1}{2}$ deg.

Valve springs:

Free length—Inner	1.875
Outer	2.2343

Valve timing:

Inlet opens	5 deg. BTDC
closes	45 deg. ABDC
Exhaust opens	45 deg. BBDC
closes	5 deg. ATDC

Pistons:

Type	Aluminium solid skirt
Clearance at bottom of skirt	.0036 to .0043

Piston rings:

Number	3 compression (1 chrome, 2 tapered) 2 oil control
Width—Compression	.0771 to .0781
Oil control	.1552 to .1562
Gap—Top	.012 to .020
Others	.008 to .013
Clearance—Top	.0035 to .0055
2nd and 3rd	.0025 to .0045
Oil control	.002 to .004

Gudgeon pins:

Type	Floating, located by circlips
Fit—in piston	.00035 clearance to .00005 interference
in rod	.0002 to .0009
Diameter	.9998 to 1.000
Length	2.360 to 2.375

FUEL SYSTEM

Carburetter:

Type—1489 cc	Solex B26HN	
Choke	20 mm	
Main jet	115	
Air correction jet	142	
Auxiliary jet	50	
Needle...	2.1 mm	
Air cleaner	Burgess oil wetted	
Type—1622 cc	Solex 30AHG	B30AHG
Choke	26	26
Main jet	115	115
Air correction jet	100	170
Auxiliary jet	60	50
Starter fuel jet	140	140
Starter air jet	6 mm	6 mm
Air bleed	.8	100
Needle...	2 mm	2 mm
Air cleaner	Cooper dry element	
Petrol lift pump	AC-Delco mechanical	
Diesel lift pump	AC mechanical, type 'U'	
Type	U	
Injection pump	CAV	
1st type	DPA 3246446	
2nd type	DPA 3246786 or 3246786B	
3rd type	DPA 3246857	
4th type	DPA 3246E 857	
5th type	DPA 3246F 857	

Injectors	CAV Pintaux
Nozzle—early engines	BDN.O.SPC.6209
later engines	BDN.O.SPC.6389
Nozzle holder—early	BKB.35.SD.5091
later	BKB.35.SD.5188
Opening pressure...	135 atmospheres. Add 5 atmospheres for new injectors or new springs

Main filter...	CAV bowl-less
Type	FS5836020
Static injection timing	22 deg. BTDC fully retarded

COOLING SYSTEM

Type	Pressurized radiator. Thermo-siphon, pump and fan assisted
Pressure	4 lb/sq in
Water pump:	
Spindle diameter	.6262 to .6267
Impeller bore	.6244 to .6252
Pulley hub bore	.6239 to .6247

IGNITION SYSTEM

Distributor	Lucas 25 D.4
Gap	.014 to .016, dwell angle 60 deg. ± 3 deg.
Timing—1489 cc	$7\frac{1}{2}$ deg. BTDC
1622 cc	5 deg. BTDC
Direction of rotation	Anticlockwise
Sparking plugs	Champion N5
Sparking plug gap	.025

CLUTCH

Make and type	Borg and Beck. Single dry plate
Diameter—Petrol models	8
Diesel models	9
Number and colour of thrust spring—Petrol models	6 light grey
Diesel models	9 cream
Thickness of lining	.150

GEARBOX

Number of speeds	4 Forward and Reverse
Synchromesh	2nd, 3rd and 4th
Ratios—Top	1 : 1
Third	1.49 : 1
Second	2.403 : 1
First	3.944 : 1
Reverse	5.159 : 1

REAR AXLE

Type	Hypoid ¾ floating
Ratio	4.875 : 1
Number of gearteeth	8/39

STEERING

Type	Cam and lever
Ratio	13 : 1
Turning circle	33 feet
Toe-in	Parallel (unladen)
Castor angle	3½ deg.
Camber angle	1 deg.
Kingpin inclination	6½ deg.

SUSPENSION

Front	Independent, coil springs
Spring—free length	10.3
fitted length	7.7 at 1658 lb (±30 lb)
identification	3 stripes of green paint
Rear	Semi-elliptic
Dampers	Armstrong lever type

BRAKES

Type	Girling hydraulic, drum
Drum diameter	9
Lining type	AM3 Ferodo
Fluid	Castrol Girling Brake and Clutch Fluid (Crimson)

WHEELS AND TYRES

Wheels—type	Steel disc with well base rim
size	4.50 J x 14
Tyres—type...	Tubeless
size	5.90 x 14 or 6.40 x 14

Recommended pressures:

	Load per tyre:	
	5.90	6.40
18 lb/sq in	680 lb	755 lb
24 lb/sq in	803 lb	895 lb
28 lb/sq in	880 lb	980 lb
36 lb/sq in	1025 lb	1135 lb

ELECTRICAL

Battery	Lucas 12-volt
Polarity	Positive earth
Starter motor—Petrol engines	Lucas M35G (early models)
	Lucas M35J (later models)
Diesel engines	Lucas M418G (early)
	Lucas M45G (late)
Generator—Petrol engines	Lucas C40
Diesel engines	Lucas C40 or C40L
Control box	RB106/2 or RB340
Alternator	Lucas 11AC, later 16 ACR
Output	43 amps, 34 amps on 16 ACR at 6000 alternator rev/min
Minimum brush length	$\frac{5}{32}$, $\frac{5}{16}$ on 16 ACR
Heater plugs	KLG GS103L or Champion AG32
Brush spring pressure:	
Type 11AC	$\frac{25}{32}$ compressed length under 4 to 5 oz $\frac{13}{32}$ compressed length under $7\frac{1}{2}$ to $8\frac{1}{2}$ oz
Type 16ACR	9 to 13 oz when brush is pushed in flush with box face

CAPACITIES

Engine sump	$8\frac{1}{4}$ pints (including filter)
Cooling system (excluding heater)	$11\frac{1}{2}$ pints
Gearbox	$4\frac{1}{2}$ pints
Automatic transmission	$11\frac{1}{4}$ pints (including 5 pints in torque converter)
Rear axle	2 pints
Steering box	$\frac{1}{2}$ pint
Fuel tank	8 gallons

TORQUE WRENCH SETTINGS

Figures are in lb ft unless otherwise stated

Petrol models:

Cylinder head nuts	40
Rocker bracket nuts	25
Main bearing nuts	70
Big-end bolts	35
Gudgeon pin clamp bolts	25
Sparking plugs	30
Flywheel bolts	40
Distributor clamp bolt:	
Fixed nut type	50 lb in
Fixed bolt type	30 lb in
Timing cover set screws—$\frac{1}{4}$ inch...	6
$\frac{5}{16}$ inch	14
Engine rear plate set screws—$\frac{5}{16}$ inch	20
$\frac{3}{8}$ inch	30
Water pump bolts	17
Water outlet elbow	8
Manifold nuts	15
Crankshaft pulley nut	70 to 80
Sump set screws	6
Camshaft nut	60 to 70
Oil release valve domed nut	40 to 45
Water pump pulley set screws	18
Thermal transmitter	16
Drive pulley securing nut...	30 to 35

Automatic transmission:

Converter drive plate	25 to 30
Transmission case to converter housing	
Oil pan to case	8 to 13
Front servo to case	
Rear servo to case	13 to 27
Pump adaptor to front pump housing:	
No. 10 diameter screws	2 to 3
$\frac{5}{16}$ inch diameter screws	17 to 22
Pump adaptor to transmission case	8 to 18.5
Rear pump to case:	
$\frac{1}{4}$ inch diameter screws	4 to 7
No. 10 diameter screws	1.7 to 3
Outer lever to manual valve shaft	7 to 9
Pressure point on case	4 to 5
Oil pan drain plug	9 to 12
Oil tube collector to lower body	
Governor line plate to lower body (includes rear pump strainer)	
Lower body end plate to lower body	
Upper body end plates to upper body	
Upper body to lower body	1.7 to 2.5
Valve bodies assembly to transmission case ...	
Front pump strainer to lower body	
Rear pump strainer to lower body	
Down-shift valve cam bracket to valve body ...	
Cover plate to governor body	
Rear band adjusting screw locknut	25 to 30
Front band adjusting screw locknut	15 to 20

Inhibitor switch locknut ...	...	...	...	...	...	...	8 to 10
Filler tube connector adaptor to transmission case			...	...	...		9 to 10
Filler tube connector sleeve nut ...	...	...	...	...	...	...	17 to 18

Diesel models:

Cylinder head nuts	...	...	...	...	...	...	71
Main bearing nuts	...	...	...	...	...	...	75
Big-end bolts ...	...	...	...	...	...	...	35
Flywheel nuts ...	...	...	...	...	...	...	37
Injector securing nuts	...	...	...	...	...	...	12
Injector nozzle nut	...	...	...	...	...	...	50
Rocker bracket nuts	...	...	...	...	...	...	25
Manifold nuts ...	...	...	...	...	...	...	15
Engine rear distance piece bolts—$\frac{5}{16}$ inch		...	...	...	...		20
$\frac{3}{8}$ inch			...	...	...		30
Water pump bolts ...	...	...	...	...	...	...	17

Diesel and petrol models:

Differential bearing cap nuts	...	...	...	...	...	...	60 to 65
Crownwheel bolts ...	...	...	...	...	...	...	55 to 60
Crownwheel pinion shaft nut	...	...	...	...	...	...	135 to 140
Steering wheel nut ...	...	...	...	...	...	...	41
Road wheel nuts ...	...	...	...	...	...	...	65
Clutch assembly to flywheel bolts	...	...	...	...	...	...	25
Oil filter centre bolt ...	...	...	...	...	...	...	15

Alternator:

Brush box fixing screws ...	...	...	...	...	...	...	10 lb in
Diode heat sink fixings ...	...	...	...	...	...	...	25 lb in
Through-bolts ...	...	...	...	...	...	...	45 to 50 lb in

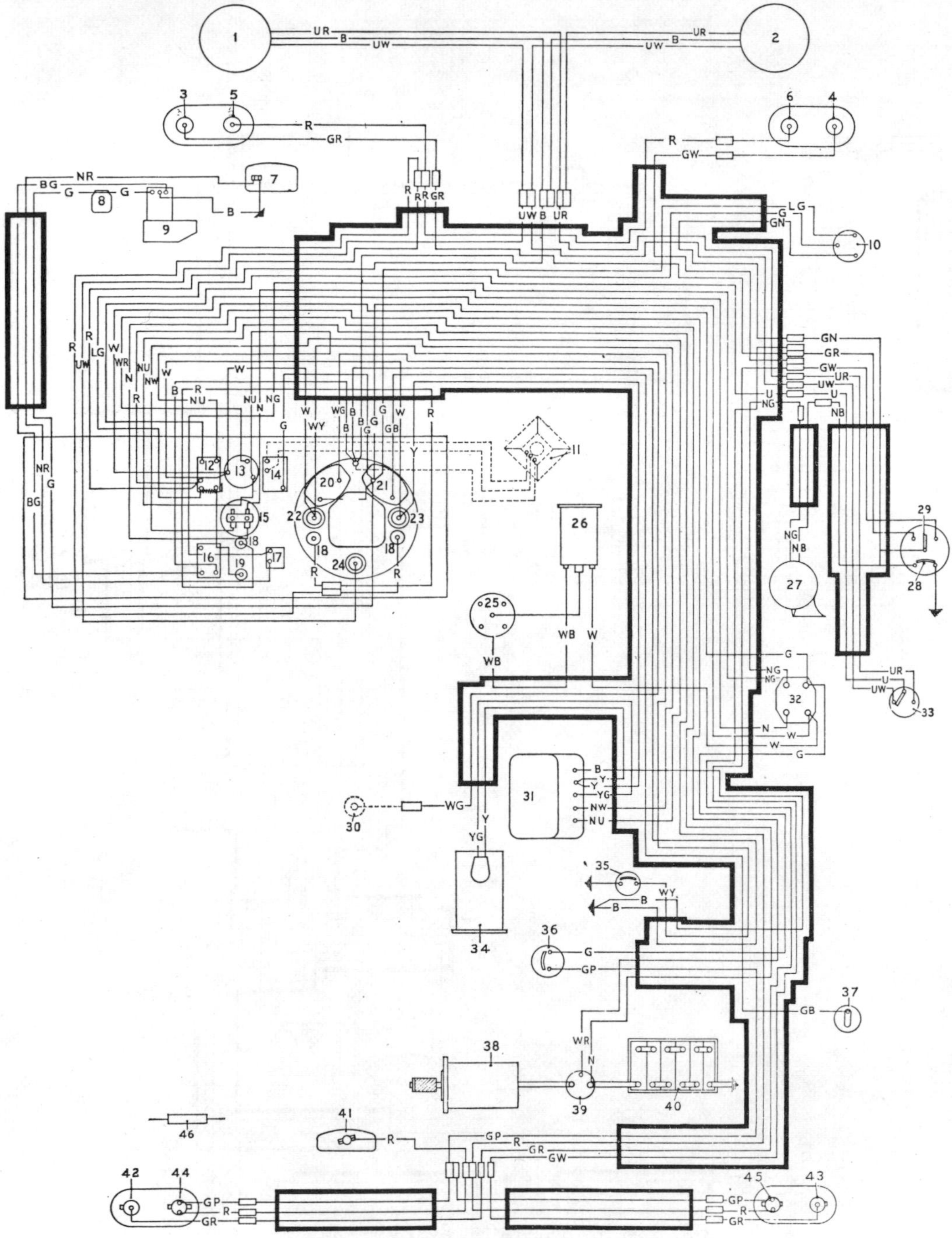

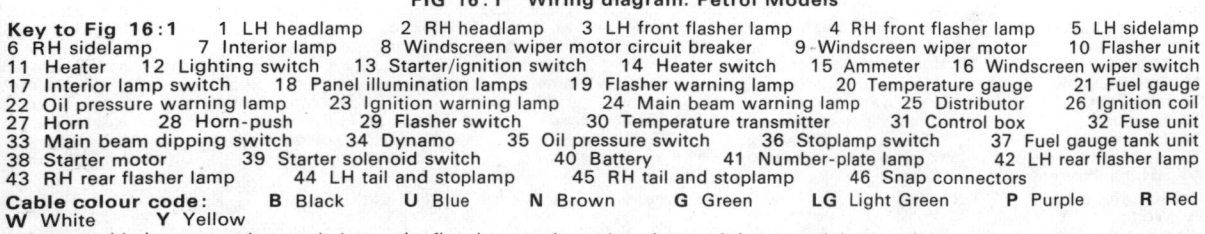

FIG 16:1   Wiring diagram. Petrol Models

Key to Fig 16:1   1 LH headlamp   2 RH headlamp   3 LH front flasher lamp   4 RH front flasher lamp   5 LH sidelamp
6 RH sidelamp   7 Interior lamp   8 Windscreen wiper motor circuit breaker   9 Windscreen wiper motor   10 Flasher unit
11 Heater   12 Lighting switch   13 Starter/ignition switch   14 Heater switch   15 Ammeter   16 Windscreen wiper switch
17 Interior lamp switch   18 Panel illumination lamps   19 Flasher warning lamp   20 Temperature gauge   21 Fuel gauge
22 Oil pressure warning lamp   23 Ignition warning lamp   24 Main beam warning lamp   25 Distributor   26 Ignition coil
27 Horn   28 Horn-push   29 Flasher switch   30 Temperature transmitter   31 Control box   32 Fuse unit
33 Main beam dipping switch   34 Dynamo   35 Oil pressure switch   36 Stoplamp switch   37 Fuel gauge tank unit
38 Starter motor   39 Starter solenoid switch   40 Battery   41 Number-plate lamp   42 LH rear flasher lamp
43 RH rear flasher lamp   44 LH tail and stoplamp   45 RH tail and stoplamp   46 Snap connectors
Cable colour code: **B** Black   **U** Blue   **N** Brown   **G** Green   **LG** Light Green   **P** Purple   **R** Red
W White   **Y** Yellow
When a cable has two colour code letters the first denotes the main colour and the second denotes the tracer colour

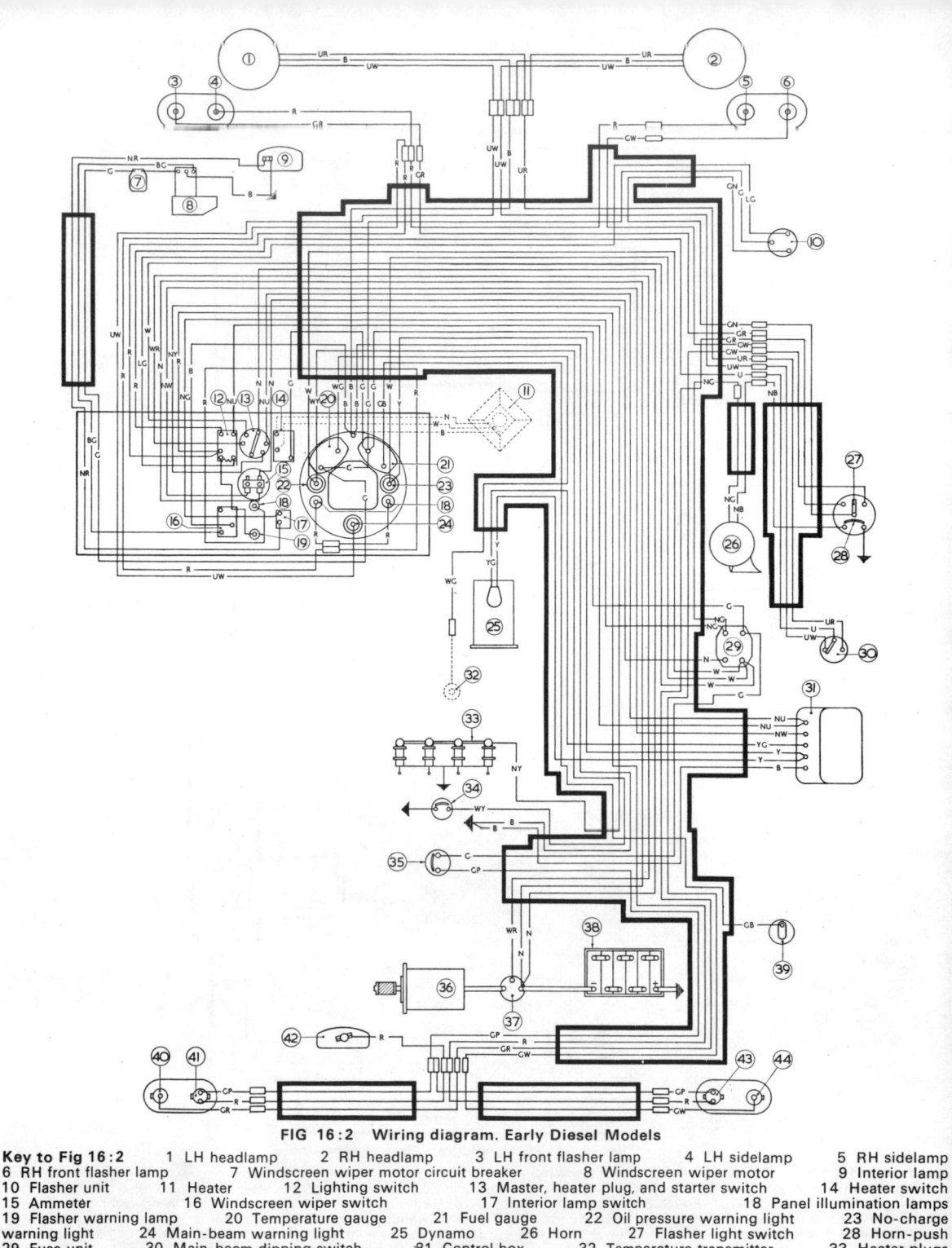

FIG 16:2 Wiring diagram. Early Diesel Models

Key to Fig 16:2   1 LH headlamp   2 RH headlamp   3 LH front flasher lamp   4 LH sidelamp   5 RH sidelamp
6 RH front flasher lamp   7 Windscreen wiper motor circuit breaker   8 Windscreen wiper motor   9 Interior lamp
10 Flasher unit   11 Heater   12 Lighting switch   13 Master, heater plug, and starter switch   14 Heater switch
15 Ammeter   16 Windscreen wiper switch   17 Interior lamp switch   18 Panel illumination lamps
19 Flasher warning lamp   20 Temperature gauge   21 Fuel gauge   22 Oil pressure warning light   23 No-charge
warning light   24 Main-beam warning light   25 Dynamo   26 Horn   27 Flasher light switch   28 Horn-push
29 Fuse unit   30 Main-beam dipping switch   31 Control box   32 Temperature transmitter   33 Heater plugs
34 Oil pressure switch   35 Stoplamp switch   36 Starter motor   37 Starter solenoid switch   38 Battery
39 Fuel gauge tank unit   40 LH rear flasher lamp   41 LH stop tail lamp   42 Number-plate lamp   43 RH stop tail lamp
44 RH rear flasher lamp

Cable colour code: **B** Black   **U** Blue   **N** Brown   **G** Green   **LG** Light Green   **P** Purple   **R** Red
W White   **Y** Yellow
When a cable has two colour code letters the first denotes the main colour and the second denotes the tracer colour

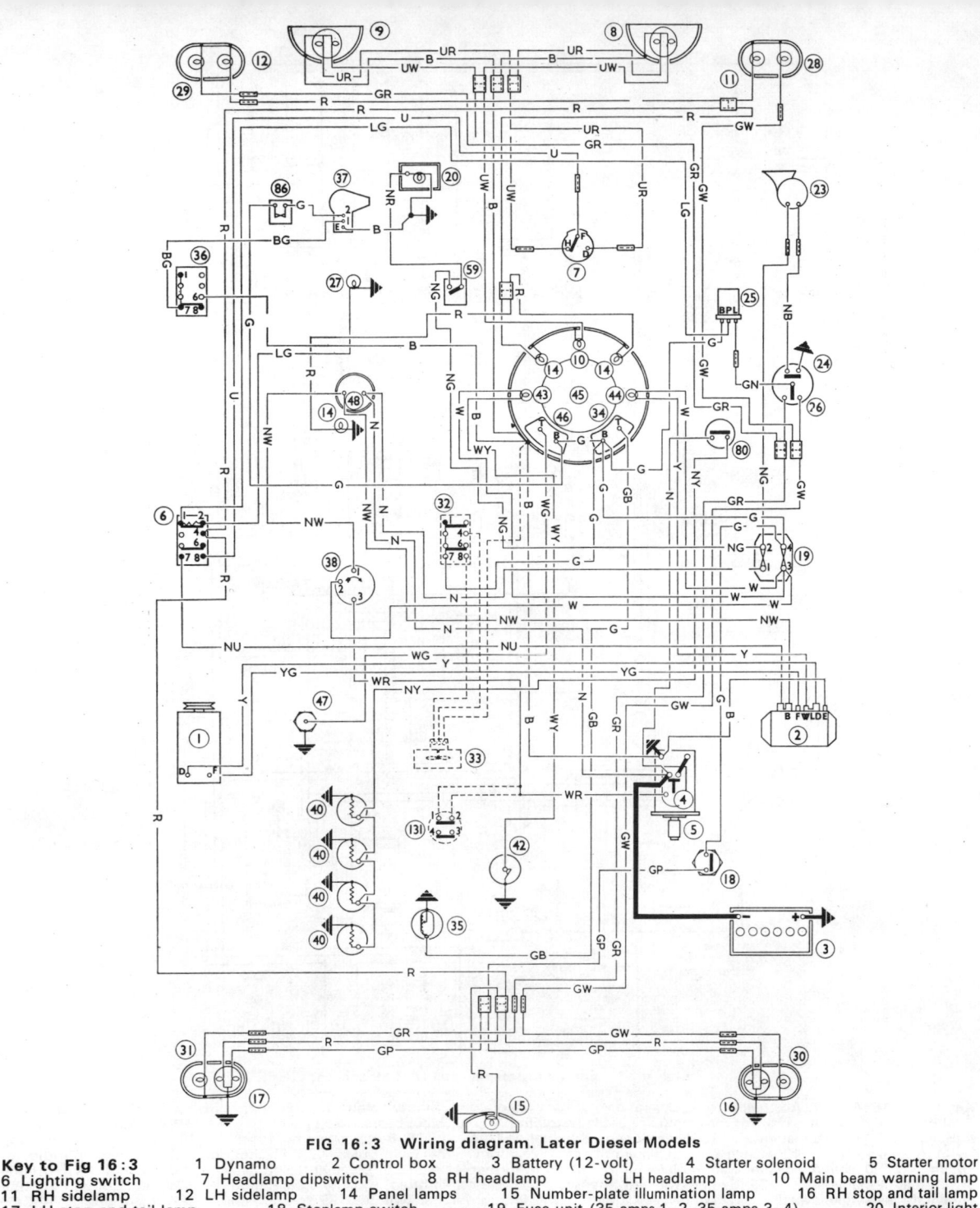

FIG 16:3 Wiring diagram. Later Diesel Models

Key to Fig 16:3 1 Dynamo 2 Control box 3 Battery (12-volt) 4 Starter solenoid 5 Starter motor
6 Lighting switch 7 Headlamp dipswitch 8 RH headlamp 9 LH headlamp 10 Main beam warning lamp
11 RH sidelamp 12 LH sidelamp 14 Panel lamps 15 Number-plate illumination lamp 16 RH stop and tail lamp
17 LH stop and tail lamp 18 Stoplamp switch 19 Fuse unit (35 amps 1–2, 35 amps 3–4) 20 Interior light
23 Horn (twin horns when fitted) 24 Horn push 25 Flasher unit 26 Direction indicator switch 27 Direction
indicator warning lamp 28 RH front flasher lamp 29 LH front flasher lamp 30 RH rear flasher lamp 31 LH rear
flasher lamp 32 Heater or fresh air motor switch (when fitted) 33 Heater or fresh air motor (when fitted) 34 Fuel gauge
35 Fuel gauge tank unit 36 Windscreen wiper switch 37 Windscreen wiper 38 Ignition/starter switch 40 Heater plug
42 Oil pressure switch 43 Oil pressure warning lamp 44 Ignition warning lamp 45 Speedometer 46 Water
temperature gauge (when fitted) 47 Water temperature transmitter (when fitted) 48 Ammeter 59 Interior light switch
80 Heater plug switch 86 Wiper motor circuit breaker 131 Automatic gearbox reverse and safety switch (when fitted)
Cable colour code: **B** Black **U** Blue **N** Brown **G** Green **LG** Light Green **P** Purple **R** Red
W White **Y** Yellow
When a cable has two colour code letters the first denotes the main colour and the second denotes the tracer colour

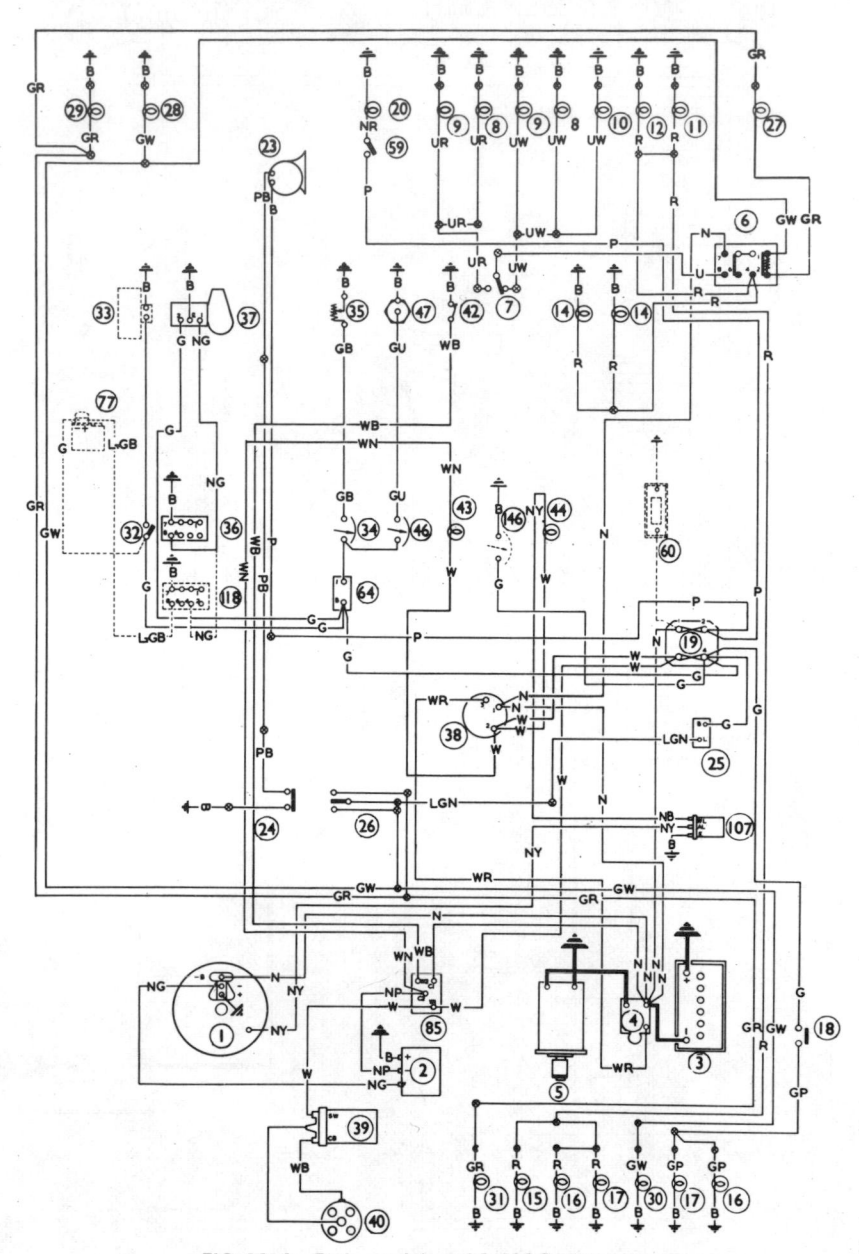

FIG 16:4 Early models, with 11AC alternator

Key to Fig 16:4 1 Alternator   2 Control box   3 Battery   4 Starter solenoid   5 Starter motor   6 Lighting switch
7 Headlamp dip switch   8 RH headlamp   9 LH headlamp   10 Main beam warning light   11 RH sidelamps   12 LH
sidelamps   14 Panel lamps   15 Number plate illumination lamp   16 RH stop and tail lamp   17 LH stop and tail lamp
18 Stop lamp switch   19 Fuse unit   20 Interior light   23 Horn   24 Horn push   25 Flasher unit   26 Direction indicator
switch   27 Direction indicator warning lamp   28 RH front flasher lamp   29 LH front flasher lamp   30 RH rear flasher lamp
31 LH rear flasher lamp   32 Heater switch (if fitted)   33 Heater (if fitted)   34 Fuel gauge   35 Fuel gauge tank unit
36 Windscreen wiper switch   37 Windscreen wipers   38 Ignition/starter switch   39 Ignition coil   40 Distributor   42 Oil
pressure switch   43 Oil pressure warning light or gauge   44 No charge warning light   46 Temperature gauge (if fitted)
47 Temperature transmitter (if fitted)   59 Interior light switch   60 Radio (if fitted)   64 Bi-metal instrument voltage stabilizer
77 Electric windscreen washer   85 Alternator isolating relay   107 Alternator charge indicator unit   118 Combined windscreen
washer and wiper switch (if fitted)   146 Battery condition indicator (if fitted)

Cable colour code: N Brown   **U** Blue   **R** Red   **P** Purple   **G** Green   **LG** Light green   **W** White   **Y** Yellow   **B** Black

When a cable has two colour code letters the first denotes the main colour and the second denotes the tracer colour

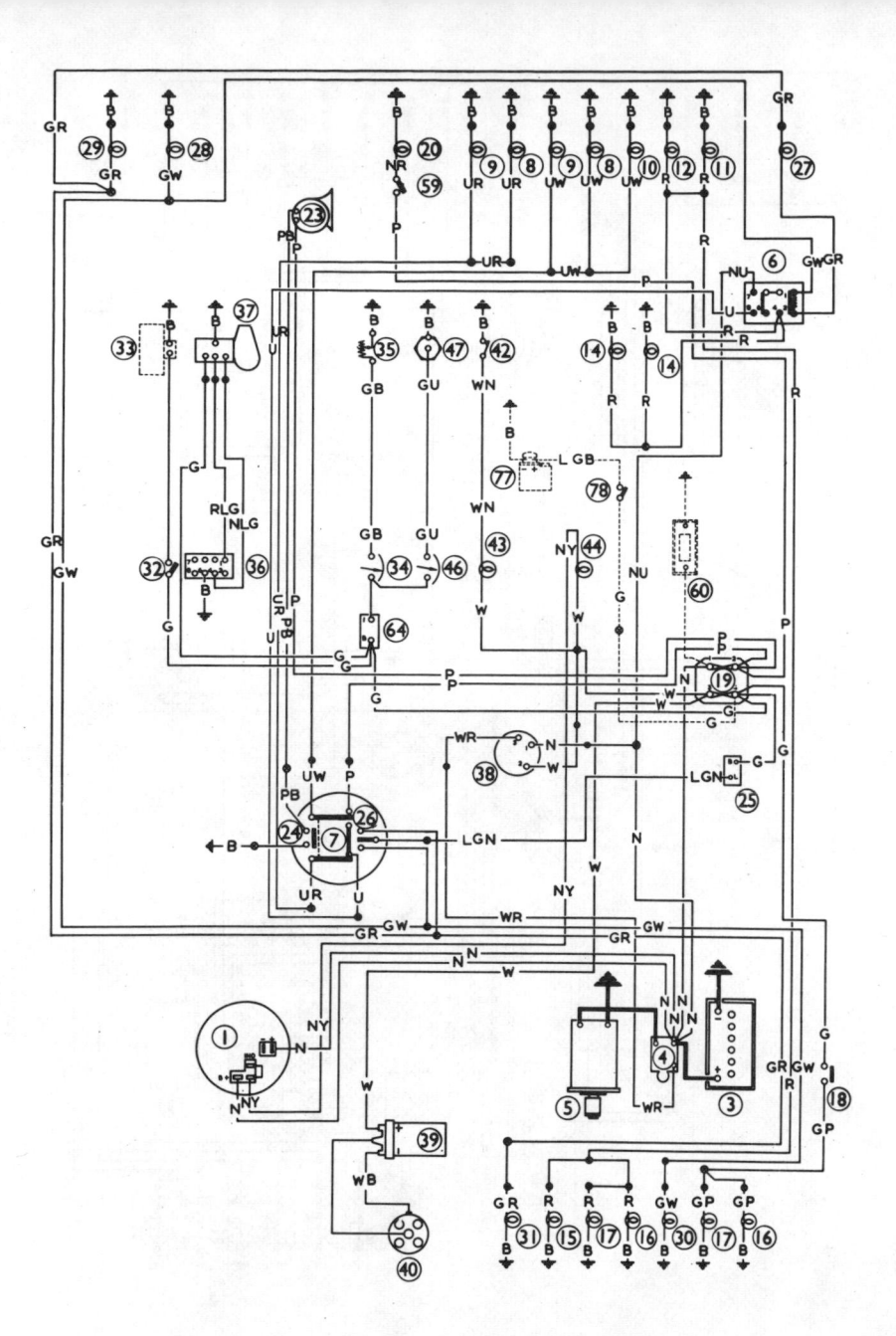

FIG 16 : 5   Later models, with 16ACR alternator

Key to Fig 16 : 5   1 Alternator (generator)   3 Battery   4 Starter solenoid   5 Starter motor   6 Lighting switch
7 Headlamp dipper and flasher switch   8 RH headlamp   9 LH headlamp   10 Main beam warning lamp   11 RH sidelamp
12 LH sidelamp   14 Panel lamps   15 Number plate illumination lamp   16 RH stop and tail lamp   17 LH stop and tail lamp
18 Stop lamp switch   19 Fuse unit   20 Interior light   23 Horn   24 Horn push   25 Flasher unit   26 Direction indicator
switch   27 Direction indicator warning lamp   28 RH front flasher lamp   29 LH front flasher lamp   30 RH rear flasher lamp
31 LH rear flasher lamp   32 Heater switch   33 Heater motor   34 Fuel gauge   35 Fuel gauge tank unit   36 Windscreen
wiper switch   37 Windscreen wiper motor   38 Ignition/starter switch   39 Ignition coil   40 Distributor   42 Oil pressure
switch   43 Oil pressure warning lamp   44 Ignition warning lamp   46 Temperature gauge   47 Temperature transmitter
59 Interior light switch   60 Radio   64 Bi-metal voltage stabilizer   77 Windscreen washer   78 Windscreen washer switch

Cable colour code: See **FIG 16 : 4**

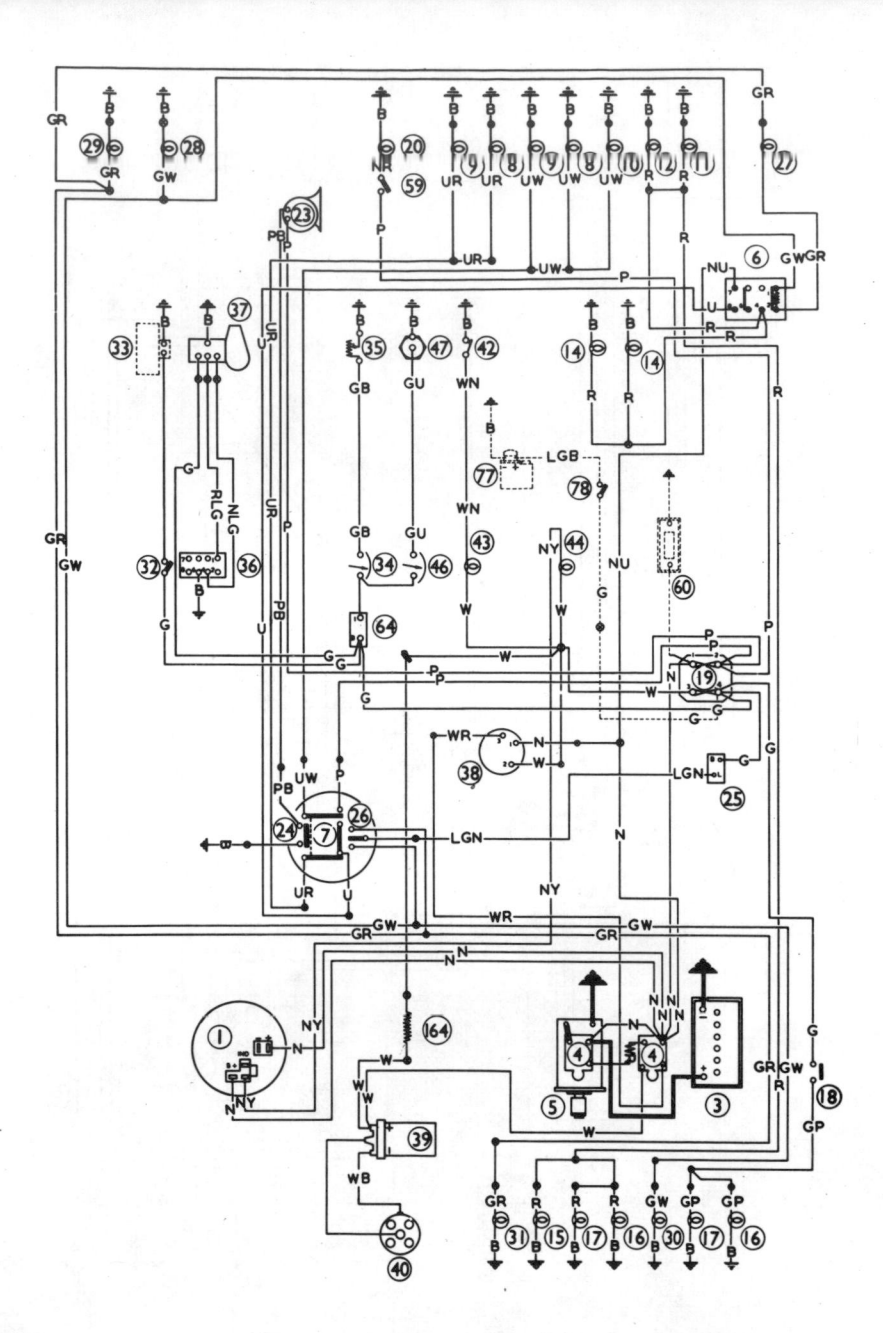

FIG 16:6   Later models, with 16ACR alternator for cold climates

Key to Fig 16:6   1 Alternator (generator)   3 Battery   4 Starter solenoid   5 Starter motor   6 Lighting switch
7 Headlamp dipper and flasher switch   8 RH headlamp   9 LH headlamp   10 Main beam warning lamp   11 RH sidelamp
12 LH sidelamp   14 Panel lamps   15 Number plate illumination lamp   16 RH stop and tail lamp   17 LH stop and tail lamp
18 Stop lamp switch   19 Fuse unit   20 Interior light   23 Horn   24 Horn push   25 Flasher unit   26 Direction indicator
switch   27 Direction indicator warning lamp   28 RH front flasher lamp   29 LH front flasher lamp   30 RH rear flasher lamp
31 LH rear flasher lamp   32 Heater switch   33 Heater motor   34 Fuel gauge   35 Fuel gauge tank unit   36 Windscreen
wiper switch   37 Windscreen wiper motor   38 Ignition/starter switch   39 Ignition coil   40 Distributor   42 Oil pressure
switch   43 Oil pressure warning lamp   44 Ignition warning lamp   46 Temperature gauge   47 Temperature transmitter
59 Interior light switch   60 Radio   64 Bi-metal voltage stabilizer   77 Windscreen washer   78 Windscreen washer switch
164 Ballast resistor

Cable colour code: See **FIG 16:4**

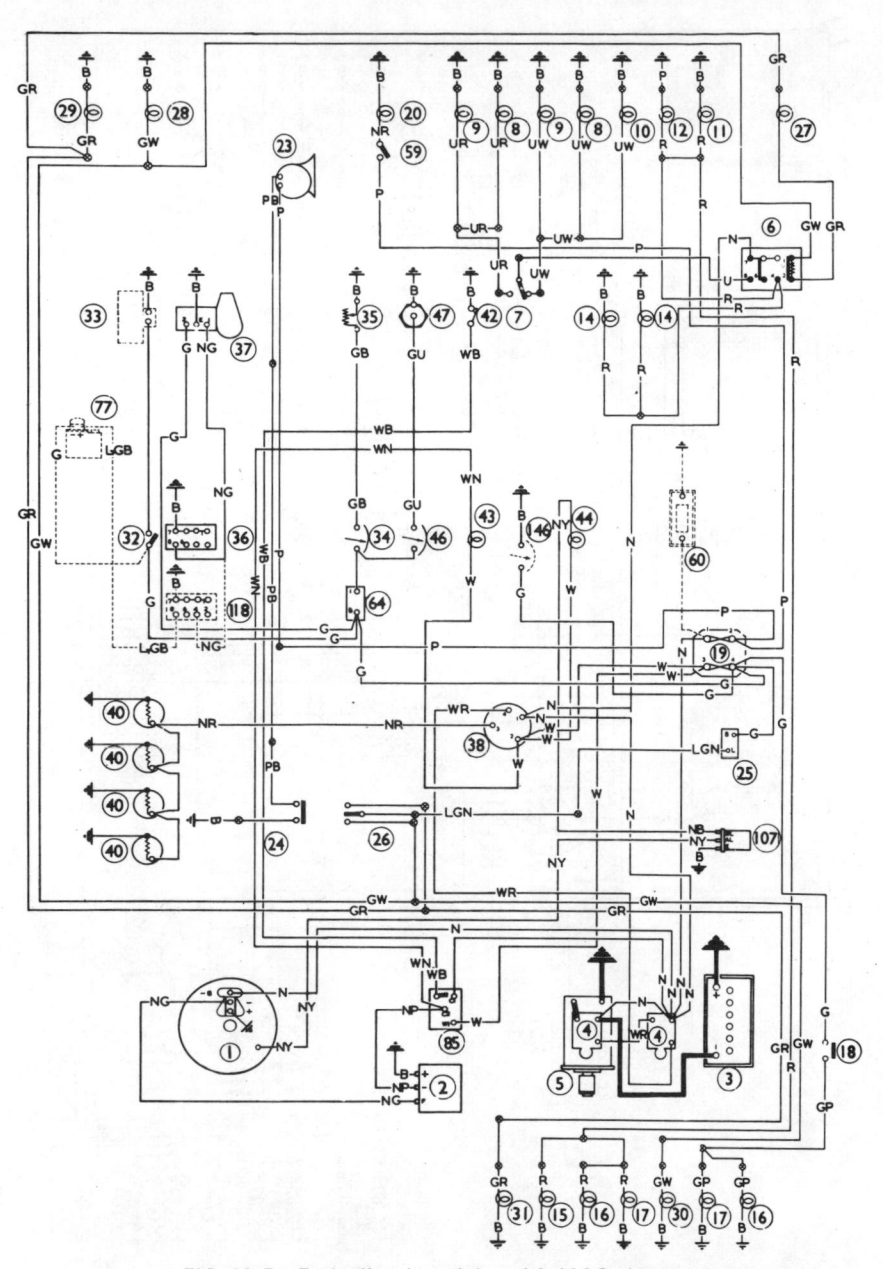

FIG 16:7 Early diesel models, with 11AC alternator

Key to Fig 16:7 1 Alternator   2 Control box   3 Battery   4 Starter solenoid   5 Starter motor   6 Lighting switch
7 Headlamp dip switch   8 RH headlamp   9 LH headlamp   10 Main beam warning light   11 RH sidelamp   12 LH
sidelamp   14 Panel lamps   15 Number plate illumination lamp   16 RH stop and tail lamp   17 LH stop and tail lamp
18 Stop lamp switch   19 Fuse unit   20 Interior light   23 Horn   24 Horn push   25 Flasher unit   26 Direction indicator
switch   27 Direction indicator warning lamp   28 RH front flasher lamp   29 LH front flasher lamp   30 RH rear flasher lamp
31 LH rear flasher lamp   32 Heater switch (if fitted)   33 Heater (if fitted)   34 Fuel gauge   35 Fuel guage tank unit
36 Windscreen wiper switch   37 Windscreen wiper   38 Master/starter switch   40 Heater plugs   42 Oil pressure switch
43 Oil pressure warning light or gauge   44 No charge warning light   46 Temperature gauge (if fitted)   47 Temperature
transmitter (if fitted)   59 Interior light switch   60 Radio (if fitted)   64 Bi-metal instrument voltage stabilizer   77 Electric
windscreen washer   85 Alternator isolating relay   107 Alternator charge indicator unit   118 Combined windscreen washer
and wiper switch (if fitted)   146 Battery condition indicator (if fitted)

Cable colour code: **N** Brown   **P** Purple   **W** White   **U** Blue   **G** Green   **Y** Yellow   **R** Red   **LG** Light green   **B** Black

When a cable has two colour code letters the first denotes the main colour and the second denotes the tracer colour

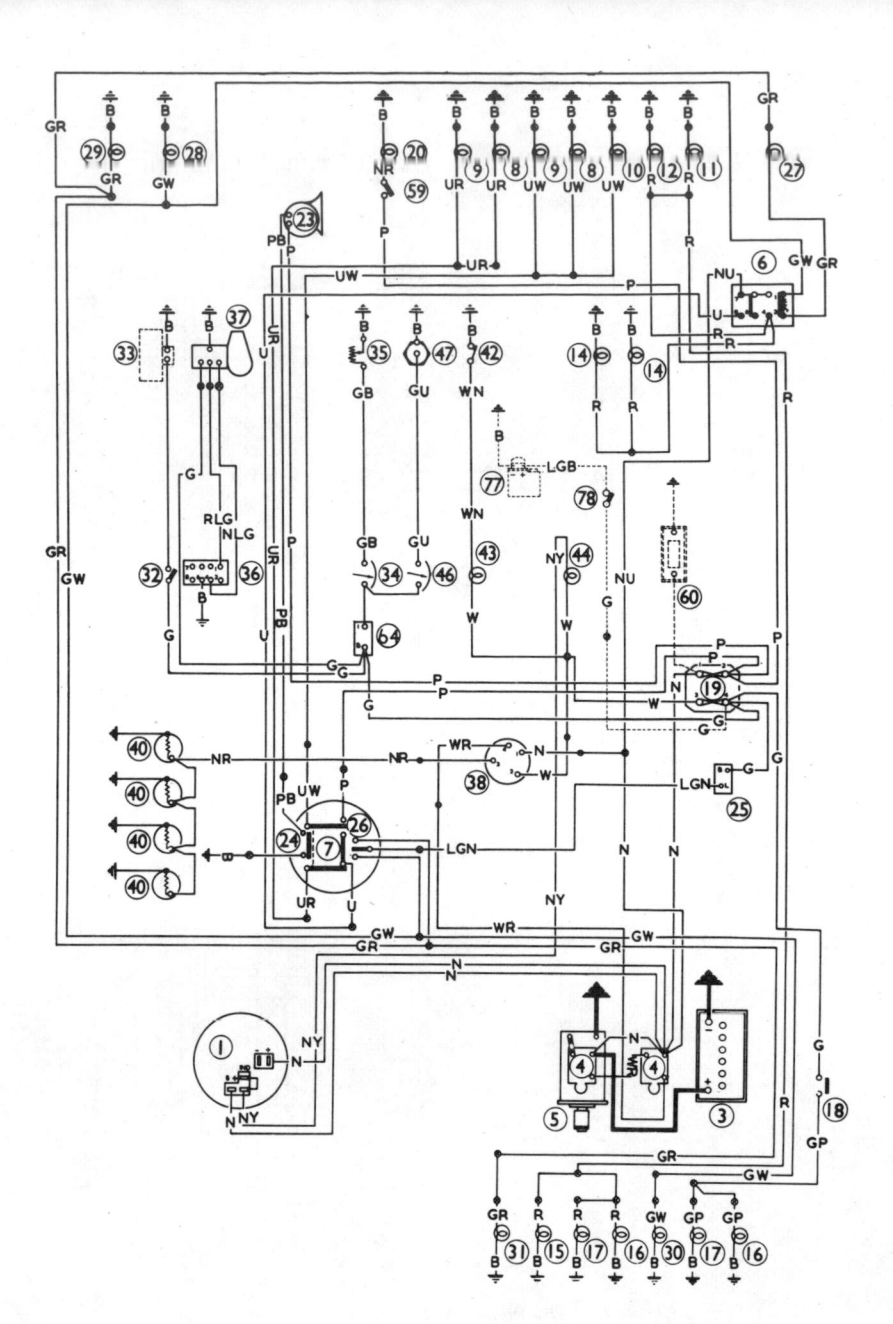

FIG 16:8   Later diesel models, with 16ACR alternator

Key to Fig 16:8   1 Alternator (generator)   3 Battery   4 Starter solenoid   5 Starter motor   6 Lighting switch
7 Headlamp dipper and flasher switch   8 RH headlamp   9 LH headlamp   10 Main beam warning lamp   11 RH sidelamp
12 LH sidelamp   14 Panel lamps   15 Number plate illumination lamp   16 RH stop and tail lamp   17 LH stop and tail lamp
18 Stop lamp switch   19 Fuse unit   20 Interior light   24 Horn push   25 Flasher unit   26 Direction indicator switch
27 Direction indicator warning lamp   28 RH front flasher lamp   29 LH front flasher lamp   30 RH rear flasher lamp   31 LH
rear flasher lamp   32 Heater switch   33 Heater motor   34 Fuel gauge   35 Fuel gauge tank unit   36 Windscreen wiper
switch   37 Windscreen wiper motor   38 Master and starter switch   40 Heater plugs   42 Oil pressure switch   43 Oil
pressure warning lamp   44 No charge warning lamp   46 Temperature gauge   47 Temperature transmitter   59 Interior light
switch   60 Radio   64 Bi-metal voltage stabilizer   77 Windscreen washer   78 Windscreen washer switch

Cable colour code: See FIG 16:4

Inches	Decimals	Milli-metres	Inches to Millimetres — Inches	Inches to Millimetres — mm	Millimetres to Inches — mm	Millimetres to Inches — Inches
1/64	.015625	.3969	.001	.0254	.01	.00039
1/32	.03125	.7937	.002	.0508	.02	.00079
3/64	.046875	1.1906	.003	.0762	.03	.00118
1/16	.0625	1.5875	.004	.1016	.04	.00157
5/64	.078125	1.9844	.005	.1270	.05	.00197
3/32	.09375	2.3812	.006	.1524	.06	.00236
7/64	.109375	2.7781	.007	.1778	.07	.00276
1/8	.125	3.1750	.008	.2032	.08	.00315
9/64	.140625	3.5719	.009	.2286	.09	.00354
5/32	.15625	3.9687	.01	.254	.1	.00394
11/64	.171875	4.3656	.02	.508	.2	.00787
3/16	.1875	4.7625	.03	.762	.3	.01181
13/64	.203125	5·1594	.04	1.016	.4	.01575
7/32	.21875	5.5562	.05	1.270	.5	.01969
15/64	.234375	5.9531	.06	1.524	.6	.02362
1/4	.25	6.3500	.07	1.778	.7	.02756
17/64	.265625	6.7469	.08	2.032	.8	.03150
9/32	.28125	7.1437	.09	2.286	.9	.03543
19/64	.296875	7.5406	.1	2.54	1	.03937
5/16	.3125	7.9375	.2	5.08	2	.07874
21/64	.328125	8.3344	.3	7.62	3	.11811
11/32	.34375	8.7312	.4	10.16	4	.15748
23/64	.359375	9.1281	.5	12.70	5	.19685
3/8	.375	9.5250	.6	15.24	6	.23622
25/64	.390625	9.9219	.7	17.78	7	.27559
13/32	.40625	10.3187	.8	20.32	8	.31496
27/64	.421875	10.7156	.9	22.86	9	.35433
7/16	.4375	11.1125	1	25.4	10	.39370
29/64	.453125	11.5094	2	50.8	11	.43307
15/32	.46875	11.9062	3	76.2	12	.47244
31/64	.484375	12.3031	4	101.6	13	.51181
1/2	.5	12.7000	5	127.0	14	.55118
33/64	.515625	13.0969	6	152.4	15	.59055
17/32	.53125	13.4937	7	177.8	16	.62992
35/64	.546875	13.8906	8	203.2	17	.66929
9/16	.5625	14.2875	9	228.6	18	.70866
37/64	.578125	14.6844	10	254.0	19	.74803
19/32	.59375	15.0812	11	279.4	20	.78740
39/64	.609375	15.4781	12	304.8	21	.82677
5/8	.625	15.8750	13	330.2	22	.86614
41/64	.640625	16.2719	14	355.6	23	.90551
21/32	.65625	16.6687	15	381.0	24	.94488
43/64	.671875	17.0656	16	406.4	25	.98425
11/16	.6875	17.4625	17	431.8	26	1.02362
45/64	.703125	17.8594	18	457.2	27	1.06299
23/32	.71875	18.2562	19	482.6	28	1.10236
47/64	.734375	18.6531	20	508.0	29	1.14173
3/4	.75	19.0500	21	533.4	30	1.18110
49/64	.765625	19.4469	22	558.8	31	1.22047
25/32	.78125	19.8437	23	584.2	32	1.25984
51/64	.796875	20.2406	24	609.6	33	1.29921
13/16	.8125	20.6375	25	635.0	34	1.33858
53/64	.828125	21.0344	26	660.4	35	1.37795
27/32	.84375	21.4312	27	685.8	36	1.41732
55/64	.859375	21.8281	28	711.2	37	1.4567
7/8	.875	22.2250	29	736.6	38	1.4961
57/64	.890625	22.6219	30	762.0	39	1.5354
29/32	.90625	23.0187	31	787.4	40	1.5748
59/64	.921875	23.4156	32	812.8	41	1.6142
15/16	.9375	23.8125	33	838.2	42	1.6535
61/64	.953125	24.2094	34	863.6	43	1.6929
31/32	.96875	24.6062	35	889.0	44	1.7323
63/64	.984375	25.0031	36	914.4	45	1.7717

UNITS	Pints to Litres	Gallons to Litres	Litres to Pints	Litres to Gallons	Miles to Kilometres	Kilometres to Miles	Lbs. per sq. In. to Kg. per sq. Cm.	Kg. per sq. Cm. to Lbs. per sq. In.
1	.57	4.55	1.76	.22	1.61	.62	.07	14.22
2	1.14	9.09	3.52	.44	3.22	1.24	.14	28.50
3	1.70	13.64	5.28	.66	4.83	1.86	.21	42.67
4	2.27	18.18	7.04	.88	6.44	2.49	.28	56.89
5	2.84	22.73	8.80	1.10	8.05	3.11	.35	71.12
6	3.41	27.28	10.56	1.32	9.66	3.73	.42	85.34
7	3.98	31.82	12.32	1.54	11.27	4.35	.49	99.56
8	4.55	36.37	14.08	1.76	12.88	4.97	.56	113.79
9		40.91	15.84	1.98	14.48	5.59	.63	128.00
10		45.46	17.60	2.20	16.09	6.21	.70	142.23
20				4.40	32.19	12.43	1.41	284.47
30				6.60	48.28	18.64	2.11	426.70
40				8.80	64.37	24.85		
50					80.47	31.07		
60					96.56	37.28		
70					112.65	43.50		
80					128.75	49.71		
90					144.84	55.92		
100					160.93	62.14		

UNITS	Lb ft to kgm	Kgm to lb ft	UNITS	Lb ft to kgm	Kgm to lb ft
1	.138	7.233	7	.967	50.631
2	.276	14.466	8	1.106	57.864
3	.414	21.699	9	1.244	65.097
4	.553	28.932	10	1.382	72.330
5	.691	36.165	20	2.765	144.660
6	.829	43.398	30	4.147	216.990

NOTES

HINTS ON MAINTENANCE AND OVERHAUL

There are few things more rewarding than the restoration of a vehicle's original peak of efficiency and smooth performance.

The following notes are intended to help the owner to reach that state of perfection. Providing that he possesses the basic manual skills he should have no difficulty in performing most of the operations detailed in this manual. It must be stressed, however, that where recommended in the manual, highly-skilled operations ought to be entrusted to experts, who have the necessary equipment, to carry out the work satisfactorily.

Quality of workmanship:

The hazardous driving conditions on the roads to-day demand that vehicles should be as nearly perfect, mechanically, as possible. It is therefore most important that amateur work be carried out with care, bearing in mind the often inadequate working conditions, and also the inferior tools which may have to be used. It is easy to counsel perfection in all things, and we recognize that it may be setting an impossibly high standard. We do, however, suggest that every care should be taken to ensure that a vehicle is as safe to take on the road as it is humanly possible to make it.

Safe working conditions:

Even though a vehicle may be stationary, it is still potentially dangerous if certain sensible precautions are not taken when working on it while it is supported on jacks or blocks. It is indeed preferable not to use jacks alone, but to supplement them with carefully placed blocks, so that there will be plenty of support if the car rolls off the jacks during a strenuous manoeuvre. Axle stands are an excellent way of providing a rigid base which is not readily disturbed. Piles of bricks are a dangerous substitute. Be careful not to get under heavy loads on lifting tackle, the load could fall. It is preferable not to work alone when lifting an engine, or when working underneath a vehicle which is supported well off the ground. To be trapped, particularly under the vehicle, may have unpleasant results if help is not quickly forthcoming. Make some provision, however humble, to deal with fires. Always disconnect a battery if there is a likelihood of electrical shorts. These may start a fire if there is leaking fuel about. This applies particularly to leads which can carry a heavy current, like those in the starter circuit. While on the subject of electricity, we must also stress the danger of using equipment which is run off the mains and which has no earth or has faulty wiring or connections. So many workshops have damp floors, and electrical shocks are of such a nature that it is sometimes impossible to let go of a live lead or piece of equipment due to the muscular spasms which take place.

Work demanding special care:

This involves the servicing of braking, steering and suspension systems. On the road, failure of the braking system may be disastrous. Make quite sure that there can be no possibility of failure through the bursting of rusty brake pipes or rotten hoses, nor to a sudden loss of pressure due to defective seals or valves.

Problems:

The chief problems which may face an operator are:
1 External dirt.
2 Difficulty in undoing tight fixings.
3 Dismantling unfamiliar mechanisms.
4 Deciding in what respect parts are defective.
5 Confusion about the correct order for reassembly.
6 Adjusting running clearances.
7 Road testing.
8 Final tuning.

Practical suggestion to solve the problems:

1 Preliminary cleaning of large parts—engines, transmissions, steering, suspensions, etc.,—should be carried out before removal from the car. Where road dirt and mud alone are present, wash clean with a high-pressure water jet, brushing to remove stubborn adhesions, and allow to drain and dry. Where oil or grease is also present, wash down with a proprietary compound (Gunk, Teepol etc.,) applying with a stiff brush—an old paint brush is suitable—into all crevices. Cover the distributor and ignition coils with a polythene bag and then apply a strong water jet to clear the loosened deposits. Allow to drain and dry. The assemblies will then be sufficiently clean to remove and transfer to the bench for the next stage.

On the bench, further cleaning can be carried out, first wiping the parts as free as possible from grease with old newspaper. Avoid using rag or cotton waste which can leave clogging fibres behind. Any remaining grease can be removed with a brush dipped in paraffin. If necessary, traces of paraffin can be removed by carbon tetrachloride. Avoid using paraffin or petrol in large quantities for cleaning in enclosed areas, such as garages, on account of the high fire risk.

When all exteriors have been cleaned, and not before, dismantling can be commenced. This ensures that dirt will not enter into interiors and orifices revealed by dismantling. In the next phases, where components have to be cleaned, use carbon tetrachloride in preference to petrol and keep the containers covered except when in use. After the components have been cleaned, plug small holes with tapered hard wood plugs cut to size and blank off larger orifices with grease-proof paper and masking tape. Do not use soft wood plugs or matchsticks as they may break.

2 It is not advisable to hammer on the end of a screw thread, but if it must be done, first screw on a nut to protect the thread, and use a lead hammer. This applies particularly to the removal of tapered cotters. Nuts and bolts seem to 'grow' together, especially in exhaust systems. If penetrating oil does not work, try the judicious application of heat, but be careful ot starting a fire. Asbestos sheet or cloth is useful to isolate heat.

Tight bushes or pieces of tail-pipe rusted into a silencer can be removed by splitting them with an open-ended hacksaw. Tight screws can sometimes be started by a tap from a hammer on the end of a suitable screwdriver. Many tight fittings will yield to the judicious use of a hammer, but it must be a soft-faced hammer if damage is to be avoided, use a heavy block on the opposite side to absorb shock. Any parts of the steering system which have been damaged should be renewed, as attempts to repair them may lead to cracking and subsequent failure, and steering ball joints should be disconnected using a recommended tool to prevent damage.

3   If often happens that an owner is baffled when trying to dismantle an unfamiliar piece of equipment. So many modern devices are pressed together or assembled by spinning-over flanges, that they must be sawn apart. The intention is that the whole assembly must be renewed. However, parts which appear to be in one piece to the naked eye, may reveal close-fitting joint lines when inspected with a magnifying glass, and, this may provide the necessary clue to dismantling. Left-handed screw threads are used where rotational forces would tend to unscrew a righthanded screw thread.

Be very careful when dismantling mechanisms which may come apart suddenly. Work in an enclosed space where the parts will be contained, and drape a piece of cloth over the device if springs are likely to fly in all directions. Mark everything which might be reassembled in the wrong position, scratched symbols may be used on unstressed parts, or a sequence of tiny dots from a centre punch can be useful. Stressed parts should never be scratched or centre-popped as this may lead to cracking under working conditions. Store parts which look alike in the correct order for reassembly. Never rely upon memory to assist in the assembly of complicated mechanisms, especially when they will be dismantled for a long time, but make notes, and drawings to supplement the diagrams in the manual, and put labels on detached wires. Rust stains may indicate unlubricated wear. This can sometimes be seen round the outside edge of a bearing cup in a universal joint. Look for bright rubbing marks on parts which normally should not make heavy contact. These might prove that something is bent or running out of truth. For example, there might be bright marks on one side of a piston, at the top near the ring grooves, and others at the bottom of the skirt on the other side. This could well be the clue to a bent connecting rod. Suspected cracks can be proved by heating the component in a light oil to approximately 100°C, removing, drying off, and dusting with french chalk, if a crack is present the oil retained in the crack will stain the french chalk.

4   In determining wear, and the degree, against the permissible limits set in the manual, accurate measurement can only be achieved by the use of a micrometer. In many cases, the wear is given to the fourth place of decimals; that is in ten-thousandths of an inch. This can be read by the vernier scale on the barrel of a good micrometer. Bore diameters are more difficult to determine. If, however, the matching shaft is accurately measured, the degree of play in the bore can be felt as a guide to its suitability. In other cases, the shank of a twist drill of known diameter is a handy check.

Many methods have been devised for determining the clearance between bearing surfaces. To-day the best and simplest is by the use of Plastigage, obtainable from most garages. A thin plastic thread is laid between the two surfaces and the bearing is tightened, flattening the thread. On removal, the width of the thread is compared with a scale supplied with the thread and the clearance is read off directly. Sometimes joint faces leak persistently, even after gasket renewal. The fault will then be traceable to distortion, dirt or burrs. Studs which are screwed into soft metal frequently raise burrs at the point of entry. A quick cure for this is to chamfer the edge of the hole in the part which fits over the stud.

5   **Always check a replacement part with the original one before it is fitted.**

If parts are not marked, and the order for reassembly is not known, a little detective work will help. Look for marks which are due to wear to see if they can be mated. Joint faces may not be identical due to manufacturing errors, and parts which overlap may be stained, giving a clue to the correct position. Most fixings leave identifying marks especially if they were painted over on assembly. It is then easier to decide whether a nut, for instance, has a plain, a spring, or a shakeproof washer under it. All running surfaces become 'bedded' together after long spells of work and tiny imperfections on one part will be found to have corresponding marks on the other. This is particularly true of shafts and bearings and even a score on a cylinder wall will show on the piston.

6   Checking end float or rocker clearances by feeler gauge may not always give accurate results because of wear. For instance, the rocker tip which bears on a valve stem may be deeply pitted, in which case the feeler will simply be bridging a depression. Thrust washers may also wear depressions in opposing faces to make accurate measurement difficult. End float is then easier to check by using a dial gauge. It is common practice to adjust end play in bearing assemblies, like front hubs with taper rollers, by doing up the axle nut until the hub becomes stiff to turn and then backing it off a little. Do not use this method with ballbearing hubs as the assembly is often preloaded by tightening the axle nut to its fullest extent. If the splitpin hole will not line up file the base of the nut a little.

Steering assemblies often wear in the straight-ahead position. If any part is adjusted, make sure that it remains free when moved from lock to lock. Do not be surprised if an assembly like a steering gearbox, which is known to be carefully adjusted outside the car, becomes stiff when it is bolted in place. This will be due to distortion of the case by the pull of the mounting bolts, particularly if the mounting points are not all touching together. This problem may be met in other equipment and is cured by careful attention to the alignment of mounting points.

When a spanner is stamped with a size and A/F it means that the dimension is the width between the jaws and has no connection with ANF, which is the designation for the American National Fine thread. Coarse threads like Whitworth are rarely used on cars to-day except for studs which screw into soft aluminium or cast iron. For this reason it might be found that the top end of a cylinder head stud has a fine thread and the lower end a coarse thread to screw into the cylinder block. If the car has mainly UNF threads then it is likely that any coarse threads will be UNC, which are not the same as Whitworth. Small sizes have the same number of threads in Whitworth and UNC, but in the $\frac{1}{2}$ inch size for example, there are twelve threads to the inch in the former and thirteen in the latter.

7 After a major overhaul, particularly if a great deal of work has been done on the braking, steering and suspension systems, it is advisable to approach the problem of testing with care. If the braking system has been overhauled, apply heavy pressure to the brake pedal and get a second operator to check every possible source of leakage. The brakes may work extremely well, but a leak could cause complete failure after a few miles.

Do not fit the hub caps until every wheel nut has been checked for tightness, and make sure the tyre pressures are correct. Check the levels of coolant, lubricants and hydraulic fluids. Being satisfied that all is well, take the car on the road and test the brakes at once. Check the steering and the action of the handbrake. Do all this at moderate speeds on quiet roads, and make sure there is no other vehicle behind you when you try a rapid stop.

Finally, remember that many parts settle down after a time, so check for tightness of all fixings after the car has been on the road for a hundred miles or so.

8 It is useless to tune an engine which has not reached its normal running temperature. In the same way, the tune of an engine which is stiff after a rebore will be different when the engine is again running free. Remember too, that rocker clearances on pushrod operated valve gear will change when the cylinder head nuts are tightened after an initial period of running with a new head gasket.

Trouble may not always be due to what seems the obvious cause. Ignition, carburation and mechanical condition are interdependent and spitting back through the carburetter, which might be attributed to a weak mixture, can be caused by a sticking inlet valve.

For one final hint on tuning, never adjust more than one thing at a time or it will be impossible to tell which adjustment produced the desired result.

NOTES

GLOSSARY OF TERMS

llen key   Cranked wrench of hexagonal section for use with socket head screws.

lternator   Electrical generator producing alternating current. Rectified to direct current for battery charging.

mbient emperature   Surrounding atmospheric temperature.

nnulus   Used in engineering to indicate the outer ring gear of an epicyclic gear train.

rmature   The shaft carrying the windings, which rotates in the magnetic field of a generator or starter motor. That part of a solenoid or relay which is activated by the magnetic field.

xial   In line with, or pertaining to, an axis.

acklash   Play in meshing gears.

alance lever   A bar where force applied at the centre is equally divided between connections at the ends.

anjo axle   Axle casing with large diameter housing for the crownwheel and differential.

endix pinion   A self-engaging and self-disengaging drive on a starter motor shaft.

evel pinion   A conical shaped gearwheel, designed to mesh with a similar gear with an axis usually at 90 deg. to its own.

hp   Brake horse power, measured on a dynamometer.

nep   Brake mean effective pressure. Average pressure on a piston during the working stroke.

rake cylinder   Cylinder with hydraulically operated piston(s) acting on brake shoes or pad(s).

rake regulator   Control valve fitted in hydraulic braking system which limits brake pressure to rear brakes during heavy braking to prevent rear wheel locking.

amber   Angle at which a wheel is tilted from the vertical.

apacitor   Modern term for an electrical condenser. Part of distributor assembly, connected across contact breaker points, acts as an interference suppressor.

astellated   Top face of a nut, slotted across the flats, to take a locking splitpin.

astor   Angle at which the kingpin or swivel pin is tilted when viewed from the side.

Cubic centimetres. Engine capacity is arrived at by multiplying the area of the bore in sq cm by the stroke in cm by the number of cylinders.

Clevis   U-shaped forked connector used with a clevis pin, usually at handbrake connections.

Collet   A type of collar, usually split and located in a groove in a shaft, and held in place by a retainer. The arrangement used to retain the spring(s) on a valve stem in most cases.

Commutator   Rotating segmented current distributor between armature windings and brushes in generator or motor.

Compression ratio   The ratio, or quantitative relation, of the total volume (piston at bottom of stroke) to the unswept volume (piston at top of stroke) in an engine cylinder.

Condenser   See capacitor.

Core plug   Plug for blanking off a manufacturing hole in a casting.

Crownwheel   Large bevel gear in rear axle, driven by a bevel pinion attached to the propeller shaft. Sometimes called a 'ring gear'.

'C'-spanner   Like a 'C' with a handle. For use on screwed collars without flats, but with slots or holes.

Damper   Modern term for shock-absorber, used in vehicle suspension systems to damp out spring oscillations.

Depression   The lowering of atmospheric pressure as in the inlet manifold and carburetter.

Dowel   Close tolerance pin, peg, tube, or bolt, which accurately locates mating parts.

Drag link   Rod connecting steering box drop arm (pitman arm) to nearest front wheel steering arm in certain types of steering systems.

Dry liner   Thinwall tube pressed into cylinder bore

Dry sump   Lubrication system where all oil is scavenged from the sump, and returned to a separate tank.

Dynamo   See Generator.

Electrode   Terminal, part of an electrical component, such as the points or 'Electrodes' of a sparking plug.

Electrolyte   In lead-acid car batteries a solution of sulphuric acid and distilled water.

End float   The axial movement between associated parts, end play.

EP   Extreme pressure. In lubricants, special grades for heavily loaded bearing surfaces, such as gear teeth in a gearbox, or crownwheel and pinion in a rear axle.

Fade — Of brakes. Reduced efficiency due to overheating.

Field coils — Windings on the polepieces of motors and generators

Fillets — Narrow finishing strips usually applied to interior bodywork.

First motion shaft — Input shaft from clutch to gearbox.

Fullflow filter — Filters in which all the oil is pumped to the engine. If the element becomes clogged, a bypass valve operates to pass unfiltered oil to the engine.

FWD — Front wheel drive.

Gear pump — Two meshing gears in a close fitting casing. Oil is carried from the inlet round the outside of both gears in the spaces between the gear teeth and casing to the outlet, the meshing gear teeth prevent oil passing back to the inlet, and the oil is forced through the outlet port.

Generator — Modern term for 'Dynamo'. When rotated produces electrical current.

Grommet — A ring of protective or sealing material. Can be used to protect pipes or leads passing through bulkheads.

Grubscrew — Fully threaded headless screw with screwdriver slot. Used for locking, or alignment purposes.

Gudgeon pin — Shaft which connects a piston to its connecting rod. Sometimes called 'wrist pin', or 'piston pin'.

Halfshaft — One of a pair transmitting drive from the differential.

Helical — In spiral form. The teeth of helical gears are cut at a spiral angle to the side faces of the gearwheel.

Hot spot — Hot area that assists vapourisation of fuel on its way to cylinders. Often provided by close contact between inlet and exhaust manifolds.

HT — High Tension. Applied to electrical current produced by the ignition coil for the sparking plugs.

Hydrometer — A device for checking specific gravity of liquids. Used to check specific gravity of electrolyte.

Hypoid bevel gears — A form of bevel gear used in the rear axle drive gears. The bevel pinion meshes below the centre line of the crownwheel, giving a lower propeller shaft line.

Idler — A device for passing on movement. A free running gear between driving and driven gears. A lever transmitting track rod movement to a side rod in steering gear.

Impeller — A centrifugal pumping element. Used in water pumps to stimulate flow.

Journals — Those parts of a shaft that are i contact with the bearings.

Kingpin — The main vertical pin which carries th front wheel spindle, and permits steer ing movement. May be called 'steerin pin' or 'swivel pin'.

Layshaft — The shaft which carries the laygear i the gearbox. The laygear is driven b the first motion shaft and drives th third motion shaft according to th gear selected. Sometimes called th 'countershaft' or 'second motion shaf

lb ft — A measure of twist or torque. A pull 10 lb at a radius of 1 ft is a torque 10 lb ft.

lb/sq in — Pounds per square inch.

Little-end — The small, or piston end of a connectir rod. Sometimes called the 'small-enc

LT — Low Tension. The current output fro the battery.

Mandrel — Accurately manufactured bar or rc used for test or centring purposes.

Manifold — A pipe, duct, or chamber, with sever branches.

Needle rollers — Bearing rollers with a length mar times their diameter.

Oil bath — Reservoir which lubricates parts immersion. In air filters, a separate supply for wetting a wire mesh eleme to hold the dust.

Oil wetted — In air filters, a wire mesh eleme lightly oiled to trap and hold airborr dust.

Overlap — Period during which inlet and exhau valves are open together.

Panhard rod — Bar connected between fixed point chassis and another on axle to cont sideways movement.

Pawl — Pivoted catch which engages in t teeth of a ratchet to permit moveme in one direction only.

Peg spanner — Tool with pegs, or pins, to engage holes or slots in the part to be turnec

Pendant pedals — Pedals with levers that are pivoted the top end.

Phillips screwdriver — A cross-point screwdriver for use w the cross-slotted heads of Philli screws.

Pinion — A small gear, usually in relation another gear.

Piston-type damper — Shock absorber in which damping controlled by a piston working in closed oil-filled cylinder.

Preloading — Preset static pressure on ball or rol bearings not due to working loads.

Radial — Radiating from a centre, like the spol of a wheel.

adius rod	Pivoted arm confining movement of a part to an arc of fixed radius.
atchet	Toothed wheel or rack which can move in one direction only, movement in the other being prevented by a pawl.
ng gear	A gear tooth ring attached to outer periphery of flywheel. Starter pinion engages with it during starting.
nout	Amount by which rotating part is out of true.
mi-floating le	Outer end of rear axle halfshaft is carried on bearing inside axle casing. Wheel hub is secured to end of shaft.
rvo	A hydraulic or pneumatic system for assisting, or, augmenting a physical effort. See 'Vacuum Servo'.
tscrew	One which is threaded for the full length of the shank.
ackle	A coupling link, used in the form of two parallel pins connected by side plates to secure the end of the master suspension spring and absorb the effects of deflection.
ell bearing	Thinwalled steel shell lined with anti-friction metal. Usually semi-circular and used in pairs for main and big-end bearings.
ock absorber	See 'Damper'.
entbloc	Rubber bush bonded to inner and outer metal sleeves.
cket-head ew	Screw with hexagonal socket for an Allen key.
enoid	A coil of wire creating a magnetic field when electric current passes through it. Used with a soft iron core to operate contacts or a mechanical device.
ur gear	A gear with teeth cut axially across the periphery.
b axle	Short axle fixed at one end only.
hometer	An instrument for accurate measurement of rotating speed. Usually indicates in revolutions per minute.

TDC	Top Dead Centre. The highest point reached by a piston in a cylinder, with the crank and connecting rod in line.
Thermostat	Automatic device for regulating temperature. Used in vehicle coolant systems to open a valve which restricts circulation at low temperature.
Third motion shaft	Output shaft of gearbox.
Threequarter floating axle	Outer end of rear axle halfshaft flanged and bolted to wheel hub, which runs on bearing mounted on outside of axle casing. Vehicle weight is not carried by the axle shaft.
Thrust bearing or washer	Used to reduce friction in rotating parts subject to axial loads.
Torque	Turning or twisting effort. See 'lb ft'.
Track rod	The bar(s) across the vehicle which connect the steering arms and maintain the front wheels in their correct alignment.
UJ	Universal joint. A coupling between shafts which permits angular movement.
UNF	Unified National Fine screw thread.
Vacuum servo	Device used in brake system, using difference between atmospheric pressure and inlet manifold depression to operate a piston which acts to augment brake pressure as required. See 'Servo'
Venturi	A restriction or 'choke' in a tube, as in a carburetter, used to increase velocity to obtain a reduction in pressure.
Vernier	A sliding scale for obtaining fractional readings of the graduations of an adjacent scale.
Welch plug	A domed thin metal disc which is partially flattened to lock in a recess. Used to plug core holes in castings.
Wet liner	Removable cylinder barrel, sealed against coolant leakage, where the coolant is in direct contact with the outer surface.
Wet sump	A reservoir attached to the crankcase to hold the lubricating oil.

NOTES

INDEX

NOTES

Alfa Romeo Giulia 1600,
  1750, 2000 1962 on
Aston Martin 1921-58
Auto Union Audi 70, 80,
  Super 90, 1966-72
Audi 100 1969 on
Austin, Morris etc.
  1100 Mk. 1 1962-67
Austin, Morris etc. 1100
  Mk. 2, 3, 1300 Mk. 1, 2, 3
  America 1968 on
Austin A30, A35, A40
  Farina 1951-67
Austin A55 Mk. 2, A60
  1958-69
Austin A99, A110 1959-68
Austin J4 1960 on
Austin Allegro 1973 on
Austin Maxi 1969 on
Austin, Morris 1800
  1964 on
Austin, Morris 2200 1972 on
Austin Kimberley, Tasman
  1970 on
Austin, Morris 1300, 1500
  Nomad 1969 on
BMC 3 (Austin A50, A55
  Mk. 1, Morris Oxford
  2, 3 1954-59)
Austin Healey 100/6,
  3000 1956-68
Austin Healey, MG
  Sprite, Midget 1958 on
Bedford CA Mk. 2 1964-69
Bedford CF Vans 1969 on
Bedford Beagle HA Vans
  1964 on
BMW 1600 1966 on
BMW 1800 1964-71
BMW 2000, 2002 1966 on
Chevrolet Corvair 1960-69
Chevrolet Corvette V8
  1957-65
Chevrolet Corvette V8
  1965 on
Chevrolet Vega 2300
  1970 on
Chrysler Valiant V8
  1965 on
Chrysler Valiant Straight
  Six 1963 on
Citroen DS 19, ID 19
  1955-66
Citroen ID 19, DS 19, 20,
  21 1966 on
Citroen Dyane Ami 1964 on
Daf 31, 32, 33, 44, 55
  1961 on
Datsun Bluebird 610 series
  1972 on
Datsun Cherry 100A, 120A
  1971 on
Datsun 1000, 1200 1968 on
Datsun 1300, 1400, 1600
  1968 on
Datsun 240C 1971 on

Datsun 240Z Sport 1970 on
Fiat 124 1966 on
Fiat 124 Sport 1966 on
Fiat 125 1967-72
Fiat 127 1971 on
Fiat 128 1969 on
Fiat 500 1957 on
Fiat 600, 600D 1955-69
Fiat 850 1964 on
Fiat 1100 1957-69
Fiat 1300, 1500 1961-67
Ford Anglia Prefect 100E
  1953-62
Ford Anglia 105E, Prefect
  107E 1959-67
Ford Capri 1300, 1600 OHV
  1968 on
Ford Capri 1300, 1600,
  2000 OHC 1972 on
Ford Capri 2000 V4, 3000 V6
  1969 on
Ford Classic, Capri
  1961-64
Ford Consul, Zephyr,
  Zodiac, 1, 2 1950-62
Ford Corsair Straight
  Four 1963-65
Ford Corsair V4 1965-68
Ford Corsair V4 2000
  1969-70
Ford Cortina 1962-66
Ford Cortina 1967-68
Ford Cortina 1969-70
Ford Cortina Mk. 3
  1970 on
Ford Escort 1967 on
Ford Falcon 6 1964-70
Ford Falcon XK, XL
  1960-63
Ford Falcon 6 XR/XA
  1966 on
Ford Falcon V8 (U.S.A.)
  1965-71
Ford Falcon V8 (Aust.)
  1966 on
Ford Pinto 1970 on
Ford Maverick 6 1969 on
Ford Maverick V8 1970 on
Ford Mustang 6 1965 on
Ford Mustang V8 1965 on
Ford Thames 10, 12,
  15 cwt 1957-65
Ford Transit V4 1965 on
Ford Zephyr Zodiac Mk. 3
  1962-66
Ford Zephyr Zodiac V4,
  V6, Mk. 4 1966-72
Ford Consul, Granada
  1972 on
Hillman Avenger 1970 on
Hillman Hunter 1966 on
Hillman Imp 1963-68
Hillman Imp 1969 on
Hillman Minx 1 to 5
  1956-65
Hillman Minx 1965-67

Hillman Minx 1966-70
Hillman Super Minx
  1961-65
Jaguar XK120, 140, 150,
  Mk. 7, 8, 9 1948-61
Jaguar 2.4, 3.4, 3.8 Mk.
  1, 2 1955-69
Jaguar 'E' Type 1961-72
Jaguar 'S' Type 420
  1963-68
Jaguar XJ6 1968 on
Jowett Javelin Jupiter
  1947-53
Landrover 1, 2 1948-61
Landrover 2, 2a, 3 1959 on
Mazda 616 1970 on
Mazda 808, 818 1972 on
Mazda 1200, 1300 1969 on
Mazda 1500, 1800 1967 on
Mazda RX-2 1971 on
Mazda R100, RX-3 1970 on
Mercedes-Benz 190b,
  190c, 200 1959-68
Mercedes-Benz 220
  1959-65
Mercedes-Benz 220/8
  1968 on
Mercedes-Benz 230
  1963-68
Mercedes-Benz 250
  1965-67
Mercedes-Benz 250
  1968 on
Mercedes-Benz 280
  1968 on
MG TA to TF 1936-55
MGA MGB 1955-68
MGB 1969 on
Mini 1959 on
Mini Cooper 1961-72
Morgan Four 1936-72
Morris Marina 1971 on
Morris (Aust) Marina
  1972 on
Morris Minor 2, 1000
  1952-71
Morris Oxford 5, 6 1959-71
NSU 1000 1963-72
NSU Prinz 1 to 4 1957-72
Opel Ascona, Manta
  1970 on
Opel GT 1900 1968 on
Opel Kadett, Olympia 993 cc
  1078 cc 1962 on
Opel Kadett, Olympia 1492,
  1698, 1897 cc 1967 on
Opel Rekord C 1966-72
Peugeot 204 1965 on
Peugeot 304 1970 on
Peugeot 404 1960 on
Peugeot 504 1968 on
Porsche 356A, B, C 1957-65
Porsche 911 1964 on
Porsche 912 1965-69
Porsche 914 S 1969 on
Reliant Regal 1952-73

Renault R4, R4L, 4 1961 on
Renault 5 1972 on
Renault 6 1968 on
Renault 8, 10, 1100 1962-71
Renault 12, 1969 on
Renault 15, 17 1971 on
Renault R16 1965 on
Renault Dauphine
  Floride 1957-67
Renault Caravelle 1962-68
Rover 60 to 110 1953-64
Rover 2000 1963-73
Rover 3 Litre 1958-67,
Rover 3500, 3500S 1968 on
Saab 95, 96, Sport
  1960-68
Saab 99 1969 on
Saab V4 1966 on
Simca 1000 1961 on
Simca 1100 1967 on
Simca 1300, 1301, 1500,
  1501 1963 on
Skoda One (440, 445, 450)
  1955-70
Sunbeam Rapier Alpine
  1955-65
Toyota Carina, Celica
  1971 on
Toyota Corolla 1100,
  1200 1967 on
Toyota Corona 1500 Mk. 1
  1965-70
Toyota Corona Mk. 2
  1969 on
Triumph TR2, TR3, TR3A
  1952-62
Triumph TR4, TR4A
  1961-67
Triumph TR5, TR250,
  TR6 1967 on
Triumph 1300, 1500
  1965-73
Triumph 2000 Mk. 1, 2.5 PI
  Mk. 1 1963-69
Triumph 2000 Mk. 2, 2.5 PI
  Mk. 2 1969 on
Triumph Dolomite 1972 on
Triumph Herald 1959-68
Triumph Herald 1969-71
Triumph Spitfire, Vitesse
  1962-68
Triumph Spitfire Mk. 3, 4
  1969 on
Triumph GT6, Vitesse
  2 Litre 1969 on
Triumph Stag 1970 on
Triumph Toledo 1970 on
Vauxhall Velox, Cresta
  1957-72
Vauxhall Victor 1, 2, FB
  1957-64
Vauxhall Victor 101
  1964-67
Vauxhall Victor FD 1600,
  2000 1967-72

Continued on following page

THE AUTOBOOK SERIES OF WORKSHOP MANUALS

Vauxhall Victor 3300,
  Ventora 1968-72
Vauxhall Victor FE
  Ventora 1972 on
Vauxhall Viva HA 1963-66
Vauxhall Viva HB 1966-70

Vauxhall Viva, HC Firenza
  1971 on
Volkswagen Beetle 1954-67
Volkswagen Beetle 1968 on
Volkswagen 1500 1961-66

Volkswagen 1600 Fastback
  1965-73
Volkswagen Transporter
  1954-67
Volkswagen Transporter
  1968 on

Volkswagen 411 1968-72
Volvo 120 series 1961-70
Volvo 140 series 1966 on
Volvo 160 series 1968 on
Volvo 1800 1960-73

NOTES

NOTES